Queen Elizabeth I

Queen Elizabeth I

Selected Works

Edited by

Steven W. May

WSP

WASHINGTON SQUARE PRESS

New York   London   Toronto   Sydney

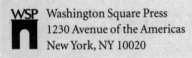

Washington Square Press
1230 Avenue of the Americas
New York, NY 10020

ISBN: 0-7434-7081-8
    0-7434-7644-1 (Pbk)

54781465

First Washington Square Press trade paperback edition January 2005

10 9 8 7 6 5 4 3 2 1

WASHINGTON SQUARE PRESS and colophon are
registered trademarks of Simon & Schuster, Inc.

Manufactured in the United States of America

For information regarding special discounts for bulk purchases,
please contact Simon & Schuster Special Sales at 1-800-456-6798 or
business@simonandschuster.com.

Contents

Chronology

1533	January 25	Henry VIII marries Anne Boleyn
	September 7	Princess Elizabeth born at Greenwich Palace
1547	January 29	Death of Henry VIII; accession of Edward VI
1553	July 6	Death of Edward VI; accession of Mary I
1558	November 17	Death of Mary I; accession of Elizabeth I
1559		Elizabeth declared Supreme Governor of the Church of England by act of her first Parliament
1568	May 16	Mary, Queen of Scots, flees Scotland to seek refuge in England
1569–70	November–February	The "Northern Rebellion"
1585	December	Robert Dudley, earl of Leicester, leads an English expeditionary force to oppose the Spanish conquest of the Low Countries
1586	August	Revelation of the "Babington Plot," a Catholic attempt to assassinate Queen Elizabeth
1587	February 8	Execution of Mary, Queen of Scots, at Fotheringay Castle

1588	July–August	Defeat of the Spanish Armada
	August 8–9	Elizabeth visits the army assembled at Tilbury Camp
1596		The "Cádiz Raid"; the English navy and army capture the Spanish town of Cádiz
1597		The "Islands Voyage"; the English navy and army fail to intercept Spain's New World treasure fleet
1601	February 8	Robert Devereux, earl of Essex's abortive coup d'état
	February 21	Essex beheaded at the Tower of London
	November 30	Elizabeth delivers her "Golden Speech" to representatives of her tenth Parliament
1603	March 24	Elizabeth dies at Richmond Palace; James VI of Scotland becomes James I of England

Abbreviations

C   Cambridge University Library
CSPD   Great Britain, Public Record Office, *Calendar of State Papers, Domestic Series,* ed. Robert Lemon and Mary Anne Everett Green (London, 1856–1871)
Hartley   *Proceedings in the Parliaments of Elizabeth I,* ed. T. E. Hartley, 3 vols. (London, 1981–95)
HMC   Great Britain, Historical Manuscripts Commission, various publications
L   British Library, London
NLW   National Library of Wales, Aberystwyth
O   Bodleian Library, Oxford
OED   *Oxford English Dictionary*
PRO   Public Record Office, Kew
STC   *A Short-Title Catalogue of English Books,* ed. W. A. Jackson, F. S. Ferguson, and Katherine F. Pantzer, 2nd ed., 2 vols. (London, 1976–86)
Y   Beinecke Rare Books and Manuscripts Library, Yale University

Introduction

Elizabeth's Life and Reign

Henry VIII, the second Tudor king, lacked a male heir as he approached age forty in 1531. His twenty-odd years of wedlock with Catherine of Aragon had produced only one child who survived into adolescence, his daughter Mary. When Pope Clement VII refused to dissolve Henry's marriage with Catherine, the King renounced papal authority, arranged for the annulment of his marriage by authority of the newly autonomous English Church, and married Anne Boleyn in 1533. By the Act of Supremacy (1534), Parliament proclaimed Henry the Supreme Head of the Church of England; thus, the Protestant Reformation came to England as a by-product of the King's efforts to perpetuate the Tudor dynasty. Henry was unable to hide his disappointment when Anne gave birth to their daughter Elizabeth on September 7, 1533. He could not foresee that this baby girl was destined to rule England for nearly forty-five years as a successful, indeed illustrious, queen.

Elizabeth learned early in life that her status as a potential successor to the crown could be dangerous. After her father's death in 1547, when her brother Edward came to the throne, she spent a year in the household of her stepmother, the dowager Queen Catherine Parr. Catherine's new husband, the Lord Admiral, Thomas Seymour, was handsome, dashing, and influential. His nephew, King Edward VI, was titular ruler of England under the protectorship of Seymour's brother, Edward, duke of Somerset. The teenage Princess found Thomas attractive, and his initial flirtation with her turned to open courtship when Catherine died just after childbirth in September 1548. Given Elizabeth's claim to the throne, this or any other match would have been treasonous without consent of the King and Privy Council. While Elizabeth escaped punishment, the Lord Admiral was in 1549 beheaded at his brother's command for, among other offenses, his designs on the Princess.

Elizabeth avoided any appearance of rivalry for the throne when Edward VI died in July 1553 and their half-sister, Mary, acceded as queen. But Mary reinstated Catholicism as the state religion and on July 25, 1554, married Philip II of Spain. During the preceding winter, English Protestants had launched a rebellion against the new regime. Sir Thomas Wyatt actually led troops into London in February, but his uprising was crushed. The government implicated Elizabeth in the failed coup and sent her to the Tower of London. Although once again her life was spared, she was held prisoner for more than a year, at first in the Tower and then at Woodstock Manor, Oxfordshire.

Elizabeth became Queen of England when Mary died on November 17, 1558. The country was deeply divided along religious lines as well as being economically and militarily weak; it was thus a tempting prey for the two great Catholic powers, Spain and France. Moreover, the new Queen was the last direct heir of the Tudor dynasty (though her legitimacy was not entirely certain even by English law). For the sake of England's future it was vital that either she marry and produce an heir or designate a successor who could then be legally ratified by Parliament. The alternative was an unregulated succession; at Elizabeth's death, civil war on behalf of rival contenders for the crown would be the most likely outcome.

The members of Elizabeth's first Parliament probably felt that the succession dilemma would be resolved soon enough by an appropriate marriage. Their foremost legislation in 1559, the Acts of Supremacy and Uniformity, restored the Protestant state church founded by Henry VIII and maintained under Edward VI. Their religious "settlement," confirmed in 1563 by adoption of the Thirty-Nine Articles of Church doctrine, termed Elizabeth the Supreme Governor of the realm in both ecclesiastical and temporal affairs. However, her status as a Protestant queen failed to discourage Catholic suitors; indeed, the formally recognized candidate who came closest to marrying her was Francis, duke of Alençon (later, duke of Anjou) and brother to the King of France. His off-and-on courtship of the Queen, begun in 1570, concluded without success in 1582 when Elizabeth was nearly fifty.

At the beginning of her reign, however, Elizabeth had engaged in open warfare with France, both in Scotland and over the French seaport of Calais, England's last Continental holding from the Hundred Years' War. The crisis intensified when Mary Stuart, Henry VII's great-granddaughter and widow of Francis II of France, returned to her native Scotland as queen in 1561. Mary was a staunch Catholic who held a viable claim to the English throne. During the 1560s and 1570s, Elizabeth's Privy Council and Parliament exhorted her with increasing fervor to marry or name an heir, but in the first decade of her reign she rejected perhaps a dozen suitors. She undoubtedly would have married her longtime favorite, Robert Dudley, were personal preference the only criterion. But the death of Lord Robert's wife under mysterious circumstances in 1560 made any match with Elizabeth politically impossible on grounds of the scandal it would cause. She instead created Dudley earl of Leicester in 1564 and offered him as a husband of suitable rank for the Queen of Scots in an effort to secure England's northern border. But in July 1565, this rival queen married another of Elizabeth's own subjects, Henry Stuart, Lord Darnley, and in the following June gave birth to a male heir, the future King James VI of Scotland.

Ironically, Mary's apparent successes as queen and mother led to the most glorious triumph of Elizabeth's reign and resulted as well in a Protestant successor to her throne. Mary's indiscreet love life implicated her lover, Bothwell, in Darnley's assassination in 1567. In the wake of this crime, most of Mary's subjects turned against her. She fled to England in May 1568, where she was arrested and where she remained a prisoner until her death. For nearly twenty years Elizabeth dealt with the crisis of a rival queen on English soil whose mere existence served as a constant incitement to Elizabeth's Catholic subjects and the Catholic powers of Europe to place her on the English throne by force. During the winter of 1569–70, Elizabeth's armies quickly suppressed the "Northern Rebellion," the first uprising on Mary's behalf. Yet there followed a series of plots to assassinate Elizabeth, among them the Ridolfi plot of 1571, the Throckmorton plot of 1583, and William Parry's conspiracy in 1585. Not until the Babington plot of 1586, however, was the government able to implicate Mary directly in a scheme to kill Elizabeth. In the fall of that year, the Queen of Scots was tried and found guilty. Parliament demanded the death sentence, but Elizabeth could not bring herself to give final approval for Mary's execution. When Mary was, nevertheless, beheaded on February 8, 1587, it was by authority of a duly signed royal warrant, yet Elizabeth insisted that she never meant to dispatch the warrant, and she made Secretary William Davison the scapegoat for her rival's death.

Mary's execution brought to a head England's conflict with

Spain and the papacy. England had sparred for years with its Catholic opponents: in Ireland, in the Netherlands, on the high seas, and in Spain's New World colonies. Spain might have launched an armada against England in 1587 had not Sir Francis Drake burned the shipping in Cádiz harbor that spring. The Great Armada sailed the following summer, its purpose to crush Elizabeth's regime and return England to the Catholic faith. Instead, the English navy routed this flotilla, and nearly half its ships and men never returned to Spain. The defeat of the Armada was Elizabeth's greatest victory on the international front, although hostilities with Spain continued to the end of her reign, draining the royal coffers and distracting the English from both their domestic needs and efforts to establish overseas colonies of their own.

The very fact, however, that Elizabeth could challenge so great a power as Spain raised England's international prestige to its highest level since the days of Henry VIII. The last dozen years of Elizabeth's reign were also a golden age of English literature, created by such writers as Edmund Spenser, Christopher Marlowe, William Shakespeare, and Ben Jonson. But the Queen who managed England's problems during these years no doubt found the age substantially less glorious. Virulent outbreaks of plague from 1592 to 1594 were followed by several years of bad weather, poor harvests, and near famine in some parts of the country. The harmonious functioning of the central government was upset by the growing influence of Robert Devereux, second earl of Essex. By1587 he had eclipsed Sir Walter Ralegh as the Queen's chief favorite. Elizabeth delighted in this exuberant nobleman who was less than half her age. But Essex's ambitions soon pitted him against Lord Treasurer Burghley and Burghley's son, Sir Robert Cecil; the result was years of bitter struggle for control of royal favor and national policy. The earl's miscalculated coup attempt and subsequent beheading early in 1601 cast a sombre pall over Elizabeth's final years. Festivities at court were often sparsely attended in the latter years of her reign, while even her most trusted courtiers secretly corresponded with her eagerly expectant successor, King James VI of Scotland. Elizabeth never lost the love of the majority of her subjects, however, just as her love for them was a constant theme of her public oratory from the time of her coronation. Her accession day, November 17, was celebrated spontaneously and publicly decades after her death. The transition to Stuart rule under King James took place smoothly in 1603, yet the new dynasty never produced a ruler as effective and popular as the queen it superseded.

Queen Elizabeth, a Writer's Life

Shortly after her birth at Greenwich Palace on September 7, 1533, Elizabeth was transferred from the royal court to a separate household where she was nurtured apart from her parents and the central government. She spent most of her childhood at royal manors north of London, often in the company of her half-siblings, Mary and Edward. Elizabeth was just four years older than the Prince, and they shared much the same education and even the same tutors, among them Richard Cox, John Cheke, Jean Belmain, and Roger Ascham. The Princess received a rigorous education in the new humanism and reformed religion. Her studies included classical Greek and Latin secular literature as well as the works of Protestant theologians, selections from the Bible, and writings of the Church Fathers. It is clear that she undertook prodigious amounts of handwritten exercises from quite an early age. In addition to Latin and Greek, she was sufficiently adept at French by age eleven to translate into English the Queen of Narvarre's *Miroir de l'âme Pécheresse*. She dedicated her carefully transcribed rendering of this religious meditation to Queen Catherine Parr as a gift for New Year's, 1545 (see Letter 1). British Library Royal MS 7 D.10 is Elizabeth's fair copy of Catherine's *Prayers and Meditations* (1545), which the Princess translated from English into Latin, French, and Italian to present as a New Year's gift to her father in 1546. In 1552 she translated Bernardino

Ochino's "Sermon on the Nature of Christ" from Italian into Latin as a New Year's gift for King Edward (O: Bodl. MS 6).

As a writer, Elizabeth stands in sharp contrast to her father. Henry VIII apparently found the physical act of handwriting distasteful, even to the point of resenting the need to affix his signature to official documents. Elizabeth, however, seems to have written constantly and voluntarily from her girlhood to shortly before her death. Beyond her school exercises, translations, and carefully inscribed New Year's gifts, Elizabeth's early writings include more than a score of extant letters. These works are set forth in her neat, italic script for the most part, but this legible hand all but disappeared after she ascended the throne. Nearly all her handwriting as queen is transcribed in a broad, cursive italic that she seldom took pains to make neat or easily readable. Her apologies in her letters for her "scribbling" do not appear coy to those who attempt to transcribe them.

Throughout her literate lifetime, Elizabeth divided her writings between official and private compositions. Her letters to the Lord Protector, Edward Seymour, for instance, especially those defending her conduct with his brother, the Lord Admiral (Letters 3–7), were motivated by political necessity. In these formal epistles she was not merely defending her reputation; as a potential heir to the throne her freedom, perhaps even her life, was at stake. In contrast, her letters to her half-siblings Edward and Mary before either took the throne are familiar and voluntary compositions. After taking the throne, the bulk of Elizabeth's correspondence was necessarily formal, dedicated to the business of rule. It was generated for the most part by her secretariats, yet she personally composed much of that sent to foreign rulers. A number of "hybrid" letters—that is, documents that mix formal and familiar elements—survive as well, for the Queen sometimes attached personal notes in her own handwriting to secretarial letters at the time of dispatch (see Letters 16 and 37).

A characteristic of Elizabeth's prose style appears in nearly all but the most formal and serious examples of her original writings. The Queen embellishes her prose with figurative language in ways almost wholly lacking in the secretarial prose of her formal correspondence or official pronouncements. Her early letters, for example, are full of similes. She begins Letter 8 to Edward VI, "Like as the rich man that daily gathereth riches to riches . . ." She followed up a few years later in Letter 11 with "Like as a shipman in stormy weather plucks down the sails, tarrying for better wind"—this to explain why she didn't travel to London to visit Edward. She employs figurative language throughout her correspondence with James VI, as in Letter 39 where she warns him that "Weeds in fields if they be suffered will quickly overgrow the corn," just as overindulged subjects will stifle his sovereignty over them. She adds metaphor even to her most serious addresses to Parliament, as in Speech 9 where she chides those who imagine that she has delayed sentencing Mary, Queen of Scots, "thereby to set my praises to the wire-drawers to lengthen them the more."

Beyond the writing required by her status as sovereign, Elizabeth undertook a variety of linguistic and literary compositions that were apparently motivated by her love of languages and desire to remain proficient in them. Among Lord Burghley's papers is a summary of her translations made toward the end of her reign. The list includes her lost rendering of part of Sallust's *De bello Iugurthino* and her complete translation of Boethius's *Consolation of Philosophy* (1593). She is credited with translating in 1598 both an excerpt from Horace's *Ars poetica* and Plutarch's essay *De curiositate* (Translations, Poetry 2).[1] In 1567 she gave her translation of Seneca's *Epistle 107* to John Harington, gentleman of her Privy Chamber, although this may not be the same rendering of Seneca mentioned by Sir Christopher Hatton in a letter of 1579.[2] In that same year, Elizabeth gave Harington a copy of her translation from Cicero's *Letters* (published, as was the Seneca, in Harington's *Nugae Antiquae*).[3]

From the political and religious topics dealt with in these works it could be argued that Elizabeth translated them as part of her duty to govern well. Yet she could have learned whatever lessons in statecraft they conveyed without translating them. Such intimate involvement with the texts grew out of her love of learning—tinged, no doubt, by a just pride in her command of the languages involved. Why she chose to translate these particular works is not always obvious. Plutarch's diatribe against prying busybodies is perhaps the easiest to explain, for Elizabeth was acutely aware of her lack of privacy as a monarch. As she expressed it before Parliament, "we princes, I tell you, are set on stages in the sight and view of all the world duly observed" (Speech 8). She allegedly turned to Boethius's *Consolation* to console herself on learning that Henry IV of France had converted to Catholicism; yet she faced many other problems at the time, including an especially lethal outbreak of plague and the growing realization that the defeat of the Armada signaled the beginning, not the end, of hostilities with Spain. Her translation of Cicero's *Pro Marcello* (Translations, Prose 1) reflects to a degree the kinds of oratorical strategies she often invoked before Parliament. As Cicero attempts to make palatable Caesar's reluctant reinstatement of a former enemy, so Elizabeth constantly placed in the best possible light before her Parliaments her refusal either to marry or to name a successor to the throne. Less obvious is the motive behind her renderings of Horace and Seneca, her "essays" on friendship, or the 280 lines of French verse, whether original or translated, that amount to a personal meditation on overcoming some serious difficulty.[4]

This survey of the Queen's devotion to literary pursuits in her spare time reveals her lifelong concern with composition. Although many works of her royal predecessors may have been lost, Elizabeth qualifies as the most prolific author among English sovereigns since the reign of King Alfred.

Original Poems

Elizabeth may have written verse as a part of her early schooling when she translated classical poetry into English, and we have several indications of her long-standing interest in vernacular poetry. Before she came to the throne Elizabeth personalized a book she presented to her lady-in-waiting, Anne Poyntz, by inscribing in it four lines of contemporary English verse.[5] The Queen's courtier favorite, Sir Christopher Hatton, paraphrased the first line of a poem from Richard Tottel's *Songs and Sonnets* in a letter he addressed to her in 1573, clearly anticipating that she would recognize the allusion.[6] Elizabeth's earliest surviving poetry dates from her confinement at Woodstock in 1555 under Queen Mary (Poems 1 and 2). Most of her verse is occasional, written in response to such immediate events as the Northern Rebellion of 1569–70, or the lyric complaint that Ralegh addressed to her in 1587. As a technician, Elizabeth's style evolved in keeping with broad trends in poetic form and prosody during her lifetime. The meter of her poem on fortune (Poem 1), for instance, is rough tetrameters, yet she writes regular iambic hexameters and heptameters some fifteen years later in her verses on the Northern Rebellion (Poem 4), and her rhythms thereafter are for the most part regular accentual-syllabic. She attempted a variety of stanzas, including such popular contemporary forms as rhyming couplets, the poulter's measure of Poem 4, and the "sixain" stanzas of her lament for "Monsieur" (Poem 6). In addition to her English poetry, Elizabeth wrote at least one Latin poem (Poem 5a) and it is possible that some 280 lines of French verse in her handwriting are also original.[7]

Overall, Elizabeth's poetry exerted the least long-term influence of any of the genres of writing she nurtured. Poem 2 was reprinted under her name in subsequent editions of John Foxe's *Acts and Monuments,* a compendium of Protestant propaganda commonly known as the "Book of Martyrs" that saw at least eight editions by 1632. The Queen's only other canonical verses to reach print in the century after her death were Poems 8 and 9, the Armada hymns published by John Rhodes in 1637. Poem 6 circulated under her name in a handful of seventeenth-century manuscript anthologies of verse, but even Poem 4, a popular anthology piece during her lifetime, soon fell out of favor with Stuart collectors. Despite the nineteenth-century editions of her verse published by Thomas Park (1806) and Ewald Flügel (1892), the Queen has been primarily understood and studied as a poet through the canon established by her later editors, Caroline Pemberton and Leicester Bradner.[8]

Speeches

In 1549, the Privy Council instructed Sir Robert Tyrwhitt, who had served in Queen Catherine Parr's household, to interrogate Elizabeth about the nature of her relationship with Thomas Seymour (see the Commentary to Letters 3–7).[9] Tyrwhitt purported to record in his letters to the Council exactly what Elizabeth said to him during their interviews. It is tempting to edit these passages as samples of Elizabeth's conversation, for Tyrwhitt's transcriptions are probably as accurate a record of what Elizabeth said as many other third-party reports of Elizabeth's words as princess and queen. Yet there is no way of knowing how accurate Tyrwhitt's memory may have been. At best, he captured the essence of her remarks, as did many later scribes in their attempts to preserve their sovereign's precise words in an age before workable systems of shorthand or electronic recordings.

The parliamentary historian Sir John Neale concluded that the Queen's speeches to that body "were always composed and written by herself."[10] A dozen of them survive in more or less complete manuscript copies, of which three are holograph in whole or part while two more are secretarial copies that she personally revised and corrected.[11] These last two drafts concerned the execution of Mary, Queen of Scots, and they were officially published in 1586 (see Speeches 8 and 9). The speeches of 1563 and 1567 that come down to us in the Queen's hand, however, were not published by the government. Yet Elizabeth lavished considerable care on their wording, repeatedly changing her drafts for the sake of purely stylistic rather than substantive effects. In the text prepared for January 2, 1567, for example, she replaced "clokes" with "vissars" (vizards) to describe what had blinded the eyes of her parliamentarians. She changed "huge scroles" to "peticions" in her draft of the address for April 10, 1563, then changed "fruict" to "trees blossomes" to develop the metaphor of an heir to the throne. And a few lines later, she crossed out "mete" (fitting) and replaced it with "ripe," apparently in an effort to extend the vegetative imagery. The evidence of these drafts argues that Elizabeth was extremely sensitive to how her words would affect her parliamentary audience. Her care in this regard was, of course, only good sense, for Parliament not only enacted laws and influenced official policy—it alone could approve substantial sources of the additional funding her government required virtually throughout her reign.

Several of Elizabeth's speeches were regularly reprinted and recopied throughout the seventeenth century and beyond. Foremost among them is her address to Parliament of November 30, 1601, termed the "Golden Speech" in a pamphlet of 1659 (Speech 11). In its third state, according to Hartley's classification,[12] the speech survives in more than a dozen manuscripts and at least four printings between about 1628 and the end of the century; a 1749 reprint was duly titled *The Golden Speech of Queen Elizabeth, To Her Last Parliament.*[13] Her speech at the adjournment of Parliament in 1576 (Speech 7) is extant in eleven manuscript copies, while Speeches 8 and 9 concerning the execution of Mary, Queen of Scots, circulated widely in print and manuscript well into the Stuart era. The "Tilbury Speech" (Speech 10) was reprinted at least five times in the second half of the seventeenth century.[14] Finally, we must not forget Elizabeth's peppery and extemporaneous reply in Latin to the Polish ambassador on July 25, 1597. The speech's most recent editor cites fifteen manuscripts and four printed texts, including several English translations.[15] The Queen's public speaking remained widely available in print and manuscript for generations after her death.

Letters

While the bulk of royal correspondence was transcribed and no doubt composed by royal secretaries, three important groups of the Queen's holograph letters survive. These are, first, the letters she wrote as Princess Elizabeth before 1559, including her dedicatory letter to Queen Catherine Parr at New Year's, 1545 (Letter 1). Second, her letters dispatched to the French court during the 1570s and 1580s, especially those to her suitor, Francis, duke of Anjou, form a distinct body of holograph correspondence, nearly all of it written in French. Her letters to James VI of Scotland during the last two decades of her reign form a third collection, much of it preserved in a single volume, L: Add. MS 23240. This is the largest single collection of Elizabeth's holograph letters in English; ten of its thirty-two letters in her hand are included in this anthology.

Where letters in the Queen's hand have not survived, certain types of scribal copies have a strong claim to authenticity. These include what might today be termed "in-house" memoranda (represented in this anthology by Letters 30 and 44); they are brief notes concerning official business addressed to various court officials. The crucial subjects treated in these memoranda, and Elizabeth's use of pet names for the addressees, argue that they convey her own words even if they do not come down to us in her own handwriting. Similarly, we know that the Queen read and at times annotated at least some of the royal correspondence that she signed. For example, the scribal copy of a letter sent to the earl of Ormond in 1597 includes a marginal note assuring us that the original was "Written with her Majesty's owne hand."[16] Similarly, the postscripts appended to the otherwise secretarial contents of Letters 16 and 37 were added personally by the Queen to the lost letters for which only copies survive. Finally, but least convincingly, perhaps, her letters to individuals about such intimate matters as death of a loved one or marital difficulties seem likely to be Elizabeth's original compositions. Letters 21 and 43 represent this type of missive, along with the playful but tender message to Burghley in 1591 (Letter 33), issued as letters patent but granting him the "right" to end his mourning for his wife's death two years earlier.

Apparently, the recipients of a few of these private letters shared them with friends and they entered the networks of manuscript circulation. These documents saw widespread circulation in manuscript during the first half of the seventeenth century. The textual notes to Letter 28, Elizabeth's praise of Sir Amias Paulet, and Letter 43, her first condolence addressed to Lady Norris, undoubtedly list only a sample of the surviving copies of these letters.

Prayers

By act of her first Parliament in 1559, Elizabeth was designated Supreme Governor of the Church of England. She had herself substituted this phrase for her father's title of "Supreme Head" of the Church. The Queen took her religious responsibilities very seriously. The Protestant Reformation had, if possible, intensified the level of religious fervor in the lives of Christians on either side of the dispute. The Queen attended religious services at court and heard sermons there, often on a daily basis. She prayed publicly and she composed original prayers, some of which circulated long and widely in manuscript and in print. In her name as well, the government issued official prayers to be said throughout all the parishes of England to implore God's aid for specific difficulties or to offer him thanks for national triumphs.

In addition, Elizabeth may have sanctioned several volumes of her collected prayers, three in print and one in manuscript.[17] The *Precationes privatae. Regiae E. R.* (1563), *Christian Prayers and Meditations in English, French, Italian, Spanish, Greek, and Latin* (1569), and *Variae meditationes et preces piae* (1582) present religious devotions in the first-person voice of the Queen. The *Precationes* even includes a very personal prayer of thanksgiving for recovery from the attack of smallpox Elizabeth had suffered in 1562.[18] The *Christian Prayers* volume was published with the royal arms and printed by John Day, who held the official patent for printing the Psalms in English. Elizabeth's personal copy of this book, with its ornamental borders on each page painstakingly hand-colored, is preserved at Lambeth Palace in the library of the archbishops of Canterbury.[19] These printed volumes were apparently published with royal approval. The fourth, untitled collection has been termed "Queen Elizabeth's Prayer Book"; it survives only in a facsimile copy of the lost manuscript original.[20] The facsimile includes a miniature portrait of Elizabeth (f. 38) and another said to represent her last and most serious suitor, Francis, Duke of Anjou (f. 1v). Its six prayers, in English, French, Italian, Latin, and Greek, are also tailored to the Queen's voice.

Despite the presumptive evidence that Elizabeth wrote all the prayers in these volumes, there is room for doubt. First, the manuscript "Prayer Book" has been routinely described as entirely in Elizabeth's hand, yet its italic script features rounded letter forms unlike the angular italic hand she wrote from at least 1549.[21] The "Prayer Book" text lacks as well her characteristic spellings. This manuscript has every appearance of being a gift prepared for presentation to the Queen rather than her own work. To be sure, Elizabeth could have written all of these printed and manuscript prayers but left preparation of their texts to others, whether printers or scribes. Significant evidence suggests, however, that the Queen considered the prayers she composed herself to be personal communications with the Deity that were not to be made public. Even her prayers at the time of the Spanish Armada— Prayer 2 and her poetic prayers, Poems 8 and 9—saw no official dissemination. Nor did she send a copy of Prayer 4 to Essex and Lord Admiral Howard, commanders of the 1596 "Cádiz Raid." One authoritative text of the prayer affirms that this is "Her Majesty's private meditation upon the present expedition, sent from Sir Robert Cecil to the generals of her Highness' army at

Plymouth."²² In the letter, Secretary Cecil emphasizes the risk he has taken to acquaint them with the prayer: "That which was only meant a secret sacrifice to one I have presumed out of trust to participate with two. It came to my hands accidently; I dare scarce justify the sight, much less the copy."²³ He concludes by asking them to keep what he has shared with them in the strictest confidence. Similarly, when Elizabeth learned that her prayer for the good success of the following year's naval expedition had been published by her archbishop of Canterbury, she demanded not only that the printing cease but that her prayer be removed from all copies of the tract already in print (see the commentary to Prayer 5). It is worth noting that this prayer was not published under Elizabeth's name, but merely appeared in the pamphlet opposite the royal arms and in a different font from the other prayers in the volume. Although John Norden published a copy of Prayer 4 in at least three editions of his *Progresse of Pietie* (reprinted in *The Pensive Mans Practise*) between 1596 and 1603, no official publication of any prayer unquestionably by Elizabeth is known to have taken place during her reign. She apparently did not object to the composition and publication of prayers for her use, including prayers worded in her person. But she distinguished these from her own prayers to God, prayers she considered too personal for widespread circulation.

Ironically, several of Elizabeth's prayers saw widespread circulation, and the prayer for the "Cádiz Raid" may qualify as her best known, most widely disseminated composition in the century and a half after her death. The "Armada" prayer (Prayer 2), along with her prayers for the naval expeditions of 1596 and 1597 (Prayers 4 and 5), appeared in forty-five editions of Thomas Sorocold's *Supplications of Saints* between 1612 and 1754. The "Armada" prayer was also reprinted in a 1688 broadside, while Prayer 5 survives in the censored printing of 1597 and a handful of manuscript copies. But her prayer for the "Cádiz Raid" saw even wider circulation. Beyond the Sorocold reprints and its appearance in the 1688 broadside, Prayer 4 appeared, as already mentioned, in at least three editions of devotional works by John Norden as well as in Camden's *Annals* (1634); and it survives in at least a dozen manuscript copies.

Essays

The earliest original texts of the works included here as Essays 1 and 2 categorize them as letters. One set of copies in the Elizabethan State Papers, but written in a post-Elizabethan, seventeenth-century hand, is endorsed "A Couple of Letters of the Queen endited and written at one time."[24] The set of copies printed in *Nugae Antiquae,* derived from the Harington family papers, describe both texts as "The Letter the Queene's Majesty wrote, whylest she gave instructions for the other that followith, and hearing a tale which she made answer unto."[25] From these complementary descriptions we can reconstruct the circumstances under which both texts were composed. The Queen wrote out Essay 1 in response to being asked "what grief encumbered my breast, together with the remedy that may cure the sore?" At the same time, she responded in Essay 2 to the question, "Must ought be denied a friend's request?" This is "The Letter dictated by the Queen," according to the *Nugae Antiquae* draft. Thus, her essays were "endited and written at one time" as the State Papers endorsement indicates. The context that emerges here is a courtly discussion of the nature of friendship as related to a specific cause for sorrow in Elizabeth's private life. Friendship was one of the most popular subjects of moral inquiry during the English Renaissance. Elizabeth demonstrated her versatility as thinker and writer on the subject by responding to both questions simultane-ously: she dictated one text as she wrote out the other. The results are thus not letters in the sense of royal correspondence but writ-ten exercises on a given theme posed by her companions at court.[26]

Translations

As a normal part of her schooling in foreign languages, Elizabeth learned to translate Latin, Greek, French, Italian, and eventually Spanish into English. She composed as well original works in foreign tongues in order to sharpen her skills as a linguist. If Elizabeth's prose style can be fairly judged to range between competent and elegant, the same cannot be said for most of her translations from foreign languages into English. Whether in prose or verse, these are frequently so awkward in syntax, so remote from idiomatic expression, as to be at times incomprehensible. Unaware that they criticized the work of a former sovereign, the editors of the catalogue of Royal manuscripts in the British Library described Elizabeth's translation of Plutarch (Translations, Poetry 2), as "A would-be Poem, without rhyme, or sense." [27] We are left to wonder how the Queen could write such felicitous English prose of her own, but then produce such tortured discourse as a translator.

Part of the answer may lie in her concern for speed in translating some of these works. The time she spent on the excerpts from Plutarch and Horace, and on her translation of Boethius's *Consolation of Philosophy,* is calculated to the day and hour in the contemporary manuscripts of these works. Although these calculations flatter the Queen by underestimating the time involved, it is clear from the rough state of these manuscripts that she worked rapidly.[28] Another influence on the idiosyncratic style of Elizabeth's translations was the way she learned Latin and Greek under the supervision of Roger Ascham, who guided her study of these languages even after she became queen. Praising his royal pupil in *The Scholemaster* (1570), Ascham affirmed that "beside her perfit readines, in *Latin, Italian, French,* and *Spanish,* she readeth here now at Windsore more Greeke every day, than some Prebendarie of this Chirch doth read *Latin* in a whole weeke."[29] As her translations of Horace and Plutarch in 1598 witness, Elizabeth maintained her facility in foreign languages virtually to the end of her reign. But what form did this practice take? Ascham's method required his pupil first to construe a passage from the classics into English, then "parse it ouer againe: so, that it may appeare, that the childe douteth in nothing" about its meaning. After at least an hour's wait, the student would then "translate his owne Englishe into latin againe."[30] Working in this fashion, Elizabeth translated the chief classical authors, including significant portions of the works of Cicero, Horace, Virgil, Hesiod, Homer, and Plutarch. The second half of the task, retranslation into the original tongue, would have been immeasurably complicated had Elizabeth rendered the Latin or Greek into smooth and idiomatic English. It was far easier—indeed, a practical necessity—to work backward from an English version that followed as closely as possible the syntax of the original. Thus Elizabeth learned to translate, and to understand as a linguistic medium, expression that mimicked the syntax and idiom of her classical models, however alien to a clear and graceful English style. The influence of this training, moreover, appears in some of Elizabeth's original compositions. In Poem 4, for example, "Their dazzled eyes with pride" and "My rusty sword through rest" (for "eyes dazzled with pride" and "sword rusty through rest") show the Queen imposing Latinate syntax on her English expression. The awkward convolutions and syncopations of Elizabeth's translation style result largely from her years of work with foreign languages under Ascham's tutelage.

Notes

1. L: Lansdowne MS 253, f. 200.

2. Sir John Harington, *Nugae Antiquae,* ed. Henry Harington, ed. Thomas Park (London, 1804), 1:109–14; Sir Harris Nicolas, *Memoirs of the Life and Times of Sir Christopher Hatton* (London, 1847), p. 127.

3. Harington, *Nugae Antiquae,* 1:140–43.

4. For the text and English translation of the latter work, see Steven W. May and Anne Lake Prescott, "The French Verses of Elizabeth I," *English Literary Renaissance* 24 (1994): 9–43.

5. This copy of Coverdale's New Testament (1538) is now L: printed book, shelfmark C.45.a.13, flyleaf 9 verso.

6. In Tottel's anthology, the poem begins, "The lyfe is long that lothsumly doth last." Hatton reminded Elizabeth that "The life (as you well remember), is too long that loathsomely lasteth," in the letter edited in Nicolas, *Memoirs,* p. 26.

7. Leicester Bradner, *The Poems of Queen Elizabeth I* (Providence, R.I., 1964), pp. 77–78, categorized as doubtful the Queen's alleged response to Latin verses addressed to her by "Melissus," the German humanist Paul Schede. The French poem is edited in May and Prescott, "French Verses."

8. Thomas Park attempted the first collected edition of the Queen's poetry in his completion of Horace Walpole's *Catalogue of the Royal and Noble Authors of England, Scotland, and Ireland* (London, 1806). Ewald Flügel's "Die Gedichte der Königin Elisabeth," *Anglia* 14 (1892): 346–61, expanded the canon but added spurious works as well. In addition to the

Queen's verse translations of Boethius, Horace, and Plutarch, Caroline Pemberton's *Queen Elizabeth's Englishings of Boethius, Plutarch, and Horace,* Early English Text Society, original ser. 113 (London, 1899), includes the prose text of her *Consolation of Philosophy.* Bradner's 1964 edition, *The Poems of Queen Elizabeth I,* contains only her poetry. Fifteen original poems attributed to the Queen appear in *Elizabeth I: Collected Works,* ed. Leah S. Marcus, Janel Mueller, and Mary Beth Rose (Chicago, 2000). This anthology omits Elizabeth's verse translations, however.

9. C. R. Manning, "State Papers Relating to the Custody of the Princess Elizabeth at Woodstock," *Norfolk Archaeology* 4 (1855): 133–231.

10. J. E. Neale, *Elizabeth I and Her Parliaments, 1559–1581* (1953; reprint, Norwich, 1969), p. 50.

11. The holographs are L: Lansdowne 94, f. 30 (April 10, 1563); L: Cotton Charter 4.38, ff. 2–2v (January 2, 1567); and PRO: SP 12/41, f. 8 (opening of the speech delivered November 5, 1567). L: Lansdowne 94, ff. 84–85 (November 12, 1586) and ff. 86–88v (November 24, 1586) are scribal drafts corrected by Elizabeth.

12. Hartley, 3:294–97. In addition to ten manuscripts of the text cited here, this version was also copied into Folger MSS X.d.152, ff. 4–8v, and V.a.142, ff. 2–4v, and in O: Rawl. MS D.1045, pp. 84–91.

13. *The Golden Speech of Queen Elizabeth, To Her Last Parliament* (London: Printed for Richard Offtey, in the Year 1749). See also STC 7579 (ca. 1628), *Queene Elizabeths Speech to her Last Parliament* (editions in 1642, 1647, 1659, and later but undated), and the text in *Historical Collections . . . Proceedings of the Four Last Parliaments of Q. Elizabeth* (1680).

14. See the textual notes to these speeches and Hartley's lists of sources.

15. Janet M. Green, "Queen Elizabeth I's Latin Reply to the Polish Ambassador," *Sixteenth Century Journal* 31 (2000): 987–1008.

16. Guildhall Library, London, MS 1752, f. 287.

17. For a useful survey of the prayers attributed to Elizabeth, see Tucker Brooke, "Queen Elizabeth's Prayers," *Huntington Library Quarterly* 2 (1938): 69–77.

18. For an English translation of this prayer and other foreign language prayers in both the printed and transcribed collections, see Marcus, Mueller, and Rose, eds., *Collected Works*, pp. 135–63.

19. Lambeth Palace MS 1049. For analysis of the adaptation for Elizabeth's use of prayers in this copy of the book, see John N. King, *Tudor Royal Iconography* (Princeton, 1989), pp. 112–14.

20. L: MS Facs. 218, with an introduction signed J. W. (John Southwood), 1893 (f. iii verso). The facsimile was edited by Adam Fox with a translation of the foreign-language prayers as *A Book of Devotions Composed by Her Majesty* (Gerrards Cross, 1970).

21. The surviving examples of her italic script after 1558 are rare, yet in them Elizabeth's usage is consistent with her hand as princess (see, for example, her subscription to Letter 18, Lambeth Palace MS 3197, f. 41; figure 11 in Marcus, Mueller, and Rose, eds., *Collected Works*, p. 213).

22. L: Cotton MS Otho E.9, f. 209.

23. The letter itself is preserved in O: Tanner 76, f. 30. Here, "participate" means "share," and "justify the sight" expresses his doubt that he can defend as proper having so much as seen the prayer (let alone sending a copy to Essex and Howard).

24. PRO: SP 12/235, f. 4Av.

25. Harington, *Nugae Antiquae*, 1:115.

26. The *OED* classifies as obsolete this definition of "letters" as "writings, written records," but cites one example as late as 1789 (s.v. "letter," II.3.b).

27. Sir George F. Warner and Julius P. Gilson, *Catalogue of Western Manuscripts in the Old Royal and King's Collections* (London, 1921), 2:224. That this is the work of Queen Elizabeth has not heretofore been noticed.

28. See my *Elizabethan Courtier Poets: The Poems and Their Contexts* (Columbia, Mo., 1991), p. 135, for a summary of these calculations. Pemberton (*Queen Elizabeth's Englishings*, p. viii) found it barely possible to copy out a page of Elizabeth's text as rapidly as the Queen was said to have translated it.

29. Roger Ascham, *English Works,* ed. William Aldis Wright (1904; reprint, Cambridge, 1970), p. 219.

30. Ibid., p. 183.

Editorial Procedures

This representative selection of the writings of Queen Elizabeth I provides reliable texts with emphasis in the commentary and textual notes on the transmission and relative popularity of her works. The question of authenticity is, of course, crucial to understanding Elizabeth as a writer. As with any author, we can assess her writing talents only to the extent that we can study the words she herself generated. This question extends equally to her translations, where we recognize that the substance belongs to someone else while the immediate expression, with its unique tone and style, characterizes the author we are studying. Beyond normal and predictable problems of determining what anyone wrote or said in the sixteenth century, Elizabeth I confronts her editors with unusual difficulties in the quest for authenticity simply because she was born a princess and became a queen. Much that she wrote before 1559 has come down to us in her own handwriting, yet holograph texts do not necessarily guarantee that these are her own words. About 1555, for example, she presented her lady-in-waiting Anne Poyntz with a printed copy of the New Testament in which she inscribed four lines of verse. But what appears to be a quatrain that Princess Elizabeth composed for this particular occasion turns out to be excerpted from an anonymous poem that circulated in manuscript while she was a child and that was later printed in Tottel's *Songs and Sonnets* (1557).[1]

The greatest threat to retrieving her authentic writings, however, is posed by the fact that Elizabeth was surrounded throughout her life by an entourage of servants, tutors, and secretaries prepared to help her with the varied kinds of writing demanded by her station in life. As princess and queen she could always delegate, in whole or part, whatever she needed to write to members of her household staff. We know that she entrusted her governess, Catherine Ashley, with composing letters for her on several occasions as Princess Elizabeth. In Letter 4 she states that instead of writing to Lord Admiral Seymour herself, "I bade her [Ashley] write as she thought best, and bade her show it me when she had done." In addition, in writing to William Cecil on her mistress's behalf, Ashley apologized that Elizabeth was busy studying and had asked her to draft the letter to him.[2] Again, we cannot know the extent to which her early holograph letters were planned, phrased, or composed outright by members of her household staff.

After Elizabeth's ascent to the throne, moreover, she signed her name to thousands of official letters, warrants, grants, and bills written for her in whole or part by others. The Crown secretariat included not only her principal secretaries—men such as William Cecil, Francis Walsingham, and Thomas Smith—but secretaries to write in the Latin and French tongues, work ably performed during the reign by Roger Ascham, Charles Yetsweirt, and Thomas Edmonds, among others.[3] Their role in the drafting of official correspondence is revealed by the Queen's conclusion to a personal letter she wrote to Sir Henry Sidney in 1565, for she orders him to conceal the fact that she has written to him directly: "Seem not to have had but Secretaries' Letters from me."[4] Elizabeth here defines the gulf between a mere secretary's letter, a formal missive signed by the Queen, and Elizabeth's own words to the recipient, a "familiar letter." The degree to which court employees could interfere with a document overtly authored by the

Queen is illustrated by a letter endorsed "To Sir Ro. Williams from her Majesty 5º July 1592" (PRO: SP 78/28, ff. 254–55). The text itself concerns redeployment of English troops in France. The much-crossed out and corrected draft is largely in Lord Burghley's handwriting, but concludes with the note that its ending "as it is contained in the letter [is] written with Mr. Yetsweirt's hand." Indeed, a quite different hand interrupts the letter's last sentence and finishes the draft. It is possible—but unlikely, I think—that the Queen dictated the original text and all its revisions to Burghley and then ordered Yetsweirt to make the final copy and send it to Williams. It seems more likely that she approved the letter's general contents in advance. Burghley and Yetsweirt then worded the draft and Elizabeth signed the final copy for dispatch. If so, analysis of this document will reveal much about Lord Burghley's compositional skills, and perhaps something about those of Charles Yetsweirt, but little if anything at all about the Queen as a writer. When Elizabeth reviewed a document generated by one or more of her officers, then signed her name to it, she expressed her political understanding and will but served at best as a collaborator in the final product.

I have selected the following texts from among those I judged the most likely to be the Queen's original compositions in English. They constitute a wide range of expression, from original poetry to letters of condolence and rebuke to prayers that stand among her most widely circulated works. While it is true that most of her poetry, letters, and translations survive in one or two copies preserved in private or official archives, a few, including several of her speeches to Parliament, saw considerable circulation in both print and manuscript long after her death. Elizabeth prided herself on being a monarch accessible to her people. She intentionally used some of her personal writings to fulfill this agenda while in other instances texts escaped official control and disseminated her words independently or even against her will.

This edition presents texts in modern spelling and punctuation that seek to transmit Elizabeth's meanings as faithfully as possible for today's readers. I have retained original punctuation and paragraphing where that does not seem to obstruct understanding of the Queen's intentions, but for the most part these accidentals of the text are editorial.

Notes

1. British Library printed book, shelfmark C.45.a.13, flyleaf 9 verso. Besides Tottel, a complete text of this anonymous poem (beginning "If right be racked and overrun"), occurs in Trinity College Dublin MS 160, f. 179.

2. Cited by James Daybell, "Women's Letters and Letter Writing in England, 1540–1603: An Introduction to the Issues of Authorship and Construction," *Shakespeare Studies* 27 (1999): 165.

3. See, e.g., the Queen's letter to the earl of Shrewsbury, October 21, 1572, drafted and corrected entirely in the hand of William Cecil, Lord Burghley (PRO: SP 12/89, f. 128).

4. Arthur Collins, *Letters and Memorials of State* (London, 1746), vol. 1, second p. 8.

Queen Elizabeth I

I

Original Poems

Poem 1

Woodstock, 1555.
From Universitätsbibliothek Basel MS Λ, 7–8,
the diary of Thomas Platter.

A[t] Woodstock Manor. 1555.

Oh fortune, thy wresting,[1] wavering state
Hath fraught[2] with cares my troubled wit,[3]
Whose witness this present prison late[4]
Could bear, where once was joy flown quite.
Thou caused'st the guilty to be loosed   [5
From bands where innocents were enclosed,
And caused the guiltless to be reserved,[5]
And freed those that death had well deserved.
But herein can be nothing wrought.[6]
So God send to my foes as they have thought.   [10
    Finis. Elisabetha the prisoner, 1555

Notes

1. *wresting:* turning
2. *fraught:* burdened
3. *wit:* mind
4. *late:* lately
5. *reserved:* set apart, restrained
6. *wrought:* performed, accomplished

Commentary

Elizabeth wrote these lines in charcoal on a wall at Woodstock Palace, where she was imprisoned by Queen Mary from June 1554 until April 17, 1555. The only extant contemporary texts were transcribed by Continental visitors to the palace (see the textual notes).

Textual Notes

Platter's text has been reprinted in Clare Williams, *Thomas Platter's Travels in England, 1599* (London, 1937), pp. 220–21, and in Thomas Platter, *Beschreibung der Reisen durch Frankreich, Spanien, England und die Niederlande 1595–1600,* ed. Rut Keiser (Basel, 1968), 2:859. I am grateful to Dr. Lukas Erne for checking this transcription against the original manuscript at Basel. See G. W. Groos, ed., *The Diary of Baron Waldstein* (London, 1981), pp. 117, 119, for the text copied at Woodstock by this nobleman in 1600. A third foreign visitor, Paul Hentzner, copied the poem on September 13, 1598. A corrupt version of his transcription was published in *Itinerarivm Germaniae, Galliae; Angliae; Italiae; Scriptum a Paulo Hentznero J C* (1612), sig. S4v–T1. A mutilated version of the poem in an eighteenth-century hand is found in British Library Add. MS 4457, f. 6.

Poem 2

Woodstock, 1555. John Foxe,
Actes and Monuments (1563), sig. 2nd 4N7v.

Much suspected by[1] *me,*
Nothing proved can be.
Quod[2] *Elisabeth the prisoner.*

Notes
1. *by:* about.
2. *quod:* quoth

Commentary

According to Foxe, Elizabeth wrote these lines "with her dia-
mond in a glass window" at Woodstock Palace, where, with Poem
1, they were routinely shown to visitors. Unlike Poem 1, however,
this couplet was widely disseminated in England during the
Queen's reign. It was printed in Foxe's "Book of Martyrs" (six editions during Elizabeth's reign, between 1563 and 1597), as well as
in Holinshed's *Chronicles* (1587), vol. 3, sig. 5S2; in Anthony
Munday's *A Watch-Woord to Englande* (1584), sig. I1; and in the
notes to Sir John Harington's translation of *Orlando Furioso*
(1591), sig. 2L2. Manuscript copies include Harington's draft of
the *Orlando Furioso* (British Library Add. MS 18920, f. 322) and
two seventeenth-century texts in NLW, Sotheby MS B2, f. 59v.

Poem 3

Royal Library, Windsor Castle,
holograph on the last page of text in a copy
of a French Psalter published in Paris ca. 1520.

No crooked leg, no bleared eye,
No part deformed out of kind,[1]
Nor yet so ugly half can be
As is the inward,[2] suspicious mind.
   Your loving mistress,
     Elizabeth

Notes

1. *out of kind:* so as to be unnatural
2. *inward:* secret

Commentary

Elizabeth inscribed these lines when she presented the psalter to a servant or friend at some time before November 17, 1558. Her signature establishes the approximate date, for after her name she drew a square knot with four loops. It mimics the knot that Henry VIII added to his signatures, and was the symbol Elizabeth ordinarily used as princess. She replaced the knot with the letter "R" (for *Regina*) upon becoming queen.

Textual Notes

The text as transcribed here is published by gracious permission of Her Majesty Queen Elizabeth II. The verse and signature occupy most of the bottom half of the printed page and Elizabeth made no effort to present her work as a verse stanza: the lines break at "bleared," "out," "ugly," and "inward."

Poem 4

Folger MS V.b.317, f. 20v.

The doubt[1] of future foes exiles my present joy,
And wit[2] me warns to shun such snares as threatens
  mine annoy,[3]
For falsehood now doth flow, and subjects' faith
  doth ebb,
Which should not be if reason ruled or wisdom
  weaved the web.
But clouds of joys untried do cloak aspiring minds,   [5
Which turns to rain of late repent[4] by changèd course
  of winds.
The top[5] of hope supposed, the root of rue[6] shall be,
And fruitless all their grafted[7] guile as shortly you
  shall see.
Their dazzled eyes with pride,[8] which great ambition
  blinds
Shall be unsealed[9] by worthy wights[10] whose foresight
  falsehood finds.   [10
The daughter of debate, that discord aye[11] doth sow
Shall reap no gain where former rule still[12] peace hath
  taught to know.
No foreign, banished wight shall anchor in this port;
Our realm brooks no seditious sects, let them elsewhere
  resort.
My rusty sword through rest shall first his[13] edge
  employ   [15
To poll[14] their tops who seek such change or gape for[15]
  future joy.

Notes

1. *doubt:* fear
2. *wit:* intellect, reason
3. *annoy:* annoyance, trouble
4. *repent:* repentance
5. *top:* flowering head
6. *rue:* sorrow, regret (with likely pun on the bitter shrub of the same spelling)
7. *grafted:* implanted
8. That is, "Their eyes dazzled with pride." This construction is influenced by Elizabeth's knowledge of Latin syntax, as is "My rusty sword through rest" (l. 15), for "My sword, rusty through rest."
9. *unsealed:* opened
10. *wights:* persons
11. *aye:* continuously
12. *still:* continuously
13. *his:* its
14. *poll:* cut off
15. *gape for:* are eager to obtain

Commentary

The Catholic Mary, Queen of Scots, had been held captive in England since 1568 when she fled Scotland after the scandal of her husband's murder. In the fall of 1569, English Catholics led by the earls of Northumberland and Westmorland attempted to free Mary by force and overthrow the Elizabethan regime. Their uprising, termed the "Northern Rebellion," was effectively suppressed early in the new year. Elizabeth's prophetic and anxious response to this victory saw widespread circulation after Lady Willoughby copied the poem from the Queen's tablet.[1]

1. Steven W. May, *Elizabethan Courtier Poets: The Poems and Their Contexts* (Columbia, Mo., 1991), pp. 47–48. For further comment, see Jennifer Summit, " 'The Arte of a Ladies Penne': Elizabeth I and the Poetics of Queenship," *English Literary Renaissance* 26 (1996): 395–422.

Textual Notes

This poem circulated in both manuscript and print. Contemporary transcribed copies include the *Arundel Harington Manuscript of Tudor Poetry* (f. 164v), ed. Ruth Hughey, 2 vols. (Columbus, Oh., 1960); another text from Harington family papers was published in Sir John Harington, *Nugae Antiquae,* ed. Henry Harington (London, 1769), 1:58–59; London, Inner Temple Petyt MS 538.10, f. 3v; L: Egerton MS 2642, f. 237v; Harleian MS 6933, f. 8; Harleian MS 7392(2), f. 27v; NLW, Ottley Papers; O: Digby MS 138, f. 159; Rawlinson Poet. MS 108, f. 44v. George Puttenham published a version of the poem in *The Arte of English Poesie* (1589), sig. 2E2v. The copy text has been emended at line 6, "rain" for "rage," and line 16, "poll" for the scribe's possible spelling variant, "pul."

Poems 5a, 5b

Pierpont Morgan Library, PML 7768, first flyleaf, recto.

5a

Genus infoelix vitae
Multum vigilavi, laboravi, presto multis fui,
Stultitiam multorum perpessa sum,
Arrogantiam pertuli, Difficultates exorbui,
Vixi ad aliorum arbitrium, non ad meum.   [5

5b

A hapless kind of life is this I wear,[1]
Much watch I dure,[2] and weary, toiling days,
I serve the rout,[3] and all their follies bear,
I suffer pride, and sup[4] full hard assays,[5]
To others' will my life is all addressed,   [5
And no way so as[6] might content me best.

Notes
   1. *wear:* endure
   2. *watch I dure:* wakefulness I undergo
   3. *rout:* rabble
   4. *sup:* taste, experience
   5. *assays:* trials, tribulations
   6. *no . . . as:* no course of action that

Commentary

Both poems were transcribed in Sir Thomas Heneage's copy of Henry Bull's *Christian Prayers and Holy Meditations* (1570).[1] As a gentleman of the Privy Chamber from the beginning of Elizabeth's reign, Heneage was an esteemed favorite whose testimony about the Queen's authorship of these poems is almost certainly reliable. The English translation (Poem 5b) is subscribed, "This above was written in a booke by the Queenes Majestie." Elizabeth apparently wrote the Latin version with its unusual cross-rhyme, then translated it into English.

1. These poems, with Heneage's sonnet in response to the Queen's lament, were discovered and first published by Curt F. Bühler in "Libri Impressi cum Notis Manuscriptis," *Modern Language Notes* 53 (1938): 245–49.

Poem 6

O: Tanner MS 76, f. 94.

Sonetto

I grieve and dare not show my discontent;
I love and yet am forced to seem to hate;
I do, yet dare not say I ever meant,[1]
I seem stark mute, but inwardly do prate,
   I am, and not; I freeze, and yet am burned,   [5
   Since from myself another self I turned.

My care is like my shadow in the sun,
Follows me flying, flies when I pursue it,
Stands and lies by me, doth what I have done,
His too-familiar care doth make me rue it.   [10
   No means I find to rid him from my breast,
   Til by the end of things it[2] be suppressed.

Some gentler passion slide into my mind,
For I am soft and made of melting snow;
Or be more cruel, Love, and so be kind,   [15
Let me or[3] float, or sink, be high or low,
   Or let me live with some more sweet content,
   Or die and so forget what love e'er meant.
     Eliz. Regina.

Notes

   1. *meant:* intendèd (with an implied object related to the grief and love of ll. 1–2)

2. *it:* i.e., her care for him

3. *or:* either

Commentary

Three of the five manuscripts of this poem associate it with Elizabeth's parting from "Monsieur"—Francis, duke of Anjou, her last suitor.[1] After protracted marriage negotiations and months of courtship in London during the winter of 1581–82, Anjou left England in February without a nuptial agreement; he died in May 1584. All five texts of this poem are closely related, and all postdate the occasion for which it was written by more than thirty years. The lack of contemporary copies of this love lament casts some doubt on its authenticity, yet each of the extant manuscripts attributes it to the Queen; it is possible that this very personal composition was discovered only after her death.

1. The others are O: Ashmole MS 781, p. 142; Leeds University MS Lt q 57, f. 3v; and L: Stowe MS 962, f. 231v. The fifth text occurs in NLW: MS 12443A, part 2, pp. 50–51.

Textual Notes

Water damage has largely obliterated the Ashmole MS 781 text. As transcribed by John Nichols (*Progresses and Public Processions of Queen Elizabeth,* new ed. [London, 1823], 2:346), this version differs from the Tanner MS in only two readings: "my other" for "another" (l. 6), and "passions" for "passion" (l. 13). Among other variants from the Tanner text, the Leeds MS *(L),* Stowe MS *(S),* and NLW MS *(W)* record the following corrupt readings:

3 yet dare] yet I dare *W*
8 pursue it] pursue *W*
12 things] living *S*
13 some] come *L;* gentler] greater *S*

Poem 7. Sir Walter Ralegh to the Queen and Her Answer

Wiltshire Record Office MS 865/500, f. 27.

7a. Sir Walter Ralegh to the Queen

A sonnet

Fortune hath taken thee away, my love,
My life's joy and my soul's heaven above;
Fortune hath taken thee away my princess,
My world's delight and my true fancy's mistress.

Fortune hath taken all away from me,   [5
Fortune hath taken all by taking thee;
Dead to all joys, I only live to woe,
So Fortune now becomes my fancy's foe.

In vain mine eyes, in vain you waste your tears,
In vain my sighs, the smokes of my despairs,   [10
In vain you search the earth and heavens above,
In vain you search, for fortune keeps my love.

Then will I leave my love in Fortune's hands,
Then will I leave my love in worthless bands,[1]
And only love the sorrow due to me;   [15
Sorrow, henceforth that shall my princess be,

And only joy that Fortune conquers kings,
Fortune that rules on earth and earthly things

Hath ta'en my love in spite of virtue's might:
So blind a goddess did never virtue right.   [20

With wisdom's eyes had but blind Fortune seen,
Then had my love my love forever been;
But love, farewell, though Fortune conquer thee,
No Fortune base shall ever alter me.

Notes

1. *bands:* bonds, restraints

7b. The Queen's answer

An answer

Ah silly pug,[1] wert thou so sore[2] afraid?
Mourn not, my Wat,[3] nor be thou so dismayed;
It passeth[4] fickle Fortune's power and skill
To force my heart to think thee any ill.[5]

No Fortune base, thou sayest, shall alter thee;   [5
And may so blind a wretch then conquer me?
No, no, my pug, though Fortune were not blind,
Assure thyself she could not rule my mind.

Ne chose I thee[6] by foolish Fortune's rede,[7]
Ne[8] can she make me alter with such speed,   [10
But must thou needs[9] sour sorrow's servant be,
If that to try[10] thy mistress jest with thee.

Fortune, I grant, sometimes doth conquer kings,
And rules and reigns on earth and earthly things,
But never think that Fortune can bear sway,   [15
If virtue watch[11] and will her not obey.

Pluck up thy heart, suppress thy brackish tears,
Torment thee not, but put away thy fears,
Thy love, thy joy, she loves no worthless bands,[12]
Much less to be in reeling Fortune's hands.   [20

Dead to all joys and living unto woe,
Slain quite by her that never gave wiseman blow,
Revive again and live without all dread,
The less afraid the better shalt thou speed.[13]

Notes

1. *pug:* (a term of endearment)
2. *sore:* sorely, intensely
3. *Wat:* nickname for Walter
4. *passeth:* surpasses, goes beyond
5. *think . . . ill:* think any ill of you
6. *Ne . . . thee:* I did not choose you
7. *rede:* counsel
8. *Ne:* nor
9. *must . . . needs:* you must necessarily
10. *If . . . try:* If to test that (i.e., her commitment to him)
11. *watch:* be vigilant
12. *bands:* bonds, restraints
13. *speed:* succeed

Commentary

The text of Ralegh's poem in L: Additional MS 63742 suggests that it was circulating by 1587, just at the time that Robert Devereux, second earl of Essex, eclipsed Ralegh as the Queen's leading favorite. By complaining that fortune had robbed him of Elizabeth's favor, Ralegh may have intended to remind her of her own vulnerability to a social superior, her half-sister Mary, and the verses she wrote (Poem 1) to lament her confinement at Woodstock by Mary's command. Elizabeth's response to Ralegh, however, consistently treats fortune as the blind goddess of fate, not the rival nobleman whose inroads into her favor elicited Ralegh's complaint.

Ralegh's verse lament apparently entered widespread manuscript circulation not long after he wrote it, for a ballad of "Fortune hath taken thee awaye my love, beinge the true dittie thereof" was entered in the Stationers' Register on June 13, 1590. A two-part ballad on the subject was also entered in the Register on September 22, 1604—no doubt a source text for the much-altered versions of these companion poems that were published as broadside ballads in the seventeenth century. For further analysis of the textual history of both poems in print and manuscript see my *Elizabethan Courtier Poets: The Poems and Their Contexts* (Columbia, Mo., 1991), pp. 319–20.

Poem 8

John Rhodes, *The Countrie Mans Comfort* (1637), sig. D6–6v.

8.

Two most excellent songs or Ditties, made by Queene Elizabeth, as it is credibly reported (and as it is very likely by some
words in it) in the yeare 1588. When the Spaniard came to possess this land and is in manner of a prayer to God.

Deliver me, O Lord my God, from all my foes that be:
And eke[1] *defend all Christian souls that put their trust*
  in thee.
Preserve us now and evermore from all the wicked
  train,[2]
Who long and thirst for Christians' blood and never will
  refrain.

Mine enemies, O Lord, be strong, and thou the same
  dost know,   [5
And that without offence in me, they seek mine
  overthrow.
My hope and help in all distress hath ever been in
  thee:
And thou, O Lord, of[3] *thy goodness didst still*[4]
  deliver me.
Come now and end this strife likewise, the cause is
  wholly thine:
Wherefore to thee myself and suit,[5] *I wholly do resign.*   [10

Notes

1. *eke:* also
2. *train:* crowd
3. *of:* through
4. *still:* always
5. *suit:* personal service

Commentary, Poems 8 and 9

These songs work together as a prayer to God for deliverance from the Spanish Armada and a prayer of thanksgiving after its defeat. The National Maritime Museum MS was described among the "Manuscripts of John Henry Gurney, Keswick Hall, Norfolk," before the dispersal of that collection.[1] A version of Poem 9 was also printed in Rhodes's book, which, he claimed, was originally published in 1588. An entry for *The Countrie Mans Comfort* in the Stationers' Register in that year confirms the assertion, although no copy of the first edition is known. Insofar as the National Maritime Museum manuscript supports Rhodes's attribution of Poem 9 to the Queen, there is no reason to doubt that the first hymn he attributes to her is also authentic. Use of the archaic "eke" in Poem 8, line 2, is matched, for example, by seven uses of the word in her translation of Plutarch.[2] Her protest in lines 5–6 that her enemies have attacked her without provocation is a common theme in Elizabeth's prayers and speeches.

Both Poems 8 and 9 are indebted in their language and sentiments to the Old Testament Psalms tradition without being translations or close adaptations of any one of them. Poem 8, however, resembles Psalm 59 in its appeal to God to "deliver me from mine enemies," its insistence on the power of these "bloodie men," and on the innocence of the singer: "the mightie men are gathered against me, not for mine offense, nor for my sinne, O Lord" (Geneva Bible, 1560, p. 247). Psalm 140 likewise opens with a plea to "Deliver me, O Lord, from the evil man," and emphasizes the adversary's power and cruelty. Psalm 86 begins, "Incline thine eare, O Lord, and heare me," and represents the singer as God's "servant." Verse 10 echoes line 6, "For thou art great and doest wonderous things," and the reference in verse 16 to saving "the sonne of thine handmaid" recalls Elizabeth as God's handmaid in line 2 of Poem 9.

1. HMC, *Twelfth Report, Appendix,* part 9 (London, 1891), p. 128.

2. See below, Plutarch, *De curiositate* (Translations, Poetry 2), ll. 14, 39, 70, 90, 271, 278, 378.

Poem 9

National Maritime Museum, Greenwich, MS SNG/4.

A song made by her Majesty and sung before her at her coming from Whitehall to Paul's through Fleetstreet in Anno Dmi 1588. Sung in December after the scattering of the Spanish Navy.

Look and bow down thine ear, O Lord, from thy bright
    sphere behold and see,
Thy handmaid and thy handiwork[1] amongst thy priests
    offering to thee,
Zeal for incense reaching the skies,
Myself and scepter, sacrifice.

My soul ascend his holy place, ascribe him strength
    and sing him praise,   [5
For he refraineth[2] princes' spirits, and hath done
    wonders in my days:
He made the winds and waters rise
To scatter all mine enemies.[3]

This Joseph's Lord and Israel's God, the fiery pillar and
    day's cloud,[4]
That saved his saints from wicked men and drenched
    the honor of the proud,   [10
And hath preserved in tender love
The spirit of his turtle dove.[5]

Notes

1. *handiwork:* Elizabeth, as part of God's creation

2. *refraineth:* restrains, holds back

3. Violent storms plagued the Spanish Armada after it had been forced into the North Sea by the English fleet.

4. The reference here is to the pillar of cloud by day and pillar of fire by night by which God conducted the Israelites out of Egypt (Exodus 13.21).

5. Elizabeth may allude here to Psalm 74.19, where the psalmist prays that God "Give not the soule of thy turtle doove unto the beast." A marginal gloss in the Geneva Bible (1560) identifies the dove as "the Church of God, which is exposed as a pray [prey] to the wicked."

Poems Possibly by Elizabeth

Possible Poem 1

Cardiff Central Library MS 3.42, p. 26.

Sir Walter Ralegh wrote this verse in the Queen's garden:
  Fain would I climb but am afraid to fall
The Queen coming by, knowing whose inditing it was,
    wrote under as followeth:
  If thou art afraid climb not at all.

Commentary

In his *Worthies of England* (1662), Thomas Fuller gives quite a different version of the circumstances of the exchange between Ralegh and Elizabeth as described in Cardiff MS 3.42. Ralegh, he writes,

> found some hopes of the queen's favours reflecting upon him. This made him write in a glass window, obvious to the queen's eye,

> *"Fain would I climb, yet fear I to fall."*

> Her majesty, either espying or being shown it, did underwrite,

> *"If thy heart fails thee, climb not at all."*

Fuller's story is very late, but is corroborated by the Cardiff MS, an anthology of verse and prose compiled by a Thomas Powell in the 1630s. Powell places the exchange in the Queen's garden but says nothing of the substance on which Sir Walter and Elizabeth wrote these lines. Powell's account, while predating Fuller's by at least twenty years, comes more than a decade after Ralegh's death and some half century after the alleged exchange took place. The Cardiff manuscript's testimony raises the odds of this text's authenticity from improbable to merely doubtful.

Possible Poem 2

L: Harl. MS 7392 (2), f. 21v.

When I was fair and young then favour graced me,
Of many was I sought their mistress for to be,
But I did scorn them all and answered them therefore,
Go, go, go, seek some otherwhere,[1] importune me no more.

How many weeping eyes I made to pine in woe,   [5
How many sighing hearts, I have not skill to show;
But I the prouder grew, and still[2] this spake therefore:
Go, go, go, seek some otherwhere, importune me no more.

Then spake fair Venus' son, that brave,[3] victorious boy,
Saying 'You dainty dame, for that you be[4] so coy,   [10
I will so pull your plumes as you shall say no more:
Go, go, go, seek some otherwhere, importune me no more.'

As soon as he had said, such change grew in my breast
That neither night nor day I could take any rest;
Wherefore I did repent that I had said before: [15
Go, go, go, seek some otherwhere, importune me no more.
     Finis ELY.

Notes

1. *otherwhere:* elsewhere
2. *still:* always
3. *brave:* intrepid, gallant
4. *for . . . be:* because you are

Commentary

This lyric is ascribed to the Queen as "ELY" in the Harleian MS and to "Elizabethe regina" in an unrelated text, O: Rawl. poet. MS 85, f. 1. The text in Folger MS V.a.89, p. 12, derives from a source quite similar to the Harleian version; it is, however, subscribed "l: of oxforde," presumably indicating Edward De Vere, seventeenth earl of Oxford. Perhaps Oxford could have written this love lament from a woman's viewpoint, yet the attributions to Elizabeth on two lines of textual descent tip the scale in her favor. Fragmentary texts of the poem in C: MS Dd.5.75, f. 38v and Folger MS V.a.262, p. 169, are unattributed.

Possible Poem 3

C: MS Dd.5.75, ca. 1596, f. 44v.

Now leave and let me rest,
Dame pleasure, be content.
Go choose among the best,
My doting days be spent;
By sundry signs I see   [5
Thy proffers are but vain,
And wisdom warneth me
That pleasure asketh pain,
And Nature that doth know
How time her steps doth try,[1]   [10
Gives place to painful woe,
And bids me learn to die.
Since all fair earthly things
Soon ripe, will soon be rot,[2]
And all that pleasant springs,   [15
Soon withered, soon forgot;
And youth that yields men joys
That wanton lust desires,
In age repents the toys[3]
That reckless youth requires,   [20
All which delights I leave
To such as folly trains[4]
By pleasures to deceive
Till they do feel the pains.
And from vain pleasures past   [25

I fly, and fain would know
The happy life at last
Whereto I hope to go.
For words or wise reports,
Ne⁵ yet examples gone [30
Gan⁶ bridle youthful sports
Till age came stealing on.
The pleasant, courtly games
That I do⁷ pleasure in,
My elder years now shames [35
Such folly to begin;
And all the fancies strange
That fond⁸ delight brought forth,
I do intend to change
And count them nothing worth. [40
For I by process worn,⁹
Am taught to know the skill,¹⁰
What might have been forborne¹¹
In my young, reckless will,
By which good proof I fleet¹² [45
From will to wit again,
In hope to set my feet
In surety to remain.

Notes

1. *try:* test

2. *rot:* rotten. Proverbial; Ruth Hughey (ed., *Arundel Harington Manuscript of Tudor Poetry* [Columbus, Oh., 1960], 2:392) cites *John Heywoodes woorkes* (1562), "But soone rype soone rotten."

3. *toys:* amorous dallying

4. *trains:* allures

5. *Ne:* nor

6. *Gan:* did

7. *do:* the reading of the Arundel Harington MS, emending "did" in the Cambridge text. The Harleian version reads "That I delighted in."

8. *fond:* foolish

9. *process worn:* course of time enfeebled

10. *skill:* cause

11. *forborne:* avoided

12. *fleet:* move unsteadily, waver

Commentary

Elizabeth's claim to this poem rests solely on the subscription "Regina," to the text in L: Harl. MS 7392 (2), ff. 49v–50. Not only is this a rather corrupt text of the poem, but the original scribe attributed it to another poet, perhaps "I. M." This subscription has been rendered illegible by a second scribe, who added the ascription to Elizabeth. Another anonymous text similar to that in the Cambridge MS is found in *The Arundel Harington Manuscript of Tudor Poetry,* ed. Ruth Hughey (Columbus, Oh., 1960), 1:280–81.

II

Speeches

Speech 1. November 20, 1558

Scribal copy, PRO: SP 12/1, f. 12.

Words Spoken by her Majesty to Master Cecil[1]

I give you this charge, that you shall be of my privy
council and content yourself to take pains for me and
my realm. This judgment I have of you, that you will
not be corrupted with any manner of gift and that you
will be faithful to the state, and that without respect of   [5
my private will[2] you will give me that counsel that you
think best. And if you shall know anything necessary
to be declared to me of secrecy[3] you shall shew it to
myself only, and assure yourself I will not fail to keep
taciturnity therein, and therefore herewith I charge   [10
you.[4]

Notes

1. This title overlooks the fact that Cecil had been knighted
in 1551.

2. *respect . . . will:* regard for my personal desires

3. *of secrecy:* secret or confidential in nature

4. *charge you:* command you

Commentary

William Cecil was the Queen's most trusted counsellor and
statesman until his death in 1598. He had served the then Princess
Elizabeth as surveyor (overseer) of her estates as early as 1550. She

appointed him to her Privy Council as her Principal Secretary three days after coming to the throne on November 17. Cecil became Master of the Court of Wards in 1561, was created Baron Burghley in 1571, and was named Lord Treasurer in the following year.

Speech 2. January 1559

Scribal copy, PRO: SP 12/1, f. 12.

Words Spoken by the Queen to the Lords

My Lords, the law of nature moveth me to sorrow for my sister; the burthen[1] that is fallen upon me maketh me over-mazed.[2] And yet considering I am God's creature ordained to obey his appointment, I will thereto yield, desiring from the bottom of my [5 heart that I may have assistance of His grace to be the minister of His heavenly will in this office now committed to me. And as I am but one body naturally considered, though by His permission a body politic to govern,[3] so I shall desire you all, my Lords (chiefly you [10 of the nobility,[4] every one in his degree and power), to be assistant to me that I with my ruling and you with your service may make a good accompt[5] to Almighty God and leave some comfort to our posterity in earth. I mean to direct all my actions by good advice and [15 counsel, and therefore, considering that divers of you[6] be of the ancient nobility, having your beginnings and estates of my progenitors, kings of this realm, and thereby ought in honor to have the more natural care for maintaining of my estate and this commonwealth. [20 Some others have been of long experience in governance and enabled by my father of noble memory, my brother, and my late sister to bear office.[7] The rest of you being upon special trust lately called to her service only, and trust for your service considered and re- [25

warded, my meaning is to require of you all nothing
more but faithful hearts in such service as from time to
time shall be in your powers towards the preservation
of me and this commonwealth. And for counsel and
advice I shall accept you of my nobility and such oth-   [30
ers of you the rest[8] as in consultation I shall think meet
and shortly appoint. To the which also with their advice I will join to their aid, and for ease of their burthen,[9] others meet for my service. And they which I
shall not appoint, let them not think the same for any   [35
disability in them but for that I do consider a multitude doth make rather discord and confusion than
good counsels. And of my goodwill you shall not
doubt, using yourselves as appertaineth to[10] good and
loving subjects.   [40

Notes

1. *burthen:* burden
2. *over-mazed:* highly bewildered
3. Elizabeth here refers to the doctrine of "the king's two
bodies"—that is, her double identity as both the embodiment
of the state and as an individual woman. Edmund Spenser
described Elizabeth accordingly in the "Letter" prefixed to his
Faerie Queene (1590): "she beareth two persons, the one of a
most royall Queene or Empresse, the other of a most vertuous
and beautifull Lady" (*Works of Edmund Spenser,* ed. Edwin
Greenlaw et al. [Baltimore, 1932], 1:168).
4. Of Elizabeth's first Privy Council, only Lord Howard of
Effingham ranked as a baron, the lowest title of nobility. Next
came six earls and then the marquesses of Winchester and
Northampton, her highest-ranking councillors.
5. *accompt:* account

6. *divers of you:* some number of you

7. *father . . . office:* a reference to Henry VIII, Edward VI, and Mary I

8. *of you the rest:* of the rest of you

9. *ease . . . burthen:* relief from their burden, workload

10. *as appertaineth to:* as is fitting or appropriate for

Commentary

The State Papers leaf on which this and Speech 1 were transcribed is endorsed "Queen Elizabeth speech to her secretary and other her lords before her coronation." Yet by the time of her coronation on January 15, 1559, Elizabeth had already dismissed most of the privy councillors she had inherited from Queen Mary, and had appointed seven of her own choosing. Perhaps we should interpret "before her coronation" to mean merely at some time prior to that event. In that case, she may have delivered both Speeches 1 and 2 as early as her first meeting with the Council at Hatfield House on November 20, 1558. The audience on that occasion would have included her secretary, Sir William Cecil, and the privy councillors who had served her recently deceased sister. The new, Protestant queen emphatically reminded the "ancient nobility" of their obligation to support her regime because of their tendency, as a group, to adhere to the Catholic Church.

Textual Notes, Speeches 1 and 2

A later copy of these speeches occurs on ff. 13–13v of this same volume of State Papers. Another text of Elizabeth's address to Cecil is included in Sir John Harington, *Nugae Antiquae,* ed. Henry Harington (London, 1779), 2:311.

Speech 3. January 28, 1563

PRO: SP 12/27, ff. 143–44 with corrections from a later draft, PRO: SP 12/27, ff. 153v–54. The text on ff. 143–44 is a scribal copy with annotations by Sir William Cecil.

Williams,[1] I have heard by you the common request of my Commons which I may well term (me
thinketh[2]), the whole realm because they[3] give, as I
have heard, in all these matters of Parliament their
common consent to such as be here assembled. The   [5
weight and greatness of this matter might cause in me,
being a woman wanting both wit[4] and memory, some
fear to speak and bashfulness besides, a thing appropriate to my sex. But yet the princely seat and kingly
throne wherein God (though unworthy), hath consti-   [10
tuted me,[5] maketh these two causes[6] to seem little in
mine eyes though grievous perhaps to your ears, and
boldeneth me to say somewhat[7] in this matter, which I
mean only to touch but not presently to answer: for
this so great a demand needeth both great and grave   [15
advice. I read of a philosopher whose deeds upon this
occasion I remember better than his name, who always
when he was required to give answer in any hard question of school points,[8] would rehearse over his alphabet before he would proceed to any further answer   [20
therein, not for that he could not presently have answered, but have his wit the riper and better sharp-
ened to answer the matter withal.[9] If he, a common

man, but in matters of school took such delay the better to shew his eloquent tale, great cause may justly　　[25
move me in this so great a matter touching the benefit
of this realm and the safety of you all to defer mine answer till some other time, wherein I assure you the
consideration of my own safety (although I thank you
for the great care that you seem to have thereof) shall　　[30
be little in comparison of[10] that great regard that I
mean to have of the safety and surety of you all.

And though God of late seemed to touch me rather
like one that he chastised than one that he punished,
and though death possessed almost every joint of me,　　[35
so as I wished then that the feeble thread of life which
lasted methought all too long, might by Clotho's
hand[11] have quietly been cut off; yet desired I not then
life (as I have some witnesses here) so much for mine
own safety as for yours. For I knew that in exchanging　　[40
of this reign[12] I should have enjoyed a better reign,
where residence is perpetual. There needs no boding
of my bane.[13] I know now as well as I did before that I
am mortal. I know also that I must seek to discharge
myself of that great burthen[14] that God hath laid upon　　[45
me, for of them to whom much is committed, much is
required. Think not that I, that in other matters have
had convenient[15] care of you all will in this matter
touching the safety of myself and you all be careless.
For I know that this matter toucheth me much nearer　　[50
than it doth you all who, if the worst happen, can lose
but your bodies. But if I take not that convenient care
that it behooveth me to have therein, I hazard to lose[16]
both body and soul.

And though I am determined in this so great and　　[55
weighty a matter to defer mine answer till some other

time because I will not in so deep a matter wade with
so shallow a wit, yet have I thought good to use these
few words as well to shew you that I am neither careless
nor unmindful of your safety in this case, as I trust you   [60
likewise do not forget that by me you were delivered
whilst you were hanging on the bough ready to fall
into the mud, yea to be drowned in the dung;[17] neither
yet the promise which you have here made concerning
your duties and due obedience, wherewith I assure you   [65
I mean to charge you, as further to let you understand,
that I neither mislike any of your requests herein nor
the great care that you seem to have of the surety and
safety of your helps in this matter. Lastly because I will
discharge some restless heads[18] in whose brains the   [70
needless hammers beat with vain[19] judgment, that I
should mislike this their petition, I say that of the matter and sum thereof I like and allow very well. As to the
circumstances, if any be, I mean upon further advice
further to answer. And so I assure you all that though   [75
after my death you may have many stepdames,[20] yet
shall you never have any a more mother[21] than I mean
to be unto you all.

Notes

1. Thomas Williams, Speaker of the House of Commons

2. *me thinketh:* it seems to me

3. *they:* i.e., all her realm's citizens, who collectively
empower Parliament

4. *wanting both wit:* lacking both intelligence

5. *though . . . me:* has appointed me, though unworthy

6. *two causes:* i.e., marriage and the succession

7. *somewhat:* a certain amount

8. *school points:* academic questions

9. *withal:* therewith. This apparently refers to an anecdote related in Plutarch's *Moralia* as advice from Athenodorus to Augustus Caesar: "Sir, when you perceive your selfe to be moved with choler, neither say [nor do] ought before you have repeated to your selfe all the 24. letters in the Alphabet" (trans. Philemon Holland, 1603). Elizabeth attributed this advice to Alcibiades in Speech 9. Further evidence of her familiarity with Plutarch is her translation of the essay on curiosity from the *Moralia* (see Translations, Poetry 2).

10. *of:* with

11. *Clotho's hand:* In Greek mythology, Clotho was the youngest of three sisters known as the Fates; she was said to spin the thread of life on her distaff (Atropos, her eldest sister, cut it at death).

12. *exchanging . . . reign:* dying (giving up this life for the next)

13. *boding . . . bane:* premonition or prophecy of my death

14. *burthen:* burden

15. *convenient:* appropriate

16. *hazard to lose:* risk losing

17. Elizabeth reminds the Commons that the nation she inherited upon Queen Mary's death was militarily weak, threatened by France and Spain, plagued with a debased coinage, and torn by bitter religious turmoil.

18. *discharge . . . heads:* relieve some restless persons (from their anxieties)

19. *vain:* empty, vacant

20. *stepdames:* stepmothers

21. *any . . . mother:* anyone more of a mother

Commentary

Speaker of the House Thomas Williams presented a petition from the Commons to the Queen on the afternoon of January 28; it voiced Parliament's most pressing concern, the question of the succession to the crown. As Williams reminded his royal auditor, "almighty God to our great terror and dreadfull warning lately towched your Highnes with some danger of your most noble person by sicknes" (Hartley, 1:90), referring to an attack of smallpox she had suffered in the fall of 1562. The petition's two main points were, first, that Elizabeth ensure continuance of the Tudor dynasty by choosing "some honorable husband whom it shall please yow to joyne to you in mariag." Second, the Commons asked for a more immediate solution to the problem by having Elizabeth establish the succession in some legally binding fashion (Hartley, 1:92–93).

Textual Notes

In addition to the PRO copies, the speech occurs in four roughly contemporary manuscripts and was printed from Harington family papers in *Nugae Antiquae,* ed. Henry Harington (London, 1804), 1:80–83 (see Hartley, 1:94). Torn out or erroneous readings in PRO: SP 12/27, ff. 143–44, are supplied from PRO: SP 12/27, ff. 153v–54 with concurrence of the text in L: Add. MS 33217, f. 13, in the following passages:

l. 37. Clotho's hand] Clois hand
l. 69. helps, [torn]
l. 70. discharge some, [torn]
l. 71. needless hammers, [torn]
l. 72. should mislike, [torn]
ll. 72–3. the matter, [torn]

Speech 4. April 10, 1563

L: Lansdowne MS 94, f. 30. Holograph, endorsed by Secretary
Cecil "X April 1563 The Queen's speech in the Parliament
uttered by the Lord Keeper. Queen Elizabeth's hand."

Since there can be no duer[1] debt than princes'
word, to keep that unspotted for my part, I was one
that would be loath that the self thing[2] that keeps the
merchant's credit from craze[3] should be the cause that
princes' speech should merit blame and so their honor   [5
quail.[4] An answer therefore I will make and this it is:
the two petitions that you presented me in many
words expressed contained these two things in sum as
of your cares the greatest:[5] my marriage and my successor, of which two the last I think is best be touched[6]   [10
and of the other a silent thought may serve, for I had
thought it had been so desired as[7] none other tree's
blossoms should have been minded[8] ere hope of my
fruit had been denied you. And by the way, if any here
doubt[9] that I am, as it were by vow or determination,   [15
bent never to trade that life,[10] put out that heresy; your
belief is awry, for, as I think it[11] best for a private
woman, so do I strive with myself to think it not
meet[12] for a prince; and if I can bend my will to your
need I will not resist such a mind.   [20

But to the last, think not that you had needed this
desire[13] if I had seen a time so fit and it so ripe to be
denounced.[14] The greatness of the cause therefore and

need of your returns[15] doth make me say that which I
think the wise may easily guess, that as a short time for [25
so long a continuance ought not pass by rote, as many
telleth tales, even so, as cause by conference[16] with the
learned shall shew me matter worthy utterance for
your behoofs,[17] so shall I more gladly pursue your
good after my days than with my prayers be a mean[18] [30
to linger my living thread. And this much more than I
had thought will I add for your comfort: I have good
record[19] in this place that other means than you mentioned have been thought of, perchance for your good
as much and for my surety no less, which if presently [35
could conveniently have been executed, had not been
deferred. But I hope I shall die in quiet with *nunc
dimittis*,[20] which cannot be without[21] I see some
glimpse[22] of your following surety after my graved
bones.[23] [40

Notes
1. *duer:* more fitting, more proper
2. *self thing:* same thing, i.e., honor, integrity
3. *craze:* unsoundness
4. *their honor quail:* impair or damage their honor
5. *in . . . greatest:* in summary as the greatest of your cares
6. *be touched:* to be touched on
7. *as:* that
8. *minded:* attended to, heeded
9. *doubt:* fear
10. *trade that life:* pursue that life (i.e., marriage)
11. *it:* i.e., marriage
12. *not meet:* unfit
13. *desire:* petition

14. *denounced:* proclaimed

15. *returns:* i.e., return of the members to their homes

16. *conference:* taking counsel

17. *behoofs:* benefit, advantage

18. *mean:* instrument, agent

19. *record:* testimony

20. *nunc dimittis:* now go, depart. This Latin incipit served as an alternate title to the "Song of Simeon," an English hymn based on Luke 2.29. The hymn became part of the Evensong liturgy and was also included in every edition of the Elizabethan metrical Psalms of David.

21. *without:* unless

22. *glimpse:* Elizabeth wrote "climp[s]e," the last letters partially obscured by a tear in the margin.

23. *following . . . bones:* security after my bones have been buried

Commentary

The Queen prorogued this session of her second Parliament on the afternoon of April 10 after Speaker Williams had addressed her, again, on the subject of the succession and her marriage. The Lord Keeper, Sir Nicholas Bacon, replied on Elizabeth's behalf, thanking the Commons for its grant of a subsidy. He then read her final words regarding marriage and the succession as set forth above from her much-corrected draft. This text provides the readings she let stand in the manuscript.

Speech 5. November 1566

PRO: SP 12/41, f. 8. Holograph, endorsed in Cecil's hand:
"A part of the beginning of the Queen's Majesty's speech to the thirty
lords and thirty commoners on Tuesday the fifth of November 1566.
Ano 8 The Queen's own hand."

If the order of your cause[1] had matched the weight
of your matter the one might well have craved reward
and the other much the sooner satisfied. But when I
call to mind how far from dutiful care, yea, rather, how
nigh a traitorous trick this tumbling cast did spring,[2] I   [5]
muse how men of wit can so hardly use[3] that gift they
hold. I marvel not much that bridleless colts do not
know their rider's hand, whom bit of kingly rein did
never snaffle[4] yet. Whether it was fit that so great a
cause as this should have had his[5] beginning in such a   [10]
public place as that, let it be well weighed. Must all evil
bodings that might be recited be found little enough to
hap to my share?[6] Was it well meant, think you, that
those that knew not how fit this matter was to be
granted by the prince[7] would prejudicate[8] their prince   [15]
in aggravating[9] the matter so all their arguments
tended to my careless care of this my dear realm?

Notes

   1. *order . . . cause:* disposition of your matter of concern,
i.e., the Commons' presentation of the succession issue

2. *tumbling . . . spring:* somersault did leap

3. *so hardly use:* use so daringly

4. *snaffle:* restrain

5. *his:* its

6. *be found . . . share:* be found, however few, to fall by chance to my part

7. *the prince:* i.e., the Queen herself

8. *prejudicate:* prejudge

9. *aggravating:* exaggerating

Commentary

Elizabeth convened this second session of her second Parliament September 30, 1566, and soon found that both houses and her own Privy Council were united in their insistence that she establish the succession to the throne before the Commons would consider her request for a subsidy. On November 5, thirty members from each house assembled to hear her response to their position. This draft of her opening remarks in the speech expresses her attitude toward their behavior in unmistakable terms.

Textual Notes

At line 5 Elizabeth wrote "tumblin." PRO: SP 12/41, f. 9 is a later copy of the text. A complete account of the speech, recorded by a witness who wrote down what "I could carrye awaye by remembrans," survives in C: MS Gg. 3.34, pp. 208–12. A similar text occurs in L: Stowe MS 354, for which see Hartley, 1:145–49.

Speech 6. January 2, 1567

Queen's speech at the close of Parliament.
Holograph, L: Cotton Charter 4.38 (2).

I love so evil counterfeiting[1] and hate so much dis-
simulation that I may not suffer you[2] depart without
that my admonitions may shew your harms and cause
you shun unseen peril. Two visors[3] have blinded the
eyes of the lookers on in this present session so far-   [5
forth[4] as, under pretense of saving all, they have done
none good. And these they be: succession and liberties.
As to the first, the prince's opinion and goodwill ought
in good order have been felt in other sort[5] than in so
public a place be uttered. It had been convenient that   [10
so weighty a cause had had his[6] original from a zealous
prince's consideration, not from so lip-labored orations out of such subjects' mouths, which, what they
be, time may teach you know and their demerits will
make them acknowledge how they have done their   [15
lewd endeavor to make all my realm suppose that their
care was much when mine was none at all. Their han-
dling of this doth well shew, they being wholly ignorant, how fit my grant at this time should be to such a
demand. In this one thing their imperfect dealings are   [20
to be excused, for I think this be the first time that so
weighty a cause passed from so simple men's mouths
as began this cause.

   As to liberties, who is so simple that doubts

whether a prince that is head of all the body may not [25
command the feet not to stray when they would slip?
God forbid that your liberty should make my bondage,[7] or that your lawful liberties should anyways
have been infringed. No, no, my commandment
tended no whit to that end, the lawfulness of which [30
commandment, if I had not more pitied you than
blamed you, might easily by good right be shewed you,
perchance to their shame that bred you that colored[8]
doubt. You were sore[9] seduced. You have met with a
gentle prince, else your needless scruple[10] might per- [35
chance have bred your caused[11] blame. And albeit the
soothing of such[12] be reprovable in all, yet I would not
you should think my simplicity such as[13] I cannot
make distinctions among you, as of some that
broached the vessel not well fined,[14] and began these [40
attempts; others not forseeing well the end that re-
spected the necessary fetches[15] of the matters and no
whit understood circumstances expedient not to have
been forgotten therein; others whose ears were de-
luded by pleasing persuasions of common good when [45
the very yielding to their own inventions[16] might have
bred all your woes; others whose capacities, I suppose,
yielded their judgment to their friends' wit;[17] some
other that served an echo's place.[18]

Well, among all these sundry affects,[19] I assure you [50
there be none, the beginners only except, whom I either condemn for[20] evil-minded to me or do suspect
not to be my most loyal subjects. Therefore I conclude
with this opinion which I will you to think unfeignedly
true: that as I have tried[21] that you may be deceived, so [55
am I persuaded you will not beguile[22] the assured joy
that ever I took to see my subjects' love to me more

staunch than ever I felt the care in myself for myself to be great, which alone hath made my heavy burden light and a kingdom[23] care but easy carriage[24] for me. [60 Let this my displing stand you[25] in stead of sorer strokes never to tempt too far a prince's patience, and let my comfort pluck up your dismayed sprites[26] and cause you think that, in hope that your following be- haviors shall make amends for past actions, you return [65 with your prince's grace: whose care for you, doubt you not, to be such as she shall not need a remem- brancer for your weal.[27]

Notes

1. *love . . . counterfeiting:* despise pretending so much

2. *suffer you:* allow you to

3. *visors:* masks

4. *so far-forth:* to such an extent

5. *felt . . . sort:* found out in some other way

6. *his:* its

7. *make my bondage:* cause my servitude

8. *colored:* pretended

9. *sore:* grievously

10. *needless scruple:* unnecessary doubt

11. *caused:* well-deserved

12. *soothing of such:* maintaining of such to be true

13. *as:* that

14. *broached . . . fined:* (figuratively) broached this ill-clarified subject

15. *end . . . fetches:* conclusion pertaining to the necessary contrivances (stratagems); i.e., the unfavorable consequences of forcing the Queen to name her successor

16. *inventions:* devices, fabrications

17. *wit:* discretion

18. *served . . . place:* acted as an echo

19. *affects:* desires, appetites

20. *for:* as

21. *tried:* proved by experience

22. *beguile:* deprive me of

23. *kingdom:* kingdom's

24. *carriage:* burden. After "easy carriage for me," Elizabeth crossed through the next three lines of her draft. They read: "which if I kept not more for conscience than for glory I could willingly wish a wiser my room."

25. *displing stand you:* disciplining serve you

26. *sprites:* spirits

27. *remembrancer . . . weal:* officer to remind her about your well-being

Commentary

On November 9, 1566, just four days after her meeting with the Commons, Elizabeth sent a message to the House ordering its members not to deal further with the question of succession to the throne. This sparked days of debate about Parliament's traditional liberty to address any issue pertinent to the national wellbeing. The lower House drafted a petition to the Queen on the subject of the succession but apparently decided not to submit it to her. On the following January 2, Speaker of the House Richard Onslow addressed the closing session of the Parliament for fully two hours. After Lord Keeper Bacon had replied on the Queen's behalf, Elizabeth added these additional remarks on the foremost subjects in contention between Parliament and the Crown: the succession question itself and the right of the representatives in assembly to raise an issue of such personal consequence to the sovereign.

Textual Notes

At l.55, "deceived" is reconstructed from "deceav," the rest of the word being lost in the margin. A crease and repaired tear in the leaf makes "past actions" (l.65) a hypothetical reading confirmed by L: Harl. MS 2125 and other manuscripts. The Queen's speech circulated widely in manuscript. To the five copies listed in Hartley, 1:174, may be added that in Huntington Library MS HM 1340, ff. 84–84v, headed "A bill delivered by her Majesty unto my Lady Bacon to be delivered by her highness' commandment unto my Lord Keeper."

Speech 7. March 15, 1576

Elizabeth's speech at the close of the session.
C: MS Dd.5.75, ff. 28–29v.

Oratio Elizabethae reginae habitu in regni conventu convocato ad diem 15 Martij anno 1575

Do I see God's most sacred word and text of holy writ drawn to so divers senses,[1] being never so[2] precisely taught, and shall I hope that my speech can pass forth through so many ears without mistaking, where so many ripe and divers wits do ofter[3] bend themselves [5 to conster[4] than attain the perfect understanding? If any look for eloquence, I shall deceive their hope. If some think I can match their gift which spake before, they hold an open heresy. I cannot satisfy their longing thirst that watch for these delights, unless I should af- [10 ford them what myself had never yet in my possession. If I should say the sweetest tongue or eloquentest speech that ever was in man were able to express that restless care which I have ever bent to govern for the greatest wealth, I should wrong mine intent and [15 greatly bate[5] the merit of mine own endeavor. I cannot attribute this happy and good success to my devise[6] without detracting much from the divine providence, nor challenge to[7] my own commendation what is only due to His eternal glory. My sex permits it not, or if it [20 might be in this kind,[8] yet find I no impeachment[9] why to persons of more base estate the like proportion[10] should not be allotted.

One special favor yet I must confess I have just cause to vaunt of: that whereas variety and love of [25 change is ever so rife in servants to their masters, in children to their parents, and in private friends one to another, as that though for one year or perhaps for two they can content themselves to hold their course upright, yet after[11] (by mistrust or doubt[12] of worse), [30 they are dissevered and in time wax weary of their wonted[13] liking. Yet still I find that assured zeal amongst my faithful subjects to my special comfort which was first declared to my great encouragement. Can a prince, which of necessity must discontent a [35 number to delight and please a few, continue so long time without great offence, much mislike, or common grudge? Or haps it oft that princes' actions are conceived in so good part and favorably interpreted? No, no, my lords, how great my fortune is in this respect I [40 were ingrate if I should not acknowledge. And as for those rare and special benefits which many years have followed and accompanied my happy reign, I attribute to God alone, the prince of rule, and count myself no better than his handmaid, rather brought up in a [45 school to bide the ferula[14] than traded in[15] a kingdom to support the scepter.

If policy[16] had been preferred before truth, would I, trow you,[17] even at the first beginning of my reign have turned upside down so great affairs, or entered [50 into tossing of the greatest waves and billows of the world; that might, if I had sought mine ease, have harbored and cast anchor in more seeming security? It cannot be denied but worldly wisdom rather bade me link myself in league and fast alliance with great [55 princes, to purchase friends on every side by worldly means and there repose the trust of mine assured strength, where force could never want[18] to give assistance. Was I to seek that, to man's outward judgment this must needs be thought the safest course. No, I can [60 never grant myself so simple as not to see what all men's eyes discovered. But all these means of leagues, alliances, and foreign strengths I quite forsook and gave myself to seek for truth without respect,[19] reposing mine assured stay[20] in God's most mighty grace [65 with full assurance. Thus I began, thus I proceed, and thus I hope to end.

These seventeen years God hath both prospered and protected you with good success under my direction. And I nothing doubt but the same maintaining [70 hand will guide you still[21] and bring you to the ripeness of perfection. Consider with yourselves the bitter storms and troubles of your neighbors,[22] the true cause whereof I will not attribute to princes— God forbid I should, since these misfortunes may pro- [75 ceed as well from sins among the people—for want of plagues declare not always want of guilt, but rather prove God's mercy.[23] I know beside that private persons may find rather fault than mend a prince's state. And for my part, I grant myself too guilty to increase [80 the burden or mislike of any. Let all men therefore bear their private faults; mine own have weight enough for me to answer for. The best way, I suppose, for you and me were by humble prayers to require[24] of God that not in weening[25] but in perfect weight,[26] in being, not [85 in seeming, we may wish the best and further it with our ability. Not the finest wit, the scrapingest[27] judgment, that can rake most deeply or take up captious ears with pleasing tales hath greater care to guide you

to the safest state or would be gladder to establish you [90
where men ought to think themselves most sure and
happy than she that speaks these words.

And touching dangers chiefly feared, first to rehearse my meaning lately unfolded to you by the Lord
Keeper, it shall not be needful, though I must confess [95
mine own mislike so much to strive against the matter
as, if I were a milkmaid with a pail on mine arm
whereby my private person might be little set by,[28] I
would not forsake that single state to match myself
with the greatest monarch. Not that I condemn the [100
double knot[29] or judge amiss of such as, forced by necessity, cannot dispose themselves to another life, but
wish that none were driven to change save such as cannot keep honest limits. Yet for your behoof there is no
way so difficile[30] that may touch my private[31] which I [105
could not well content myself to take—and in this case
as willingly to spoil[32] myself quite of myself as if I
should put off mine upper[33] garment when it wearies
me, if the present state might not thereby be encumbered. [110

I speak not this for my behoof; I know I am but
mortal, which good lesson Master Speaker in his third
division, of a virtuous princes' properties, required
me with reason to remember, and so therewhilst[34] pre-
pare myself to welcome death whensoever it shall [115
please almighty God to send it, as, if others would endeavor to perform the like, it could not be so bitter
unto many as it hath been counted. Mine experience
teacheth me to be no fonder of these vain delights than
reason would,[35] nor further to delight in things uncer- [120
tain than may seem convenient. But let good heed be
taken lest in reaching too far after future good you

peril not[36] the present, or begin to quarrel and fall by dispute together by the ears[37] before it be decided who shall wear my crown. I will not deny but[38] I might be [125 thought the indifferentest[39] judge in this respect, that shall not be at all when these things be fulfilled, which none beside myself can speak in all this company. Misdeem not of[40] my words, as though I sought what heretofore to others hath been granted: I intend it not. [130 My brains be too thin to carry so tough a matter, although I trust God will not in such haste cut off my days but that according to your own desert and my desire I may provide some good way for your security. And thus as one which yieldeth you more thanks both [135 for your zeal unto myself and service in this parliament than my tongue can utter, I recommend you to the assured guard and best keeping of the Almighty who will preserve you safe I trust in all felicity, and wish withal that each of you had tasted some drops of [140 Lethe's flood[41] to deface and cancel these my speeches out of your remembrance.

Notes

Title: Oration of Queen Elizabeth made in the assembly summoned by the monarch on March 15, 1575

1. *drawn . . . senses:* stretched to such differing meanings
2. *being never so:* no matter how
3. *divers . . . ofter:* different wits do more often
4. *conster:* construe
5. *bate:* reduce, diminish
6. *devise:* contrivance, plan
7. *challenge to:* lay claim to

8. *in . . . kind:* in my feminine nature, disposition

9. *impeachment:* impediment, obstacle

10. *the . . . proportion:* an equal amount

11. *after:* afterward

12. *doubt:* fear

13. *wonted:* accustomed

14. *bide the ferula:* endure the rod

15. *traded in:* trained up in

16. *policy:* political cunning

17. *trow you:* do you believe

18. *want:* be lacking

19. *respect:* consideration (of other political expediencies)

20. *stay:* support

21. *still:* continuously

22. As Elizabeth spoke, for example, French Catholics were forming the Catholic League to prosecute more effectively their decades-old civil war with the Protestant Huguenots. In the Low Countries, Dutch forces continued their conflict with the Spanish army that occupied the southern half of the country.

23. Elizabeth invokes the widespread belief that God punished the sinful with plagues.

24. *require:* request

25. *weening:* supposing

26. *perfect weight:* full responsibility

27. *scrapingest:* perhaps, most diligently inquiring? (no *OED* citation)

28. *set by:* regarded

29. *double knot:* i.e., marriage

30. *difficile:* difficult

31. *private:* personal affairs

32. *spoil:* deprive

33. *upper:* outer

34. *therewhilst:* during that time

35. *would:* requires, persuades

36. *peril not:* endanger ("not" here emphasizes the negative in "lest")

37. *by the ears:* at variance

38. *but:* that

39. *indifferentest:* most impartial

40. *Misdeem not of:* do not mistake

41. *Lethe's flood:* the river of forgetfulness, in the classical underworld .

Commentary

On the afternoon of March 14, 1576, the Queen attended a session of both houses of Parliament where the Speaker of the House of Commons, Robert Bell, delivered a five-part speech whose third part begged Elizabeth to marry and establish the succession to the throne. She delayed her answer until the following day, when Lord Keeper Sir Nicholas Bacon responded on her behalf to each of Bell's topics. Bacon addressed Bell's third point by saying that "Albeit of her own natural disposition she is not disposed or inclined to Marriage, neither could she ever Marry were she a private Person; yet for your sakes and the benefit of the Realm, she is contented to dispose and incline her self to the satisfaction of your humble Petition."[1]

Shortly afterward, the Queen prorogued this session of Parliament, but then stepped forward to deliver her own speech, the main thrust of which was to reinforce Bacon's words with her personal testimony. She was apparently quite satisfied with her remarks, for she sent a copy of the speech to John Harington, the teenage son of her longtime servitor and gentleman of her Privy Chamber, with these words: "Boye Jacke, I have made a clerke wryte faire my poore wordes for thyne use, as it cannot be suche striplinges have entrance into parliamente assemblye as yet. Ponder theme in thy howres of leysure, and plaie wythe theme tyll they enter thyne understandinge; so shallt thou hereafter, perchance, fynde some goode frutes hereof when thy Godmother is oute of remembraunce; and I do thys, because thy father was readye to sarve and love us in trouble and thrall."[2]

1. Sir Simonds D'Ewes, *A Compleat Journal of the Votes, Speeches and Debates, Bothe of the House of Lords and House of Commons Throughout the Whole Reign of Queen Elizabeth* (London, 1693), p. 232.

2. Sir John Harington, *Nugae Antiquae,* ed. Henry Harington (London, 1804), 1:127–28.

Textual Notes

The speech circulated widely in manuscript in the late sixteenth and early seventeenth centuries. Hartley, 1:471, transcribes the texts in Cambridge Record Office Fitzwilliam of Milton Political MS 177 and Exeter College, Oxford MS 92. He cites as well copies in L: Add. MS 15891, Add. MS 29975, Add. MS 32379, Add. MS 33271, Harl. MS 787, and O: Tanner MS 169, as well as the *Nugae Antiquae* version. In addition to these sources, the speech was also copied into Durham University Library, Mickleton and Spearman MS 73, ff. 177–79v and L: Harl. MS 4808.[1] I have emended the Cambridge text (C) in the following readings based on alternatives found in Add. 15891 (A), the Durham University MS (D), Hartley's transcription of the Fitzwilliam MS (F), the *Nugae Antiquae* print (N), and Tanner MS 169 (T):

l. 17.   happy and A D T N] hap and C; happes and F
ll. 40–41. I were ingrate A F N] I twere ingrate C; I were ungrate D; it were ungrate T

l. 87. scrapingest D F] sharpest (*corrected from* scrapingest)
A; *left blank in* C; strongest N; sharpest T

1. Allison Heisch cites another manuscript copy at the
Virginia Historical Society, Richmond, MS L T 8525a3
among the Dawson Turner Papers ("Queen Elizabeth I:
Parliamentary Rhetoric and the Exercise of Power,"
Signs 1 [1975]: 40n).

Speech 8. November 12, 1586

The Queen's speech in answer to the petition from both houses of Parliament. L: Lansdowne MS 94, ff. 84–85, scribal fair copy endorsed "The former Copy of her Majesty's first speech the 12th of Novemb." The manuscript, corrected in Elizabeth's hand, has been torn and is emended from STC 6052, sig. C1–4v.

Her Majesty's most gracious Answer delivered by herself verbally to the Petitions of the Lords and Commons being the estates of Parliament.

The bottomless graces and immeasurable benefits bestowed upon me by the Almighty are, and have been, such as I must not only acknowledge them but admire them, accounting them as well miracles as benefits, not so much in respect of His divine Majesty, [5 with whom nothing is more common than to do things rare and singular, as in regard of our weakness who cannot sufficiently set forth His wonderful works and graces which to me have been so many, so diversely folded and embroidered[1] one upon another as [10 in no sort am I able to express them.

And although there liveth not any that may more justly acknowledge themselves infinitely bound unto God than I, whose life He hath miraculously preserved at sundry times (beyond my merit) from a multitude [15 of perils and dangers, yet is not that the cause for which I count myself the deepliest[2] bound to give Him my humblest thanks or to yield Him greatest recognition, but this which I shall tell you hereafter, which will

deserve the name of wonder. If rare things and seldom   [20
seen be worthy of account, even this it is: that as I came
to the crown with the willing hearts of subjects, so do I
now after twenty-eight years' reign perceive in you no
diminution of goodwills which, if happily[3] I should
want, well mought[4] I breathe but never think I live.   [25

And now, albeit I find my life hath been full dangerously sought and death contrived by such as no
desert procured it,[5] yet am I thereof so clear from malice, which hath the property to make men glad at the
falls and faults of their foes and make them seem to do   [30
for[6] other causes when rancor is the ground, yet I
protest it is and hath been my grievous thought that
one not different in sex, of like estate, and my near kin
should be fallen into so great a crime. Yea, I had so little purpose to pursue her with any color[7] of malice   [35
that, as it is not unknown to some of my lords here (for
now I will play the blab[8]), I secretly wrote her a letter,
upon the discovery of sundry treasons, that if she
would confess them and privately acknowledge them
by her letters unto myself, she never should need be   [40
called for them into so public a question. Neither did I
it of mind to circumvent[9] her, for then I knew as much
as she could confess, and so did I write.

And if, even yet, now[10] the matter is made but too
apparent, I thought she truly would repent (as perhaps   [45
she would easily appear in outward shew to do), and
that for her none other would take the matter upon
them, or that we were but as two milkmaids with pails
upon our arms, or that there were no more depend-
ency upon us but[11] mine own life were only in danger   [50
and not the whole estate of your religion and well
doings, I protest (wherein you may believe me, for

though I may have many vices, I hope I have not accustomed my tongue to be an instrument of untruth) I would most willingly pardon and remit this offence. [55 Or if by my death other nations and kingdoms might truly say that this realm had attained a ever[12] prosperous and flourishing estate, I would (I assure you) not desire to live, but gladly give my life to the end my death might procure you a better prince. [60

And for your sakes it is that I desire to live to keep you from a worse. For as for me, I assure you I find no great cause I should be fond to live; I take no such pleasure in it that I should much wish it, nor conceive such terror in death that I should greatly fear it; and yet [65 I say that not, but if the stroke were coming, perchance flesh and blood would be moved with it and seek to shun it. I have had good experience and trial of this world. I know what it is to be a subject, what to be a sovereign, what to have good neighbors, and some- [70 time meet evil-willers.[13] I have found treason in trust, seen great benefits little regarded, and instead of gratefulness, courses of purpose to cross.[14] These former re-membrances,[15] present feeling, and future expectation of evils, I say, have made me think an evil is much the [75 better the less while it dureth,[16] and so them happiest that are hence, and taught me to bear with a better mind these treasons than is common to my sex, yea, with a better heart perhaps than is in some men, which I hope you will not merely impute to my simplicity or [80 want of understanding but rather that I thus conceived that, had their purposes taken effect, I should not have found the blow before I had felt it nor, though my peril should have been great, my pain should have been but small and short, wherein, as I would be loath to die [85 so bloody a death, so doubt I not but God would have given me grace to be prepared for such an event, chance when it shall, which I refer to His good pleasure.

And now as touching their treasons and conspiracies together with the contriver[17] of them, I will not so prejudicate[18] myself and this my realm as to say or think that I might not, without the last statute,[19] by the ancient laws of this land have proceeded against her, which was not made particularly to prejudice[20] her, though perhaps it might then be suspected in respect of the disposition of such as depend that way.[21] It was so far from being intended to entrap her that it was rather an admonition to warn her from incurring the danger thereof; but sith it is made and in the force of a law, I thought good in that which might concern her to proceed according thereunto rather than by course of common law[22] wherein, if you the judges have not deceived me or that[23] the books you brought me were not false, which God forbid, I mought as justly have tried her by the ancient laws of the land.

But you lawyers are so nice[24] and so precise in sifting and scanning every word and letter, that many times you stand more upon form than matter, upon syllabs[25] than the sense of the law. For in this strictness and exact following of common form she must have been indicted in Staffordshire[26] and have been arraigned at the bar, holden up her hand,[27] been tried by a jury—a proper course, forsooth, to deal in that manner with one of her estate! I thought it better therefore, for avoiding these and more absurdities, to commit the cause to the inquisition[28] of a good number of the greatest and most noble personages of this realm, of

[90

[95

[100

[105

[110

[115

the judges and others of good account whose sentence I must approve. [120

And all little enough: for we princes, I tell you, are set on stages in the sight and view of all the world duly observed. The eyes of many behold our actions; a spot is soon spied in our garments, a blemish quickly noted [125 in our doings. It behooveth us therefore to be careful that our proceedings be just and honorable. But I must tell you one thing more: that in this late Act of Parliament you have laid an hard hand on me, that I must give direction for her death, which cannot be but most grievous and an irksome burden to me. And lest you [130 might mistake mine absence from this Parliament (which I had almost forgotten), although there be no cause why I should willingly come amongst multitudes, for that[29] amongst many some may be evil, yet hath it not been the doubt[30] of any such danger or oc- [135 casion that kept me from thence but only the great grief to hear this cause spoken of, especially that such a one of state[31] and kin should need so open a declaration,[32] and that this nation should be so spotted with blots of disloyalty, wherein the less is my grief for that I [140 hope the better part is mine,[33] and those of the worse not much to be accounted of, for that in seeking my destruction they might have spoiled[34] their own souls.

And even now could I tell you that which would make you sorry. It is a secret and yet I will tell it you (al- [145 though it be known I have the property[35] to keep counsel but too well, ofttimes to mine own peril). It is not long since, mine eyes did see it written, that an oath was taken within few days either to kill me or to be hanged themselves, and that to be performed ere [150 one month were ended. Hereby I see your danger in me and neither can or will be so unthankful or careless of your consciences as to take no care for your safety. I am not unmindful of your oath made in the Association,[36] manifesting your great goodwills and affections [155 taken and entered into upon good conscience and true knowledge of the guilt for safeguard of my person, done, I protest to God, before I ever heard it or ever thought of such a matter till a thousand obligations[37] were shewed me at Hampton Court signed and sub- [160 scribed with the names and seals of the greatest of this land, which as I do acknowledge the greatest argument of your true hearts and great zeal to my safety, so shall my bond be stronger tied to greater care for all your good. [165

But for that this matter is rare, weighty, and of great consequence, and I think you do not look for any present resolution, the rather for that as it is not my manner in matters of far less moment to give speedy answer without due consideration, so in this of such [170 importance, I think it very requisite with earnest prayer to beseech His Divine Majesty so to illuminate mine understanding and inspire me with His grace as I may do and determine that which shall serve to the establishment of His church, preservation of your es- [175 tates, and prosperity of this commonwealth under my charge. Wherein for that I know delay is dangerous, you shall have with all conveniency our resolution delivered by our message. And whatever any prince may merit of their subjects for their approved[38] testimony [180 of their unfeigned sincerity, either by governing justly, void of all partiality or sufferance of any injuries done even to the poorest, that do I assuredly promise inviolably to perform for requital of your so many deserts.

Notes

1. *folded and embroidered:* redoubled and elaborated
2. *deepliest:* most deeply
3. *happily:* perchance (haply)
4. *want . . . mought:* lack, well might
5. *no . . . it:* no deserving induced it (i.e., her assassination)
6. *do for:* act motivated by
7. *color:* show, semblance
8. *blab:* babbler, revealer of secrets
9. *of . . . circumvent:* with intent to entrap
10. *now:* now that
11. *dependency . . . but:* consequence involved with us except
12. *a ever:* In the Lansdowne text, Elizabeth wrote "ever" above the line between "a" and "prosperous," but did not correct the indefinite article. This may have been intentional; see her uses of "a" before a vowel in her holograph Letters 4 ("a earnest," l. 5) and 5 ("a opinion," l. 13). The passage from Speech 8 appeared as "an everprosperous" in the printed text.
13. *evil-willers:* ill-wishers
14. *courses . . . cross:* actions purposely set in opposition
15. *remembrances:* memories
16. *less . . . dureth:* shorter time it lasts, endures
17. In the Lansdowne text, Elizabeth crossed out "her that was" before "the contriver," in reference to Mary.
18. *prejudicate:* judge rashly
19. The Act for the Queen's Safety, passed by Parliament in 1585
20. *prejudice:* prejudge
21. *depend . . . way:* incline that way, i.e., toward favoring Mary
22. English common law is unwritten except insofar as court rulings through the ages have recognized it in writing.

Elizabeth here claims that Mary is subject to trial by the customary tenets of the common law as well as by the parliamentary statute of 1585.

23. *that:* if

24. *nice:* fussy, persnickety

25. *syllabs:* syllables

26. Mary was imprisoned at the manor of Chartley, Staffordshire, when she wrote her incriminating letters approving Babington's plan to assassinate Elizabeth.

27. *holden . . . hand:* (have) held up her hand, i.e., in order for Mary to take the oath before testifying, a formality that Elizabeth considered degrading for royalty

28. *inquisition:* official investigation (the commission sent to try Mary for her part in the Babington plot)

29. *for that:* because

30. *doubt:* fear

31. *state:* status

32. *declaration:* revelation (of her crimes)

33. *for . . . mine:* because I think that most of the nation supports me

34. *spoiled:* destroyed

35. *property:* character, nature. The note in the left margin of the manuscript at this point indicates that the scribal text derived from that copied down as the Queen spoke on November 12: "Her Majesty referred the further knowledge hereof to some of the lords there present whereof the Lord Treasurer seemed to be one for that he stood up to verify it."

36. The bond or instrument of Association circulated informally. It obligated its subscribers not only to kill anyone who might assassinate the Queen, but also the person for whose benefit the assassination was enacted.

37. *obligations:* written bonds or contracts of association

38. *approved:* proved by experience

Commentary, Speeches 8 and 9

Anthony Babington and his co-conspirators in a plot to assassinate Elizabeth were executed on September 20, 1586. In the following month a commission of English noblemen tried and convicted Mary, Queen of Scots, for complicity in the attempt. Their key piece of incriminating evidence was her letter to Babington in which she approved of his designs. Parliament met on October 29 with no other business than to press Elizabeth for the enactment of Mary's sentence. Provisions of the Act for the Queen's Safety, passed by Parliament in 1585, excluded Mary from the English throne in the event that Elizabeth was assassinated, and authorized all English subjects to pursue to the death anyone judged guilty of plotting to kill the Queen. This last measure legally condemned Mary to death, but the process involved, first, a royal proclamation of her guilt and, second, a death warrant sealed with the Great Seal of England.

On Saturday, November 12, representatives of both houses of Parliament met with the Queen at Richmond Palace, where they presented her with their unanimous petition for Mary's execution. Elizabeth replied with Speech 8, quite probably an extemporaneous response.[1] To this she added a verbal message that Lord Chancellor Hatton conveyed to Parliament when it reconvened on Monday. Elizabeth asked the representatives to determine if her safety and that of the realm could be ensured by any other means than Mary's death. Both houses concluded, unanimously, that the Queen of Scots' death was a political necessity. A joint delegation traveled again to Richmond to present their findings to the Queen, whose extemporaneous reply follows as Speech 9. The government published a full account of these proceedings, including texts of both speeches, in *The Copie of a Letter to the Right Honourable the Earle of Leycester* (1586), STC 6052, sig. C1–4v, D4v–E3.

1. J. E. Neale, *Elizabeth I and Her Parliaments, 1584–1601* (London, 1957), p. 116.

Speech 9. November 24, 1586

The Queen's second speech. L: Lansdowne MS 94, ff. 86–8v,
in an italic cursive hand with Elizabeth's autograph revisions and
revisions in the hand of a third scribe. Endorsed "The 2 Copy of
her Majesty's Second Speech 24 November Before her Majesty
Corrected it. Touching the Queen of Scotts."

Full grievous is the way whose going on and end
breeds cumber for the hire[1] of a laborious journey. I
have strived more this day than ever in my life whether
I should speak or use silence. If I speak and not complain, I shall dissemble.[2] If I hold my peace, your labor   [5
taken were full vain. For me to make my moan[3] were
strange and rare, for I suppose you shall find few that
for their own particular will cumber[4] you with such a
care. Yet such I protest hath been my greedy desire and
hungry will that of your consultation might have   [10
fallen out some other means to work my safety, joined
with your assurance (than that for which you are become so earnest suitors), as I protest I must needs use
complaint, though not of[5] you but unto you, and of
the cause, for that I do perceive by your advices,[6]   [15
prayers, and desires, there falleth out this accident,[7]
that only my injurer's bane must be my life's surety.

But if any there live so wicked of nature to suppose
that I prolonged this time only, pro forma, to the intent to make a shew of clemency, thereby to set my   [20
praises to the wire-drawers[8] to lengthen them the

more, they do me so great a wrong as they can hardly recompense. Or if any person there be that thinks or imagines[9] that the least vainglorious thought hath drawn me furder herein, they do me as open injury as [25 ever was done to any living creature, as He that is the maker of all thoughts knoweth best to be true. Or if there be any that think that the lords appointed in commission durst do no other, as fearing thereby to displease or to be suspected to be of a contrary opinion [30 to my safety, they do but heap upon me injurious conceipts.[10] For either those put in trust by me to supply my place have not performed their duty towards me, or else they have signified unto you all that my desire was that everyone should do according to his con- [35 science, and in the course of these proceedings should enjoy both freedom of voice and liberty of opinion, and that[11] they would not openly, they might privately to myself declare. It was of a willing mind and great desire I had, that some other means might be found out [40 wherein I should have taken more comfort than in any other thing under the sun. And since now it is resolved that my surety cannot be established without a princess' head, I have just cause to complain that I, who have in my time pardoned so many rebels, winked [45 at[12] so many treasons, and either not produced them[13] or altogether slipped them over with silence, should now be forced to this proceeding against such a person.

I have besides during my reign seen and heard [50 many opprobrious books and pamphlets against me, my realm, and state, accusing me to be a tyrant—I thank them for their alms. I believe therein their meaning was to tell me news, and news it is to me in-

deed. I would it were as strange to hear of their impi-   [55
ety. What will they not now say, when it shall be
spread[14] that for the safety of her life a maiden Queen
could be content to spill the blood even of her own
kinswoman. I may therefore full well complain that
any man should think me given to cruelty, whereof I   [60
am so guiltless and innocent as I should slander God if
I should say he gave me so vile a mind. Yea, I protest I
am so far from it that, for mine own life, I would not
touch her, neither hath my care been so much bent[15]
how to prolong mine as how to preserve both, which I   [65
am right sorry is made so hard, yea so impossible.

I am not so void of judgment as not to see mine
own peril, nor yet so ignorant as not to know it were in
nature a foolish course to cherish a sword to cut mine
own throat, nor so careless as not to weigh that my life   [70
daily[16] is in hazard; but this I do consider: that many a
man would put his life in danger for the safeguard of a
king. I do not say that so will I, but I pray you think
that I have thought upon it. But sith[17] so many hath
both written and spoken against me, I pray you give   [75
me leave to say somewhat for myself and, before you
return to your countries,[18] let you know for what a one
you have passed so careful[19] thoughts, that will never
be forgetful of your exceeding cares for my safety. And
as I think myself infinitely beholding unto you all that   [80
seek to preserve my life by all the means you may, so I
protest that there liveth no prince, nor ever shall be,
more mindful to requite so good deserts wherein, as I
perceive you have kept your old wont in a general seeking the lengthening of my days, so am I sure that never   [85
shall I requite it unless I had as many lives as you all;

but forever I will acknowledge it while there is any my breath left me.

Although I may not justify but may justly condemn my sundry faults and sins to God, yet for my care in [90 this government let me acquaint you with my intents. When first I took the sceptre, my title made me not forget the Giver, and therefore began as it became me with such religion as both I was born in, bred in, and I trust shall die in, although I was not so simple[20] as not [95 to know what danger and peril so great an alteration[21] might procure me, how many great princes of the contrary opinion would attempt all they might against me, and generally what enmity I should thereby breed unto myself, which all I regarded not, knowing that He [100 for whose sake I did it might and would defend me. For which it is that ever since I have been so dangerously prosecuted as I[22] rather marvel that I am, than muse that I shall not be, if it were not God's holy hand that continueth me beyond all other expectation. [105

I was not simply trained up, nor in my youth spent my time altogether idly, and yet when I came to the crown, then entered I first into the school of experience, bethinking myself of those things that best fitted a king: justice, temper,[23] magnanimity, judgment. For I [110 found it most requisite that a prince should be endued with justice, that he should be adorned with temperance; I conceived magnanimity to beseem a royal estate possessed by whatsoever sex, and that it was necessary that such a person should be of judgment. [115 For the two latter I will not boast, but for the two first, this may I truly say: among my subjects I never knew a difference of person where right was one,[24] nor never

to my knowledge preferred for favor what I thought
not fit for worth, nor bent mine ears to credit a tale   [120
that first was told me, nor was so rash to corrupt my
judgment with my censure or [25] I heard the cause. I will
not say but many reports might fortune be [26] brought
me by such as must hear the matter whose partiality
might mar the right, for we princes cannot hear all   [125
causes ourselves. But this dare I boldly affirm, my verdict went with the truth of my knowledge.

But full well wished Alcibiades his friend [27] that he
should not give any answer till he had recited the letters of the alphabet. So have I not used over-sudden   [130
resolutions in matters that have touched me full
near—you will say that with me, I think. And therefore
as touching your counsels and consultations, I conceive them to be wise, honest, and conscionable, so
provident and careful for the safety of my life (which I   [135
wish no longer than may be for your good), that
though I never yield you of recompense your due, yet
shall I endeavor myself to give you cause to think your
goodwill not ill-bestowed, and strive to make myself
worthy for such subjects. And as for your petition,   [140
your judgment I condemn not, neither do I mistake
your reasons, but pray you to accept my thankfulness,
excuse my doubtfulness, and take in good part my answer answerless, wherein I attribute not so much to my
own judgment but that I think many particular per-   [145
sons may go before me, [28] though by my degree I go before them. Therefore if I should say I would not do
what you request, it might peradventure be more than
I thought, [29] and to say I would do it, might perhaps
breed peril of that [30] you labor to preserve, being more   [150
than in your own wisdoms and discretions would

seem convenient, circumstances of place and time being duly considered.

Notes

1. *cumber . . . hire:* difficulty in the payment

2. That is, I shall conceal my true feelings if I do not complain.

3. *make my moan:* complain

4. *particular . . . cumber:* private concerns will burden

5. *of:* about

6. *advices:* judgments

7. *accident:* unfortunate consequence

8. *set . . . wire-drawers:* place my praises with those who draw metal into wire

9. Elizabeth changed "doe thinke or imagine" to "ther be that thinkes or imagine," failing to bring the second verb into agreement with its subject.

10. *conceipts:* imaginings

11. *that:* that which

12. *winked at:* closed my eyes to

13. *produced them:* brought them to public attention

14. *spread:* made known

15. *bent:* directed, devoted to

16. *daily:* This reading from *The Copie of a Letter* replaces "darely" in the MS scribe's hand.

17. *sith:* since

18. *countries:* homes (counties)

19. *passed . . . careful:* endured such anxious

20. *simple:* foolish

21. *alteration:* a reference to the "Elizabethan Settlement," in which a Protestant state church replaced the Catholicism practiced under Queen Mary

22. *For . . . I:* deleted in the MS but retained in the printed version

23. *temper:* temperance

24. *knew . . . one:* recognized a distinction between persons where one was in the right; i.e., favored a person of higher status

25. *or:* ere, before

26. *fortune be:* happen to be

27. *wished . . . friend:* Alcibiades wished his friend. See Speech 3, n. 9, for Elizabeth's prior allusion to this anecdote from Plutarch's *Moralia.*

28. *go before me:* exceed me (in judgment)

29. *peradventure . . . thought:* perhaps indicate more than I intend, i.e., exaggerate my disinclination

30. *breed . . . that:* endanger that which

Textual Notes, Speeches 8 and 9

Torn away text and marginal damage in the Lansdowne copy of Speech 8 obscure some readings that are restored here from *The Copie of a Letter.* In so doing I have also followed the printed text in emending several contractions of "th'" with words following that begin with a vowel (e.g., "th'end," "th'ancient"), as such constructions were not Elizabeth's normal practice. *The Copie of a Letter* was reprinted in Holinshed's *First and Second Volumes of Chronicles* (1587). Presumably, a scribe or scribes wrote down Elizabeth's words as she addressed the representatives on November 12 and November 24. These drafts were then rewritten in fair copy by three different scribes in italic hands. Elizabeth personally corrected these versions of the speeches. The first (Speech 8) appeared in *The Copie of a Letter* with only minor variations from the manuscript, while Speech 9 differs significantly from the corrected manuscript in several passages.

Speech 10. August 9, 1588

The Queen's speech at Tilbury Camp.
From *Cabala* (1654), sig. 2L2v.

My loving people, we have been persuaded by some
that are careful of our safety to take heed how we commit ourself to armed multitudes for fear of treachery.
But I assure you I do not desire to live to distrust my
faithful and loving people. Let tyrants fear; I have al- [5
ways so behaved myself that, under God,[1] I have placed
my chiefest strength and safeguard in the loyal hearts
and goodwill of my subjects. And therefore I am come
amongst you as you see at this time not for my recreation and disport, but being resolved in the midst and [10
heat of the battle to live or die amongst you all, to lay
down, for my God and for my kingdom and for my
people, my honor and my blood even in the dust.

I know I have the body but of a weak and feeble
woman, but I have the heart and stomach of a king, [15
and of a king of England too, and think foul scorn that
Parma, or Spain,[2] or any prince of Europe should dare
to invade the borders of my realm, to which rather
than any dishonor shall grow by me,[3] I myself will take
up arms, I myself will be your general, judge, and re- [20
warder of every one of your virtues in the field. I know
already for your forwardness[4] you have deserved rewards and crowns, and we do assure you in the word of
a prince they shall be duly paid you. In the mean time

my Lieutenant General[5] shall be in my stead, than   [25
whom never prince commanded a more noble or worthy subject. Not doubting but by your obedience to my
general, by your concord in the camp, and your valor
in the field, we shall shortly have a famous victory over
those enemies of my God, of my kingdoms,[6] and of my   [30
people.

Notes

1. *under God:* subordinate to God

2. *Parma, or Spain:* Alexander Farnese, duke of Parma,
was the Spanish commander in the Netherlands. "Spain" here
denotes the King of Spain.

3. *by me:* because of me

4. *forwardness:* eagerness, zeal

5. *Lieutenant General:* Robert Dudley, earl of Leicester

6. *kingdoms:* Elizabeth was styled Queen of England,
France, and Ireland.

Commentary

The main English army assembled to repel the anticipated
Spanish invasion was encamped at Tilbury on the Essex coast
near the mouth of the Thames. Elizabeth visited the camp on August 8, and she returned the next day for a more extensive review
of the troops and entertainment by her officers. A text of the
speech she allegedly delivered before the army that afternoon was
reported in a letter sent to the duke of Buckingham by the earl of
Leicester's chaplain, Dr. Lionel Sharp, who was present at Tilbury.
In 1654 his version of the Queen's words found its way into print
in an anthology of letters and state papers titled *Cabala: Mysteries
of State, in Letters of the Great Ministers of King James and King*

Charles. Recent commentary on Elizabeth's visit to the camp has cast doubt on the likelihood that she addressed the army in these words, since a markedly different speech attributed to Elizabeth on the occasion survives in two texts, one subscribed to a painting in a Norfolk church and the other in a sermon printed in 1612. It has even been argued that she did not address the army at all.[1] Yet three contemporary accounts of the event affirm that she spoke to the troops on the afternoon of August 9; and while the portions of Elizabeth's speech summarized in these three narratives find little or no counterpart in the rival texts from the Norfolk church and sermon of 1612, they do echo specific passages in the *Cabala* text.

Two of these contemporary accounts were written by eyewitnesses who rushed back to London to publish them as broadside ballads. "A Joyful Song of the Royal Receiving of the Queen's most excellent Majesty . . . at Tilbury" by T.I. (STC 14067) describes Elizabeth receiving "A martial staff" on the second day of her visit and then spending two hours riding through the camp to review her army. T.I. affirms that she spoke "princely words" to the troops and promised them ample food and clothing as well as wages. This sounds like a somewhat diluted version of the "rewards and crowns" included as promises in the *Cabala* version of the speech. The second ballad, "The Queenes visiting of the Campe at Tilsburie with Her entertainment there" (STC 6565), was no doubt written by Thomas Deloney. He summarizes her afternoon address to the troops as follows:

> And then bespake our noble Queene,
>   My loving friends and countrimen
> I hope this day the worst is seene,
>   That in our wars ye shall sustain.
> But if our enimies do assaile you,
>   never let your stomackes faile you.

> For in the midst of all your troupe,
>   we our selues will be in place:
> To be your joy, your guide and comfort,
>   even before your enimies face.

Here Elizabeth's boast about having the "stomach" (that is, courage or heart) "of a king" as reported in the *Cabala* version, is perhaps transferred to her soldiers. Certainly, her vow to serve "in the midst of all your troupe" echoes the *Cabala* text's pledge to join them "in the midst and heat of the battle to live or die amongst you all," while the next to last line resembles her offer to be "your general, judge, and rewarder of every one of your virtues in the field." James Aske, who was not an eyewitness to the events at Tilbury, published a third summary of the speech in 1588.[2] Although Aske's verse narrative is filled with errors and literary fictions, he does credit Elizabeth with volunteering to lead her army into battle and to reward them handsomely for their service. All three accounts, moreover, explain why not all other accounts by those present at Tilbury mention their sovereign's speech. T.I., Deloney, and Aske are unanimous in noting that Elizabeth dismissed her following and reviewed the army accompanied only by a small band of officers and personal attendants: she "left her traine farre off to stand," in Deloney's words. Most of her courtiers and attendants were therefore not present to hear what she said.

The *Cabala* version is the longest extant account of the Queen's remarks; while many questions remain as to how accurately Sharp could have been in copying it down on site, its contents are at least partially corroborated by three independent textual witnesses. First is the *Cabala* text itself, where Elizabeth's speech was quoted as part of a letter that Sharp sent to the duke of Buckingham in 1623. This version of the speech was reprinted three times between 1654 and 1691. A broadside reprint headed *Queen*

Elizabeth's Opinion concerning Transubstantiation (1688) included the speech among other anti-Catholic writings attributed to Elizabeth; its text derives from the *Cabala* as does that in *The History of the Life and Reign of Queen Elizabeth* (London, 1740), 2:214–15. Second is a manuscript text discovered by Janet M. Green in L: Harleian MS 6978, ff. 87–87v; Green argues that this version of the speech was transcribed in Sharp's handwriting. It is subscribed, "Gathered by one that heard it, and was commanded to utter it to the whole army the next day, to send it gathered to the Queen herself." [3] Third is yet another manuscript text, heretofore unnoted, preserved among the duchess of Norfolk's Deeds (PRO: C 115/101); this was apparently copied during the second half of the seventeenth century.

While Sharp's text in the Harleian MS appears to be the obvious choice for copy text, [4] this manuscript is demonstrably in error in having Elizabeth tell her troops that she has come to Tilbury "but" (that is, only) "for my recreation and pleasure." So flippant a remark is both inappropriate to the occasion and at odds with what follows. For the Queen adds immediately that she is "resolved in the midst and heat of the battle to live and die amongst you all"—hardly an occasion of royal recreation and pleasure. The PRO text agrees with the Harleian MS in this error, but the *Cabala*'s version of this sentence removes the contradiction by having Elizabeth assert that she has come "not for my recreation and disport, but being resolved . . . to live or die amongst you all." No manifestly erroneous reading mars the *Cabala* version of the speech, which therefore serves as copy text in this edition. See the textual notes for further information about the relationships among these three texts.

1. Susan Frye, "The Myth of Elizabeth at Tilbury," *Sixteenth Century Journal* 23 (1992): 95–114, prints the speech from William Leigh's 1612 sermon (STC 15426), with the

transcription of a similar text from the painting in St. Faith's Church, Gaywood. In "Provenance and Propaganda as Editorial Stumbling Blocks," in *New Ways of Looking at Old Texts: Papers of the Renaissance English Text Society, 1985–1991,* ed. W. Speed Hill (Binghamton, N.Y., 1993), pp. 119-23, Francis Teague joins Frye in casting doubt on Sharp's testimony. Teague continues this argument in "Queen Elizabeth in Her Speeches," in *Gloriana's Face: Women, Public and Private, in the English Renaissance,* ed. S. P. Cerasano and Marion Wynne-Davies (Detroit, 1992), pp. 67–69. Moreover, a number of eyewitness accounts of the Queen's visit fail to mention her speech to the army, including Lord Burghley's (L: Lansdowne MS 103, ff. 142–45) and Sir Francis Castillion's (Y: Osborn MS fb 69, p. 221). Edward Radcliffe recalled only that the Queen "comforted many of us with her most gracious usage" (L: Cotton MS Otho E.9, f. 205v).

2. James Aske, *Elizabetha Triumphans* (STC 847), sig. E1v.

3. Janet M. Green, " 'I My Self' ": Queen Elizabeth I's Oration at Tilbury Camp," *Sixteenth Century Journal* 28 (1997): 421–45.

4. It serves as copy text for the speech in *Elizabeth I: Collected Works,* ed. Leah S. Marcus, Janel Mueller, and Mary Beth Rose (Chicago, 2000), pp. 325–26.

Textual Notes

If, as Green argues, the Harleian text (H) is in the hand of Dr. Lionel Sharp, both this and the *Cabala* version (C) derive ultimately from the same source. The PRO text (P) is dated 1688. All three sources are independent witnesses to the speech, for while both H and P agree in the erroneous reading "but for my recreation," H omits several faulty readings in P (e.g., "by your concord and your valor in the camp"). P likewise replaces the problematic reading in H, "take foul scorn," with "think it foul scorn." To "take scorn" expresses indignation about something, but the *Cabala* reading, "think scorn," expresses a slightly stronger disdain for the invasion (as the phrases are defined by the *OED*). C lacks demonstrable error and could thus derive from neither H nor P.

Speech 11. November 30, 1601

The Queen's "Golden Speech." From O: Rawl. MS A 100, ff. 97v–101.

Master Speaker, we[1] have heard your declaration and perceive your care of our estate by falling into the consideration[2] of a grateful acknowledgment of such benefits as you have received, and that[3] your coming is to present thanks unto us, which I accept with no less joy than your loves can have desire to offer such a present.   [5

I do assure you there is no prince that loveth his subjects better or whose love can countervail our love. There is no jewel, be it of never so rich a price, which I set before this jewel, I mean your love. For I do more esteem it than any treasure or riches, for that we know how to prize, but love and thanks I count unvaluable.[4] And though God hath raised me high, yet this I count the glory of my crown, that I have reigned with your loves. This makes me that[5] I do not so much rejoice that God hath made me to be a queen as to be a queen over so thankful a people. Therefore, I have cause to wish nothing more than to content the subject, and that is a duty which I owe; neither do I desire to live longer days than that I may see your prosperity, and that's my only desire. And as I am that person which still[6] (yet under God[7]) hath delivered you, so I trust by the almighty power of God that I still shall be his instrument to preserve you from envy, peril, dishonor,   [10

                [15

                [20

                [25

shame, tyranny, and oppression, partly by means of
your intended helps,[8] which we take very acceptably
because it manifesteth the largeness of your loves and
loyalties unto your sovereign. Of myself I must say this,
I was never any greedy, scraping grasper, nor a strait, [30
fast-holding[9] prince, nor yet a waster. My heart was
never set on worldly goods but only for my subjects'
good. What you do bestow on me I will not hoard it up,
but receive it to bestow on you again. Yea, my own proprieties[10] I account yours to be expended for your [35
good, and your eyes shall see the bestowing of all for
your good. Therefore render unto them[11] from me, I
beseech you, Master Speaker, such thanks as you imagine my heart yieldeth but my tongue cannot express.

Note that all this while we kneeled, whereupon her [40
Majesty said:

Master Speaker, I would wish you and the rest to
stand up, for I shall yet trouble you with longer speech.

So we all stood up and she went on in her speech,
saying: [45

Master Speaker, you give me thanks, but I doubt
me[12] that I have more cause to thank you all than you
me, and I charge you to thank them of the Lower
House from me, for had I not received a knowledge[13]
from you I might have fallen into the lapse of an error [50
only for lack of true information. Since I was Queen,
yet did I never put my pen to any grant but that upon
pretext and semblance made unto me it was both good
and beneficial to the subject in general, though a private profit to some of my ancient servants who had [55
deserved well. But the contrary being found by experience, I am exceedingly beholding[14] to such subjects as
would move the same[15] at the first. And I am not so

simple to suppose but that there be some of the Lower
House whom these grievances never touched, and for [60
them I think they spake out of zeal to their countries [16]
and not out of spleen or malevolent affection as being
parties grieved.[17] And I take it exceedingly gratefully
from them because it gives us to know that no respects
or interests had moved them other than the minds [65
they bear to suffer no diminution of our honor and
our subjects' love unto us, the zeal of which affection,
tending to ease my people and knit their hearts unto
me, I embrace with a princely care. For above all
earthly treasures I esteem my people's love, more than [70
which I desire not to merit.

That my grants should be grievous unto my people
and oppressions to be privileged under color of our
patents, our kingly dignity shall not suffer it. Yea, when
I heard it I could give no rest unto my thoughts until I [75
had reformed it. Shall they, think you, escape unpunished that have thus oppressed you and have been respectless[18] of their duty and regardless[19] of our honor?
No, no, Master Speaker, I assure you were it not more
for conscience' sake than for any glory or increase of [80
love that I desire, these errors, troubles, vexations, and
oppressions done by these varlets and lewd persons
(not worthy the name of subjects) should not escape
without condign punishment. But I perceive they dealt
with me like physicians who, ministering a drug, make [85
it more acceptable by giving it a good, aromatical
savor, or when they give pills do gild them all over.

I have ever used to set the Last Judgment Day before
my eyes and so to rule as I shall be judged to answer before a higher Judge, to whose judgment seat I do ap- [90
peal, that never thought was cherished in my heart that

tended not unto my people's good. And now if my
kingly bounty have been abused and my grants turned
to the hurts of my people, contrary to my will and
meaning, or if any in authority under me have neg-   [95
lected or perverted what I have committed to them, I
hope God will not lay their culps[20] and offences to my
charge who, though there were danger in repealing our
grants, yet what danger would I not rather incur for
your good than I would suffer them still to continue?   [100

I know the title of a king is a glorious title, but assure yourself that the shining glory of princely authority hath not so dazzled the eyes of our understanding
but that we well know and remember that we also are
to yield an account of our actions before the great   [105
Judge. To be a king and wear a crown is a thing more
glorious to them that see it than it is pleasing to them
that bear it. For myself, I was never so much enticed
with the glorious name of a king or royal authority of a
queen as delighted that God had made me His instru-   [110
ment to maintain His truth and glory and to defend
this kingdom, as I said, from peril, dishonor, tyranny,
and oppression. There will never queen sit in my seat
with more zeal to my country, care to my subjects, and
that will sooner with willingness venture her life for   [115
your good and safety than myself, for it is not my desire to live nor reign longer than my life and reign shall
be for your good. And though you have had and may
have many princes more mighty and wise sitting in
this state,[21] yet you never had nor shall have any that   [120
will be more careful[22] and loving.

Shall I ascribe anything to myself and my sexly[23]
weakness, I were not worthy to live then, and of all
most unworthy of the mercies I have had from God,

who hath ever yet given me a heart which never yet   [125
feared foreign or home enemy. I speak it to give God
the praise as a testimony before you and not to attribute anything unto myself, for I, O Lord, what am I
whom practices and perils past should not fear, or
what can I do? _(These words she spake with a great em-_   [130
phasis.) That I should speak for any glory, God forbid.
This, Master Speaker, I pray you deliver unto the
House to whom heartily recommend me, and so I
commit you all to your best fortunes and further
counsels. And I pray you, Master Comptroller, Master   [135
Secretary, and you of my Council, that before these
gentlemen depart into their countries you bring them
all to kiss my hand.

Notes

1. _we:_ the royal plural in place of "I"

2. _falling . . . consideration:_ turning to the recompense; i.e.,
Parliament turned from criticizing Crown policy to offering
Elizabeth thanks for her proclamation

3. _and that:_ i.e., and we perceive that

4. _unvaluable:_ invaluable

5. _makes me that:_ is the cause that

6. _still:_ continuously

7. _under God:_ subordinate to God

8. _helps:_ the subsidy, not yet formally approved by
Parliament

9. _fast-holding:_ hoarding, miserly

10. _proprieties:_ possessions (from the Lansdowne MS,
supported by the text in _Historical Collections_). Other texts
read "properties," but Elizabeth sold large quantities of her
jewels and plate as well toward the end of her reign in order to
meet Crown expenses.

11. *them:* the members of the House of Commons not present on this occasion

12. *doubt me:* fear

13. *a knowledge:* information

14. *beholding:* indebted, beholden

15. *move the same:* urge the same, i.e., that the Queen's grants were not beneficial to her subjects

16. *countries:* counties, shires

17. *grieved:* injured

18. *respectless:* heedless, careless

19. *regardless:* disrespectful to

20. *culps:* guilt, sin

21. *state:* the canopied throne, covered with the "cloth of estate," under which Elizabeth was sitting when the parliamentary delegation arrived

22. *careful:* full of care or concern

23. *sexly:* characteristic of one's sex

Commentary

The most inflammatory issue in the Parliament of 1601 was the question of monopolies. Over the years, Elizabeth had granted dozens of monopolies by letters patent. These allowed the patentees, royal favorites for the most part, in effect to levy extra taxes on tanning, retail sales of wine, the importing of playing cards, or the sale of starch, salt, pots, brushes, bottles, and many other items. The monopolies were greatly resented among the populace at large. In response to the Parliamentary debate, Elizabeth issued a proclamation on November 28 revoking most of the monopolies and preventing the Privy Council from taking measures to protect the patentees. On the afternoon of November 30, some 140 members of the House of Commons attended their speaker to the Council Chamber at Whitehall Palace, where they met the

Queen "sittinge under the clothe of estate at the upper end" (Hartley, 3:410). Their Speaker, John Croke, then formally thanked her Majesty for issuing the proclamation. Her response, the "Golden Speech," was so named for its expressions of love for her people and concern for their welfare above all else.

Hartley identifies four quite different versions of the speech. Its purpose, evident in all four states of the text, was twofold. The Queen began by thanking Parliament for its grant of a subsidy, the principal source of extra income for the central government. Next, she assured the representatives that she agreed to their legislation for repealing many state monopolies and leaving the rest subject to testing of their legitimacy by the law courts. She may have delivered the speech extemporaneously, yet shortly afterward she sent a text of her remarks to Henry Savile, provost of Eton College. This she followed up with a command that he neither copy the speech nor share it with anyone.[1] Whether or not any of the surviving texts of the speech represents the one Elizabeth sent to Savile cannot be determined. Version 1 purports to record only its "effect," although the parts of this text can be roughly aligned with the substance of the other versions.[2] A copy of the second version is extant among Lord Burghley's papers. It is entitled a copy of the speech "taken verbatim in wrytinge by A. B. as neer as he could possiblie set yt downe."[3] This text was published in December 1601, as the government's official account of what the Queen said.[4] The parliamentary historian J. E. Neale contends that it represents not her firsthand delivery of the address, being instead "entirely the Queen's composition" after the fact. This seems unlikely. The florid style of this version of the speech little resembles that of Elizabeth's other orations. As Neale admits, it "deservedly sank from memory under the leaden weight of its euphuistic artifice and obscurity."[5] Moreover, it conveys an error the Queen surely would not have let stand had she studied it carefully. In the text edited above (version 4), she compares, on the one hand, the suitors who urged her to grant the monopolies to, on the other hand, physicians who coat drugs with "aromatical savors" to hide their bitterness. It is an apt comparison. In version 2 of the speech, however—in both the manuscript and the printed texts—this simile is applied instead to "the vantinge boast of a kingly name" (Hartley, 3:293). The drugs are somehow to be likened to the deceitful glory of being a king. Although this second account does pick up some wording found in the other versions, it is more likely a draft that was reworded by someone other than the Queen and then published with her approval, though not her careful reading.

The third and fourth versions of the speech are closely related because version 4 is actually an amalgam of version 3 with yet another contemporary account of the "Golden Speech."[6] A number of manuscripts of Townshend's "Journal" include as an appendix a fifth summary of the Queen's address (Hartley, 3:494–96). This was combined with version 3 to create version 4. They differ in the order in which they present the topics treated in the speech, but they also mingle passages that are essentially identical in wording with passages worded very differently or, in version 4, with passages not found in version 3. I have selected version 4 as the closest approximation to what Elizabeth said on that November afternoon for several reasons. It was clearly recorded by an eyewitness: version 4 states that when Elizabeth gave her kneeling audience permission to stand, "we all stood up and she went on in her speech." It notes as well that she spoke one passage "with great emphasis." Version 4 is also the most complete text. It incorporates virtually all the subjects reported in version 3 and adds others so that it runs about a third longer than version 3. And while the third version connects the physicians and their drugs with the glory of kingship, version 4 applies this simile correctly to the courtiers who lured the Queen into granting them monopolies.

1. J. E. Neale, *Elizabeth I and Her Parliaments, 1584–1601* (London, 1957), p. 392.

2. L: Harl. MS 787, transcribed in Hartley, 3:288–91. For analysis of the speech in context see David Harris Sacks, "The Countervailing of Benefits: Monopoly, Liberty, and Benevolence in Elizabethan England," in *Tudor Political Culture,* ed. Dale Hoak (Cambridge, 1995), pp. 272–91.

3. L: Lansdowne MS 94, f. 123; quoted by Hartley, 3:292.

4. The printed text is STC 7578.

5. Neale, *Elizabeth I and Her Parliaments, 1584–1601,* p. 392.

6. Version 3 was published about 1628 (STC 7579). Its appearance in at least eleven manuscripts makes it the second most widely dispersed contemporary state of the speech. The fourth version occurs in fourteen manuscript texts of Hayward Townshend's "Journal," his eyewitness record of the 1601 session of Parliament. Townshend's narrative was first published in 1680 under the title *Historical Collections.*

Textual Notes

A greatly condensed text of version 4 was published as *A Speech Made by Queen Elizabeth (of Famous Memory) in Parliament* (1688). In addition to the manuscript copies of version 4 listed by Hartley (3:298), this state of the text is also found in L: Lansdowne MS 512, ff. 37v–41, and Lansdowne MS 515, ff. 140–44v. Both manuscripts date from the mid–seventeenth century or even later. The latter document closely follows the text of version 4 in *Historical Collections: Or an Exact Account of the Proceedings of the Four Last Parliaments of Q. Elizabeth* (1680), pp. 263–66. This printed text, and that in Lansdowne 515, are second in accuracy only to the Rawlinson manuscript, and provide four emendations to its readings: "acceptably" for "acceptable" (l.27), "proprieties" for "properties" (l.35), "state" for "seat" (l.121), and "what am I" for "what and I" (l.129).

III

Letters

Letter 1. Princess Elizabeth's dedicatory letter prefaced to the holograph "Glass of the Sinful Soul," presented as a New Year's gift to Queen Catherine Parr, December 31, 1544

O: Cherry MS 36, ff. 2–4v.

To our most Noble and virtuous Queen, Katherine, Elizabeth, her humble daughter, wisheth perpetual felicity and everlasting joy.

Not only knowing the affectuous[1] will and fervent zeal the which your Highness hath towards all godly [5 learning, as also my duty towards you (most gracious and sovereign princess), but knowing also that pusillanimity and idleness are most repugnant unto a reasonable creature, and that (as the philosopher sayeth) even as an instrument of iron or of other metal wax- [10 eth[2] soon rusty unless it be continually occupied,[3] even so shall the wit of a man or woman wax dull and unapt to do or understand anything perfitly[4] unless it be always occupied upon some manner of study, which things considered hath moved so small a por- [15 tion[5] as God hath lent me to prove[6] what I could do. And therefore have I (as for assay[7] or beginning, following the right notable saying of the proverb aforesaid), translated this little book out of French rhyme into English prose, joining the sentences together as [20 well as the capacity of my simple wit and small learning could extend themselves.

The which book is entitled or named the *miroir* or glass[8] of the sinful soul, wherein is contained how she[9]

(beholding and contempling[10] what she is) doth per- [25
ceive how of herself and of her own strength she can
do nothing that good is or prevaileth for her salvation
unless it be through the grace of God, whose mother,
daughter, sister, and wife by the scriptures she proveth
herself to be. Trusting also that through His incompre- [30
hensible love, grace, and mercy she (being called from
sin to repentance) doth faithfully hope to be saved.
And although I know that as for my part which I have
wrought in it,[11] (as well spiritual as manual[12]), there is
nothing done as it should be nor else worthy[13] to come [35
in your Grace's hands, but rather all unperfit[14] and un-
correct, yet do I trust also that albeit it is like a work
which is but new begun and shapen,[15] that the file of
your excellent wit and godly learning[16] in the reading
of it (if so it vouchsafe your Highness[17] to do) shall rub [40
out, polish, and mend (or else cause to mend[18]) the
words (or rather the order of my writing), the which I
know in many places to be rude and nothing done as it
should be. But I hope that after to have been[19] in your
Grace's hands there shall be nothing in it worthy of [45
reprehension and that in the meanwhile no other (but
your Highness only) shall read it or see it, lest my faults
be known of[20] many. Then shall they[21] be better excused (as my confidence is in your Grace's accustomed
benevolence) than if I should bestow a whole year in [50
writing or inventing ways for to excuse them. Praying
God almighty the Maker and Creator of all things to
grant unto your Highness the same New Year's Day a
lucky and a prosperous year with prosperous issue and
continuance of many years in good health and contin- [55
ual joy and all to His honor, praise, and glory. From
Ashridge the last day of the year of our Lord God 1544.

Notes

1. *affectuous:* loving, affectionate

2. *waxeth:* grows, becomes

3. *occupied:* used. Elizabeth perhaps translated this proverb from the "philosopher" Erasmus's *Similia: ut ferrum si non utaris, obducitur rubigine* (as iron, if you do not use it, is covered with rust). See R. W. Dent, *Proverbial Language in English Drama Exclusive of Shakespeare, 1495–1616* (Berkeley, 1984), p. 441, entry I91.

4. *perfitly:* completely, thoroughly (perfectly)

5. *portion:* i.e., of wit

6. *prove:* try, attempt

7. *assay:* attempt

8. *glass:* mirror, looking glass

9. *she:* i.e., the soul

10. *contempling:* contemplating

11. *part . . . in it:* the share I have performed in it; i.e., the work of translation

12. *as well . . . manual:* the spiritual as well as the physical

13. *nor else worthy:* nor otherwise worthy

14. *unperfit:* incomplete, unfinished (imperfect)

15. *shapen:* fashioned

16. *file . . . learning:* i.e., metaphorically, Catherine's keenness of mind

17. *it . . . Highness:* your Highness condescend

18. *cause to mend:* arrange to have corrected

19. *after . . . been:* after being

20. *of:* to

21. *they:* i.e., my faults

Commentary

Elizabeth was barely eleven when she undertook her translation of *Le Miroir de l'âme Pécheresse*. This pious French meditation was written in verse by the Queen of Navarre, Marguerite Angoulême. Marguerite had met the youthful Anne Boleyn at the French court and may have supplied her with a copy of the treatise that eventually found its way to her daughter's bookshelf.[1] Elizabeth's translation was edited by John Bale and published at Wesel, in northern Germany, in 1548 as *A Godly Medytacyon of the christen sowle* (STC 17320).

1. See Marc Shell, *Elizabeth's Glass* (Lincoln, Neb., 1993), pp. 3–4. Shell edits Elizabeth's text from O: Cherry MS 36, and includes a facsimile of her part of the manuscript. For a complete facsimile of the manuscript see Marguerite, *The Mirror of the Sinful Soul: A Prose Translation from the French,* ed. Percy W. Ames (London, 1897).

Letter 2. Elizabeth to Queen Catherine Parr, June (?) 1548

Holograph, PRO: SP 10/2, f. 84c.

Although I could not be plentiful in giving thanks
for the manifold kindness received at your Highness'
hand at my departure, yet I am something to be borne
withal,[1] for truly I was replete with sorrow to depart
from your Highness, especially seeing you undoubt-   [5
ful[2] of health, and albeit I answered little, I weighed it
more deeper when you said you would warn[3] me of all
evils that you should hear of me, for if your Grace had
not a good opinion of me you would not have offered
friendship to me that way that all men judge the con-   [10
trary. But what may I more say than thank God for
providing such friends to me, desiring God to enrich
me with their long life and me grace to be in heart no
less thankful to receive it than I now am glad in writing
to shew it. And although I have plenty of matter,[4] here   [15
I will stay,[5] for I know you are not quiet[6] to read.

From Cheston[7] this present Saturday.

                   Your Highness' humble daughter
                   Elizabeth

Notes

1. *borne withal:* put up with, moreover
2. *undoubtful:* without doubt, certain
3. *warn:* notify
4. *matter:* subjects (to impart to Catherine)
5. *stay:* end

6. *quiet:* free from annoyance

7. *Cheston:* Cheshunt, the home, about ten miles southeast of Hatfield, of Sir Anthony Denny and his wife Joan, Catherine Ashley's sister

Commentary

Shortly after the death of Henry VIII early in 1547, Elizabeth took up residence with Queen Catherine Parr and her new husband, Lord Admiral Thomas Seymour, whom Catherine had married in April. Elizabeth's sojourn ended abruptly in late spring or early summer of 1548. Whether or not Seymour and his stepdaughter had engaged in any overly intimate flirtation, their behavior was apparently more than the Queen, now pregnant with her first child, could endure. As Elizabeth's letter makes clear, it was at her initiative that the Princess was sent to the Dennys' home at Cheshunt. The letter, however, seems to imply that Catherine trusted Elizabeth while "all men judge the contrary."

Letter 3. Elizabeth to Edward Seymour, duke of Somerset, Lord Protector, after May 1548

Scribal copy with autograph signature,
PRO: EXT 9/42 (formerly SP 10/5, f. 8A).

My very good Lord,

Many lines will not serve to render the least part of the thanks that your Grace hath deserved of me, most especially for that[1] you have been careful for my health and sending unto me not only your comfortable[2] letters, but also physicians as Doctor Bill,[3] whose diligence and pain has been a great part of my recovery, for whom I do most heartily thank your Grace, desiring you to give him thanks for me, who can ascertain you of mine estate[4] of health wherefore[5] I will not write it. And although I be most bounden to you in this time of my sickness, yet I may not be unthankful for that your Grace hath made expedition for my patent.[6] With my most hearty thanks and commendations to you and to my good Lady your wife.[7] Most heartily fare you well, from Cheshunt this present Friday.

[5

[10

[15

> Your assured friend to my power,
> Elizabeth

Notes

1. *for that:* because

2. *comfortable:* encouraging, supportive

3. *as . . . Bill:* such as Doctor Bill; i.e., Dr. Thomas Bill, royal physician to Henry VIII and Edward VI

4. *ascertain . . . estate:* inform you of my condition

5. *wherefore:* for which reason

6. *made . . . patent:* urged the prompt issue of my letters patent. At stake were lands to the value of more than £3,000 per year granted to Elizabeth by her father's will. The patent was finally issued March 17, 1550 (*Calendar of the Patent Rolls, Edward VI,* 3:238–42). A tear in the paper has removed one or more words between "made" and "expedition."

7. Somerset's second wife, Anne, daughter of Sir Edward Stanhope and Elizabeth Bourchier.

Commentary

Queen Catherine died from complications of childbirth in September 1548, whereupon Thomas Seymour explored the feasibility of marrying the Princess. On January 16, 1549, Edward Seymour, duke of Somerset and Lord Protector, placed Thomas, his brother, under arrest. The charge against him was suspicion of treason, including an intention to marry Elizabeth without the Privy Council's approval. The Council dismissed her governess, Catherine Ashley, and her cofferer (treasurer), Thomas Parry; both were rigorously interrogated by the government. Meanwhile, authority over Elizabeth was transferred to Sir Robert Tyrwhitt and his wife, both of whom had served in Queen Catherine Parr's household. The Lord Admiral was beheaded on March 20, 1549. These matters are addressed in Letters 3–7.

Letter 4. Elizabeth to Edward Seymour, duke of Somerset, Lord Protector, January 28, 1549

Holograph, Hatfield House, Cecil Papers 133/4/2.

My Lord,

Your great gentleness and goodwill toward me as well in this thing as in other things I do understand, for the which, even as I ought, so I do give you most humble thanks. And whereas[1] your Lordship willeth and counseleth me, as a earnest friend, to declare what I   [5 know in this matter, and also to write what I have declared to Master Tyrwhitt, I shall most willingly do it.

I declared unto him first that after that the Cofferer had declared unto me what my Lord Admiral answered for Allen's matter,[2] and for Durham Place,[3] that   [10 it was appointed to be a mint, he told me that my Lord Admiral did offer me his house for my time being with the King's Majesty. And further said and asked me whether if the Council did consent that I should have my Lord Admiral, whether I would consent to it or no.   [15 I answered that I would not tell him what my mind was, and I inquired further of him what he meant to ask me that question or who bade him say so. He answered me and said, nobody bade him say so, but that he perceived (as he thought) by my Lord Admiral's in-   [20 quiring whether my patent were sealed[4] or no, and debating what he spent in his house, and inquiring what was spent in my house, that he was given[5] that way rather than otherwise. And as concerning Kat Ashley, she never advised[6] me unto it but said always (when any   [25

talked of my marriage) that she would never have me
marry neither in England nor out of England without
the consent of the King's Majesty, your Graces', and the
Council's, and after the Queen was departed,[7] when I
asked of her[8] what news she heard from London, she [30
answered merrily, "They say there that your Grace
shall have my Lord Admiral, and that he will come
shortly to woo you." And moreover I said unto him
that the Cofferer sent a letter hither that my Lord said
that he would come this way as he went down to the [35
country. Then I bade her write as she thought best, and
bade her show it me when she had done. So she writ
that she thought it not best for fear of suspicion, and so
it went forth. And my Lord Admiral, after he heard
that, asked of the Cofferer why he might not come as [40
well to me as to my sister, and then I desired Kat Ashley
to write again (lest my Lord might think that she knew
more in it than he) that she knew nothing in it but suspicion. And also I told Master Tyrwhitt that to the effect of the matter[9] I never consented unto any such [45
thing without the Council's consent thereunto.

 And as for Kat Ashley or the Cofferer, they never
told me that they would practice[10] it. These be the
things which I both declared to Master Tyrwhitt and
also whereof my conscience beareth me witness, which [50
I would not for all earthly things offend in anything,
for I know I have a soul to save as well as other folks
have, wherefore I will above all thing have respect unto
this same.

 If there be any more things which I can remember [55
I will either write it myself or cause Master Tyrwhit
to write it. Master Tyrwhitt and others have told me
that there goeth rumors abroad which be greatly both

against mine honor and honesty,[11] which above all other things I esteem, which be these, that I am in the [60 Tower and with child by my Lord Admiral. My Lord, these are shameful slanders, for the which besides the great desire I have to see the King's Majesty, I shall most heartily desire your Lordship that I may come to the court after your first determination,[12] that I may [65 shew myself there as I am. Written in haste from Hatfield this 28 of January.

> Your assured friend to my little power,[13]
> Elizabeth

Notes

1. *whereas:* considering that

2. *Allen's matter:* probably referring to Edmund Allen, who was appointed Elizabeth's chaplain this same year

3. *Durham Place:* the bishop of Durham's London residence, conveyed to Elizabeth by letters patent, March 17, 1550

4. *sealed:* affixed with the Great Seal and thus enacted

5. *given:* inclined

6. *avised:* advised

7. *after . . . departed:* i.e., after the death of Queen Catherine Parr

8. *her:* i.e., Ashley

9. *to . . . matter:* regarding the substance of the matter

10. *practice:* arrange by stealth or intrigue

11. *honesty:* chaste reputation

12. *after . . . determination:* according to your original intention

13. *to . . . power:* to my small ability

Commentary

Within days of Thomas Seymour's arrest, Elizabeth was being pressured to explain in detail her relationship with him. As she was well aware, her account would be compared with those of Ashley and Parry, now under interrogation in the Tower of London.

Textual Notes

This and other texts from the Cecil Papers are published courtesy of the Marquess of Salisbury. At l. 38, Elizabeth wrote "iuspicion" for "suspicion," and at l. 60, "thinkes" for "things."

Letter 5. Elizabeth to Lord Protector Edward Seymour, February 6, 1549

Holograph, O: Arch. F.c.39.

My Lord, I have received your gentle letter and also your message by Master Tyrwhitt for the which two things especially (although for many other things) I cannot give your Lordship sufficient thanks. And whereas your grace doth will me to credit Master Tyr- [5
whitt, I have done so and will do so as long as he willeth me (as he doth not) to nothing but to that which is for mine honor and honesty. And even as I said to him, and did write to your lordship, so I do write now again that when there doth any more things happen in my [10
mind which I have forgotten I assure your Grace I will declare them most willingly, for I would not (as I trust you have not) so evil a opinion of me that I would conceal anything that I knew, for it were to no purpose; and surely forgetfulness may well cause me to hide [15
things, but undoubtedly else[1] I will declare all that I know. From Hatfield the 6 of February.

> Your assured friend to my little
> power. Elizabeth

Notes

   1. *else:* otherwise

Textual Notes

   The letter is a bifolium endorsed in Elizabeth's hand, "To my verey good Lorde my Lorde Protector."

Letter 6. Elizabeth to Lord Protector Edward Seymour, February 21, 1549

Holograph, L: Lansdowne MS 1236, ff. 33–33v.

My Lord,

Having received your Lordship's letters, I perceive
in them your goodwill toward me because you declare
to me plainly your mind in this thing, and again for
that[1] you would not wish that I should do anything
that should not seem good unto the Council, for the   [5
which thing I give you most hearty thanks. And
whereas I do understand that you do take in evil[2] part
the letters that I did write unto your Lordship, I am
very sorry that you should take them so, for my mind[3]
was to declare unto you plainly, as I thought, in that   [10
thing, which I did also the more willingly because (as I
writ to you) you desired me to be plain with you in all
things. And as concerning that point that you writ
that I seem to stand in mine own wit[4] in being so well
assured of mine own self, I did assure me of myself[5] no   [15
more than I trust the truth shall try.[6] And to say that
which I knew of myself I did not think should have dis-
pleased the Council or your Grace.

And surely the cause why that I was sorry that there
should be any such about me[7] was because that I   [20
thought the people will say that I deserved through my
lewd demeanor to have such a one, and not that I mislike anything that your Lordship or the Council shall
think good, for I know that you and the Council are

charged with me or[8] that I take upon me to rule my-   [25
self, for I know they are most deceived that trusteth
most in themselves, wherefore I trust you shall never
find that fault in me, to the which thing I do not see
that your Grace has made any direct answer at this
time. And seeing they make so evil reports already,   [30
shall be but a increasing of their evil tongues, howbeit
you did write that if I would bring forth any that had
reported it, you and the Council would see it re-
dressed, which thing though I can easily do it, I would
be loath to do it for because[9] it is mine own cause, and   [35
again that should be but a breeding[10] of a evil name of
me that I am glad to punish them and so get the evil
will of the people, which thing I would be loath to
have.

But if it mought[11] so seem good unto your Lord-   [40
ship and the rest of the Council to send forth a proclamation into the countries[12] that they refrain their
tongues, declaring how the tales be but lies, it should
make both the people think that you and the Council
have great regard that no such rumors should be   [45
spread of any of the King's Majesty's sisters as I am,
though unworthy. And also I should think myself to
receive such friendship at your hands as you have
promised me, although your Lordship hath shewed
me great already. Howbeit I am ashamed to ask it any   [50
more because I see you are not so well minded thereunto. And as concerning that you say that I give folks
occasion to think in[13] refusing the good to uphold the
evil, I am not of so simple understanding nor I would
that your Grace should have so evil a opinion of me   [55
that I have so little respect to mine own honesty that I

would maintain it if I had sufficient promise of the same, and so your grace shall prove[14] me when it comes to the point.[15]

And thus I bid you farewell, desiring God always to   [60 assist you in all your affairs. Written in haste from Hatfield this 21 of February.

> Your assured friend to my little power,
> Elizabeth

Notes

1. *for that:* because
2. *evil:* ill
3. *mind:* intention
4. *stand . . . wit:* trust to my own judgment
5. *assure . . . myself:* assert my self-confidence
6. *try:* ascertain
7. *sorry . . . me:* i.e., objecting to the Council's appointment of Lady Tyrwhitt to replace Catherine Ashley as Elizabeth's governess
8. *charged . . . or:* responsible for me, rather than
9. *for because:* because
10. *breeding:* origination, production of
11. *mought:* might
12. *countries:* shires, counties
13. *think in:* think that in
14. *prove:* find
15. *point:* critical moment

Textual Notes

Elizabeth's "refraine ther tonges" is written with three minims that could as easily stand for "reframe ther tonges" (ll. 41–42) as there is no indication of a dotted *i*. But as she frequently failed to dot the *i*'s in this letter, I have transcribed the word as "refrain" as making the best sense in context. The letter is endorsed in Elizabeth's hand "To my verey good Lorde my Lorde Protector," with the scribal note "xxj Fbr 1548 My Lady Elizabeth to my L. P."

Letter 7. Elizabeth to Lord Protector Edward Seymour, March 7, 1549

Holograph, L: Lansdowne MS 1236, f. 35.

My Lord,

I have a request to make unto your Grace which
fear has made me omit[1] til this time for two causes, the
one because I saw that my request for[2] the rumors
which were spread abroad of me took so little place,[3]
which thing when I considered, I thought I should lit- [5
tle profit in any other suit; howbeit, now[4] I understand
that there is a proclamation for them[5] (for the which I
give your Grace and the rest of the Council most humble thanks), I am the bolder to speak for another thing.
And the other was because peradventure your Lord- [10
ship and the rest of the Council will think that I favor
her evil-doing for whom I shall speak for, which is for
Catherine Ashley, that it would please your Grace and
the rest of the Council to be good unto her, which
thing I do not to favor her in any evil (for that I would [15
be sorry to do), but for these considerations which follow, the which hope doth teach me in saying that I
ought not to doubt but that your Grace and the rest of
the Council will think that I do it for three other considerations: first because that she hath been with me a [20
long time and many years, and hath taken great labor
and pain in bringing of me up in learning and honesty,
and therefore I ought of very[6] duty speak for her, for
Saint Gregory sayeth that we are more bound to them

that bringeth us up well than to our parents, for our [25
parents do that which is natural for them, that is,
bringeth us into this world, but our bringers-up are a
cause to make us live well in it.[7] The second is because
I think that whatsoever she hath done in my Lord
Admiral's matter as concerning the marrying of me, [30
she did it because, knowing him to be one of the
Council, she thought he would not go about any such
thing without[8] he had the Council's consent thereunto, for I have heard her many times say that she
would never have me marry in any place without your [35
Grace's and the Council's consent. The third cause is
because that it shall and doth make men think that I
am not clear of the deed myself, but that it is pardoned
in me because of my youth, because that she I loved so
well is in such a place. Thus hope prevailing more with [40
me than fear hath won the battle, and I have at this
time gone forth with it. Which I pray God be taken no
other ways that[9] it is meant. Written in haste from Hatfield this 7 day of March.

Also if I may be so bold, not offending, I beseech [45
your Grace and the rest of the Council to be good to
Master Ashley her husband, which because he is my
kinsman I would be glad he should a {   }[10]

> Your assured friend to my little power,
> Elizabeth

Notes

1. *omit:* pass over
2. *request for:* request with regard to
3. *took . . . place:* elicited so little effect

4. *now:* now that

5. *them:* i.e., the rumors. If so, no copy of the document seems to have survived.

6. *very:* true

7. Elizabeth may here be thinking of St. Gregory Thaumaturgus's "Address of Thanksgiving to Origen" (ca. 220–230). Gregory writes of Origen, his mentor, that "of all the human race, let this our thanks be directed particularly to this holy man . . . who was not close to me by family or any human blood relationship" (*St. Gregory Thaumaturgus: Life and Works,* trans. Michael Slusser [Washington, D.C., 1998], pp. 97–98).

8. *without:* unless

9. *that:* than

10. The leaf is torn at this point.

Textual Notes

This letter shows signs that it was indeed written in haste as Elizabeth claims in her subscription. She no doubt copied from a draft and probably at one sitting, for her accuracy declines in the second half of the text. She wrote "brinkinge" for "bringing" at l. 22 and "brinkers" for "bringers" at l. 27. Also at l. 27, "us" is inserted above the line and "have me marry" (l. 35) is written in the right margin with a caret to indicate its placement. At l. 43, "that it is meant" stands for "than it is meant" (l. 43); and she squeezes in "to be good" between the lines in her last-minute plea for John Ashley. The letter is endorsed (f. 36v) in Elizabeth's hand "To my verey good Lorde my Lorde Protector," with a scribal note: "7 marche My Lady Elizabeth to my L. P."

Letter 8. Elizabeth to King Edward VI, May 15, 1551

Holograph, L: Cotton Vespasian MS F.3, f. 48.

Like as the rich man that daily gathereth riches to riches and to one bag of money layeth a great sort[1] till it come to infinite,[2] so methinks your majesty, not being sufficed[3] with many benefits and gentleness shewed to me afore this time, doth now increase them [5 in asking and desiring where you may bid and command, requiring a thing not worthy the desiring for itself but made worthy for[4] your Highness' request—my picture, I mean, in which if the inward good mind[5] toward your Grace might as well be declared as the out- [10 ward face and countenance shall be seen, I would nor[6] have tarried the commandment but prevent[7] it, nor have been the last to grant but the first to offer it. For the face, I grant I might well blush to offer, but the mind I shall never be ashamed to present. For though [15 from the grace of the picture the colors may fade by time, may give[8] by weather, may be spotted by chance, yet the other nor[9] time with her swift wings shall over- take, nor the misty clouds with their lourings[10] may darken, nor chance with her slippery foot may over- [20 throw.

Of this, although yet the proof could not be great because the occasions hath been but small, notwith- standing as a dog hath a day, so may I perchance have time to declare it in deeds where now I do write them [25 but in words. And further, I shall most humbly beseech your majesty that when you shall look on my picture you will vouchsafe[11] to think that as you have but the outward shadow[12] of the body afore you, so my inward mind wisheth that the body itself were oftener in your presence. Howbeit because both my so being,[13] I think, could do your Majesty little pleasure, though myself great good, and again because I see as yet not the time agreeing thereunto, I shall learn to follow this saying of Horace, *Feras non culpes quod vitari non potest.*[14]   [35

And thus I will (troubling your Majesty, I fear), end with my most humble thanks, beseeching God long to preserve you to His honor, to your comfort, to the realm's profit, and to my joy. From Hatfield, this 15 day of May.   [40

> Your Majesty's most humbly, sister and servant, Elizabeth

Notes

1. *sort:* quantity, multitude
2. *infinite:* an exceedingly large amount
3. *sufficed:* satisfied with
4. *for:* by, because of
5. *inward good mind:* inner good disposition
6. *nor:* neither
7. *prevent:* anticipated
8. *give:* fade
9. *nor:* neither
10. *lourings:* frowning, scowling
11. *vouchsafe:* correction for Elizabeth's "witsafe"
12. *shadow:* image
13. *so being:* i.e., being in your presence
14. *Feras . . . potest:* "You must endure, not blame, what cannot be avoided." This is a variant of *Feras, non culpes quod*

mutari non potest (You must endure, not blame, what cannot be changed), from the *Sententiae* of Publilius Syrus. This collection of proverbs attributed to Publilius, a mime of the first century B.C.E., became a school text early in the Christian era. The variant text Elizabeth attributes to Horace has not been identified.

Commentary

Although a compelling case has been made for Elizabeth's composition of this letter in 1547 to accompany the portrait of herself that is now part of the royal collection at Windsor Castle,[1] she signs the letter from Hatfield but was not residing there on May 15, 1547. It was apparently in 1551 that Edward asked Elizabeth to send him her portrait, for this is the only time during his reign that she was at Hatfield on May 15.[2]

1. Janet Arnold, "The Picture of Elizabeth I When Princess," *Burlington Magazine* 123 (May 1981): 303–4.
2. I am grateful to Dr. Simon Adams for supplying me with this information from his forthcoming biography of Elizabeth from Yale University Press.

Letter 9. Elizabeth to King Edward VI, April 21, 1552

Holograph, Harvard University, Houghton Library MS Typ 686.

What cause I had of sorry[1] when I heard first of
your Majesty's sickness all men might guess, but none
but myself could feel, which to declare were or might
seem a point of flattery, and therefore to write it I omit.
But as the sorrow could not be little because the occa- [5
sions were many, so is the joy great to hear of the good
escape out of the perilous diseases. And that I am fully
satisfied and well assured of the same by your Grace's
own hand I must needs give you my most humble
thanks, assuring your Majesty that a precious jewel at [10
another time could not so well have contented as your
letter in this case hath comforted me. For now do I say
with Saint Austin that a disease is to be counted no
sickness that shall cause a better health when it is past
than was assured afore it came.[2] For afore you had [15
them, every man thought that that should not be es-
chewed of you that was not scaped of many. But since
you have had them, doubt[3] of them is past and hope is
given to all men that it was a purgation by these means
for other, worse diseases which might happen this year. [20
Moreover, I consider that as a good father that loves his
child dearly doth punish him sharply, so God, favoring
your Majesty greatly, hath chastened you straitly, and
as a father doth it for the further good of his child, so
hath God prepared this for the better health of your [25
Grace. And in this hope I commit your Majesty to his
hands, most humbly craving pardon of your Grace

that I did write no sooner, desiring you to attribute the fault to my evil[4] head and not to my slothful hand.

From Hatfield this 21 of April,
Your Majesty's most humble
sister to command,
Elizabeth

Notes

1. *sorry:* sorrow
2. Perhaps alluding to the *Confessions,* book 5, chapters 9 and 10, where St. Augustine describes his recovery from a fever. Augustine writes, "Thou didst restore me then from that illness . . . that thou mightest endow [me] with a better and more certain health" (*Confessions and Enchiridion,* trans. and ed. Albert C. Outler [Philadelphia, 1955], pp. 106–7).
3. *doubt:* fear
4. *evil:* defective, flawed

Commentary

This letter fits the circumstances of April 1552; on the second of that month, the fourteen-year-old King Edward VI recorded in his "Chronicle," "I fell sick of the measles and the smallpox."[1] He recovered within weeks from these serious diseases, although their effects on his health may have opened the way for the tuberculosis that clearly afflicted him by the end of the year and led to his death in July 1553.

1. Edward VI, *The Chronicle and Political Papers,* ed. W. K. Jordan (Ithaca, N.Y., 1966), p. 117.

Letter 10. Elizabeth to Princess Mary, October 27, 1552 (?)
Holograph, L: Lansdowne MS 1236, f. 39.

Good Sister,

  As to hear of your sickness is unpleasant to me, so is
it nothing fearful for that[1] I understand it is your old
guest[2] that is wont oft to visit you, whose coming
though it be oft, yet is it never welcome, but notwithstanding it is comfortable[3] for that *Iacula praevisa*   [5
minus feriunt.[4] And as I do understand your need of Jane
Russell's service,[5] so am I sorry that it is by my man's[6] occasion letted,[7] which if I had known afore, I would have
caused his will give place to need[8] of her service, for as it
is her duty to obey his commandment, so is it his part to   [10
attend your pleasure. And as I confess it were meeter[9] for
him to go to her since she attends upon you, so indeed he
required[10] the same, but for that divers of his fellows had
business abroad,[11] that made[12] his tarrying at home.

  Good sister, though I have good cause to thank you   [15
for your oft sending to me, yet I have more occasion to
render you my hearty thanks for your gentle writing,
which how painful it is to you I may well guess by myself, and you may well see by my writing so oft how
pleasant it is to me. And thus I end to trouble you, de-   [20
siring God to send you as well to do as you can think
and wish or I desire or pray. From Ashridge scribbled
this 27th of October.

                    Your loving sister. Elizabeth

Notes

1. *for that:* because
2. *guest:* temporary condition. The exact nature of Mary's discomfort is unknown.
3. *comfortable:* reassuring
4. *Iacula . . . feriunt:* Darts foreseen strike less forcefully. In the morality play *Mankind,* Mercy explains to the title character, "The proverbe seyth: '*Iacula praestita minus laedunt*' " (in *Medieval Drama,* ed. David Bevington [Boston, 1975], 1. 882).
5. Jane served Princess Mary but was the wife of Elizabeth's Groom of the Chamber, William Russell.
6. *man's:* servant's
7. *letted:* prevented
8. *give . . . need:* to give place to your need
9. *meeter:* fitter
10. *required:* requested
11. *abroad:* out of the house
12. *made:* caused, necessitated

Commentary

Elizabeth wrote to her sister from Ashridge, Hertfordshire, a royal estate north of London. Princess Mary was afflicted with her "old illness" in late October 1552.[1] Elizabeth endorsed the letter (f. 40v) "To my welbeloued sistar Marye."

1. David Loades, *Mary Tudor: A Life* (Oxford, 1989), p. 164.

Letter 11. Elizabeth to King Edward VI, May or June (?) 1553
Holograph, L: Harl. MS 6986, f. 23.

Like as a shipman in stormy weather plucks down
the sails, tarrying for better wind, so did I, most noble
King, in my unfortunate chance a-Thursday pluck
down the high sails of my joy and comfort, and do
trust one day that as troublesome waves have repulsed   [5
me backward, so a gentle wind will bring me forward
to my haven. Two chief occasions moved me much and
grieved me greatly, the one for that I doubted[1] your
Majesty's health, the other because for all my long tarrying I went without that[2] I came for. Of the first I am   [10
relieved in a part, both that I understood of[3] your
health and also that your Majesty's lodging is far from
my Lord Marque[ss's] chamber.[4] Of my other grief I
am not eased, but the best is that whatsoever other
folks will suspect, I intend not to fear your Grace's   [15
goodwill, which as I know that I never deserved to
faint,[5] so I trust will still stick by me. For if your Grace's
advise[6] that I should return (whose will is a commandment) had not been, I would not have made the
half of my way the end of my journey. And thus as one   [20
desirous to hear of your Majesty's health, though unfortunate to see it,[7] I shall pray God forever to preserve
you. From Hatfield this present Saturday.

      Your Majesty's humble sister to commandment
      Elizabeth

Notes

1. *doubted:* feared for
2. *that:* that which
3. *both . . . of:* that I gained understanding both of
4. Both William Parr, marquess of Northampton, and William Paulet, marquess of Winchester, were members of the King's Privy Council and attending court in the spring of 1553. Paulet, however, would have been addressed by his title as Lord Treasurer; thus Elizabeth probably refers to Northampton in this passage. Presumably, Northampton or one of his attendants had been visited with some contagious disease.
5. *to faint:* to have decline (with an implied "it," referring to Edward's goodwill)
6. *advise:* advice
7. *to see it:* in not seeing it

Commentary

In the course of Edward's final illness, Elizabeth apparently set out from Hatfield to visit him in London but turned back after receiving a message to do so from the King himself.

Textual Notes

Elizabeth endorsed her letter on f. 24v, "To the Kinges most Excellent Majestie." Readings along the right margin have been slightly cropped. Percy W. Ames includes a facsimile of the Harleian text in his edition of Marguerite, *The Mirror of the Sinful Soul: A Prose Translation from the French* (London, 1897), facing p. 46.

Letter 12. Elizabeth to Lady Catherine Knollys, 1553

Scribal copy, L: Lansdowne MS 94, f. 21.

Relieve your sorrow for your far journey with joy of your short return[1] and think this pilgrimage rather a proof[2] of your friends than a leaving of your country. The length of time and distance of place separates not the love of friends nor deprives not the shew of good- [5 will. A old saying, when bale is lowest, boot is nearest,[3] when your need shall be most, you shall find my friendship greaterest.[4] Let other[5] promise and I will do, in words not mo,[6] in deeds as much. My power but small, my love as great as they whose gifts may tell their [10 friendships' tale. Let will supply all other want, and oft sending take the lieu[7] of often sights. Your messengers shall not return empty nor yet your desires unaccomplished. Lethe's flood[8] hath here no course, good memory hath greatest stream, and to conclude—a [15 word that hardly I can say, I am driven by need to write—farewell it is, which, in the sense one way I wish, the other way I grieve.

> Your loving cousin and ready friend,
> Cor rotto.[9]

Notes

    1. *short return:* return after a brief interval

    2. *proof:* test, trial

    3. *when . . . nearest:* When sorrow is worst, relief is nearest. This proverb is traced by the *OED* to ca. 1250, "When the bale

is all highest then is the boot all nighest." See M. P. Tilley, *A Dictionary of the Proverbs in England in the Sixteenth and Seventeenth Centuries* (Ann Arbor, Mich., 1950), B59.

4. *greaterest:* greatest (MS "greatrest"); an example of Elizabeth's habit of grafting superlatives onto comparative forms

5. *other:* others

6. *mo:* more

7. *lieu:* place

8. *Lethe's flood:* the mythical river of forgetfulness in Hades

9. *Cor rotto:* heart broken (Italian, misspelled)

Commentary

Catherine, the wife of Sir Francis Knollys, was Elizabeth's first cousin. Born Catherine Carey, her mother was Mary Boleyn, Queen Anne Boleyn's sister. Lady Knollys and her husband were staunch Protestants who fled to the Continent when Mary came to the throne. On Mary's death, they returned to assume important roles at Elizabeth's court: Catherine as lady of the Queen's bedchamber, and Sir Francis as privy councillor and vice-chamberlain of the household.

Textual Notes

The text is copied in a mixed script and cursive italic hand that preserves such spellings characteristic of Elizabeth's writing as "nide" for "need" (l. 7) and "the whose" for "they whose" (l. 10). The leaf is endorsed in Burghley's hand, "1553 Copy of a letter wrytten by the Lady Elizab: Grace to the Lady Knolles."

Letter 13. Elizabeth to Queen Mary I, March 17, 1554

Holograph, PRO: SP 11/4, f. 3.

If any ever did try this old saying that a king's word was more than another man's oath, I most humbly beseech your Majesty to verify it in me and to remember your last promise and my last demand[1] that I be not condemned without answer and due proof, which it [5 seems that now I am, for that[2] without cause proved I am by your Council from you commanded to go unto the Tower, a place more wonted[3] for a false traitor than a true subject which, though I know I deserve it not, yet in the face of all this realm appears[4] that it is [10 proved, which I pray God I may die the shamefullest death that ever any died afore I may mean any such thing. And to this present hour I protest afore God (who shall judge my truth whatsoever malice shall devise) that I never practised, concealed, nor consented [15 to anything that might be prejudicial to your person any way, or dangerous to the state by any mean, and therefore I humbly beseech your Majesty to let me answer afore yourself and not suffer me to trust your counsellors, yea and that afore I go to the Tower (if [20 it be possible), if not afore I be further condemned; howbeit I trust assuredly your Highness will give me leave to do it afore I go for that thus shamefully I may not be cried out on[5] as now I shall be, yea and without cause. [25

Let conscience move your Highness to take some better way with me than to make me be condemned in

all men's sight afore my desert known. Also I most
humbly beseech your Highness to pardon this my
boldness, which my innocency procures me to do, to-   [30
gether with hope of your natural kindness, which I
trust will not see me cast away without desert, which
what it is I would desire no more of God but that you
truly knew, which thing I think and believe you shall
never by report know unless by yourself you hear. I   [35
have heard in my time of many cast away for want[6] of
coming to the presence of their prince, and in late days
I heard my Lord of Somerset say that if his brother had
been suffered[7] to speak with him he had never suffered,[8] but the persuasions were made to him so great   [40
that he was brought in belief that he could not live
safely if the Admiral lived, and that made him give his
consent to his death. Though these persons are not to
be compared to your Majesty, yet I pray God as evil[9]
persuasions persuade not one sister again[10] the other,   [45
and all for that[11] they have heard false report and not
harkene[d][12] to the truth known.

Therefore once again kneeling with humbleness of
my heart because I am not suffered to bow the knees of
my body, I humbly crave to speak with your Highness,   [50
which I would not be so bold to desire if I knew not
myself most clear[13] as I know myself most true. And as
for the traitor Wyatt, he might peradventure write me
a letter, but on my faith I never received any from him,
and as for the copy of my letter sent to the French   [55
King, I pray God confound[14] me eternally if ever I sent
him word, message, token, or letter by any means, and
to this my truth I will stand in to my death.

I humbly crave but only one word of answer from
yourself.   [60

Your Highness' most faithful subject that hath been
from the beginning and will be to my end.

Elizabeth

Notes

1. *demand:* request
2. *for that:* because
3. *wonted:* customary for
4. *appears:* i.e., it appears
5. *cried out on:* loudly complained of
6. *want:* lack
7. *suffered:* allowed
8. *suffered:* i.e., suffered death. Edward Seymour, as Lord Protector Somerset, condemned to death his brother Thomas, the Lord Admiral (see commentary to Letters 3–8).
9. *as evil:* equally evil
10. *again:* against
11. *for that:* because
12. Elizabeth failed to transcribe the final *d* in this word.
13. *clear:* innocent
14. *confound:* destroy

Commentary

In February, Sir Thomas Wyatt, son of the poet, led an unsuccessful coup d'état against Queen Mary. He had written to Elizabeth in advance of his attempt, although she did not reply to him in writing. Mary suspected Elizabeth's complicity in the plot and ordered her removed to London from her house at Ashridge. Elizabeth stalled at first, pleading illness, but was forced to travel in stages to the metropolis. The case against her was aggravated because a copy of one of her letters to Mary had been discovered among papers forwarded to the King of France by his ambassador to England. Mary's government took this as evidence that Elizabeth was conspiring with the French. The Queen refused to see her half-sister, who was sent to the Tower on March 18.[1]

1. The date of this letter is established in Great Britain, Public Record Office, *Calendar of State Papers, Domestic Series, of the Reign of Mary I, 1553–1558*, ed. C. S. Knighton, rev. ed. (London, 1998), p. 53. On January 28 the bishop of Winchester wrote Sir William Petre that he was attempting to decipher the letter found in the French ambassador's packet (p. 24).

Textual Notes

A few passages in this letter are badly faded and spotted; their readings have been reconstructed from the copy in Great Britain, Public Record Office, *Fac-similes of National Manuscripts*, ed. Henry James (Southampton, 1865–68), pt. 3, no. 25. For an early transcription of the text, see Henry Ellis's *Original Letters, Illustrative of English History: Including Numerous Royal Letters*, 2nd ser. (London, 1827), 2:255–57. Elizabeth filled the space between the last sentence of her text and her final plea to Mary just above her subscription with eleven parallel strokes of the pen slanting from left to right, a ploy that would prevent unauthorized additions to her text.

Letter 14. Elizabeth to Queen Mary, August 2, 1556

Holograph, L: Lansdowne MS 1236, f. 37.

When I revolve in mind (most noble Queen) the
old love of paynims[1] to their prince and the reverent
fear of Romans to their Senate, I can but muse for my
part and blush for theirs, to see the rebellious hearts
and devilish intents of Christians in names, but Jews   [5
indeed, toward their anointed[2] king, which methinks,
if they had feared God, though they could not have
loved the state, they should for dread of their own
plague have refrained that wickedness which their
bounden duty to your Majesty hath not restrained.   [10
But when I call to remembrance that the devil, *tanquam leo rugiens circumit querens quem deuorare
potest*,[3] I do the less marvel though he have gotten such
novices into his professed house, as vessels (without
God's grace) more apt to serve his palace than meet to   [15
inhabit English land. I am the bolder to call them his
imps for that St. Paul sayeth *seditiosi filij sunt diaboli*,[4]
and since I have so good a buckler I fear the less to
enter into their judgment.

Of this I assure your Majesty though it be my part   [20
above the rest to bewail such things though my name
had not been in them, yet it vexeth me too much than[5]
the devil owen[6] me such a hate as to put me in any part
of his mischievous instigations, whom as I profess him
my foe, that is all Christians' enemy, so wish I he had   [25
some other way invented to spite me. But since it hath
pleased God thus to bewray[7] their malice afore they

finish their purpose, I most humbly thank Him both that He hath ever thus preserved your Majesty through His aid much like a lamb from the horns of these Basan's bulls,[8] and also stirs up the hearts of your loving subjects to resist them and deliver you to His honor and their shame. The intelligence[9] of which proceeding from your Majesty deserveth more humble thanks than with my pen I can render, which as infinite I will leave to number.[10] And among earthly things I chiefly wish this one, that there were as good surgeons for making anatomies of hearts that might shew my thoughts to your Majesty as there are expert physicians of the bodies able to express the inward grieves[11] of their maladies to their patient. For then I doubt not but know well that whatsoever other should suggest[12] by malice, yet your Majesty should be sure by knowledge so that the more such misty clouds obfuscates the clear light of my truth, the more my tried[13] thoughts should glister to the dimming of their hidden malice.

But since wishes are vain and desires oft fails, I must crave that my deeds may supply that[14] my thoughts cannot declare, and[15] they be not misdeemed there as the facts have been so well tried. And like as I have been your faithful subject from the beginning of your reign, so shall no wicked persons cause me to change to the end of my life. And thus I commit your Majesty to God's tuition, whom I beseech long time to preserve, ending with the new remembrance of my old suit more for that[16] it should not be forgotten than for that[17] I think it not remembered. From Hatfield this present Sunday the second day of August.

Your Majesty's obedient subject and humble sister, Elizabeth

[30

[35

[40

[45

[50

[55

Notes

1. *paynims:* pagans

2. *anointed:* editorial correction for Elizabeth's "oincted"

3. *tanquam . . . potest:* "He goeth about like a roaring lion seeking whom he may devour" (1 Peter 5.8), as translated by the Protestant reformer Hugh Latimer, who cites the same passage in his "Sermon of the Plough" (*A notable Sermon of the reverende father Maister Hughe Latemer,* 1548, sig. C5). Latimer was burned at the stake for heresy by Mary's officials on October 16, 1555.

4. *seditiosi . . . diaboli:* rebels are children of the devil. Elizabeth misquotes Scripture here; Paul terms a sorcerer the child of the devil in Acts 13.10.

5. *than:* Elizabeth's error for "that"

6. *owen:* might owe

7. *bewray:* disclose

8. *Basan's bulls:* The bulls of Bashan in Psalm 22 are the type of an aggressive enemy.

9. *intelligence:* communication

10. *leave to number:* decline to count

11. *grieves:* griefs

12. *suggest:* editorial correction for Elizabeth's "sugiect"

13. *tried:* tested by experience

14. *that:* that which

15. *and:* if

16. *for that:* in order that. It is not clear what request to her sister Elizabeth had in mind when mentioning her "old suit."

17. *for that:* because

Commentary

In May the government foiled a plot led by Henry Dudley and Sir Anthony Kingston to place Elizabeth on the throne. Again, members of Elizabeth's personal retinue, including Catherine Ashley, were arrested and interrogated. The Princess, however, merely found herself and her household placed under the control of Mary's privy councillor, Sir Thomas Pope. Mary assured her that she had full confidence in Elizabeth's innocence of any part in the intrigue.

Textual Notes

Elizabeth endorsed this letter "To the Quines most Excelent Maiestie." A scribal note adds: "Scdo Augustij 1556 The lady Elizabeth to the queens matie. 1556."

Letter 15. Elizabeth to Sir William Cecil and the Privy Council (?), November 1566

Holograph, L: Lansdowne MS 1236, ff. 42–42v.

Set these two conceivings[1] into one meaning and my counsel is all given.[2] Let not other[3] regard themselves so holy as I have no corner left for me. Let them know that I knew (though I followed not[4]) that some of them would[5] my pure conscience better served me [5 than their lewd[6] practices could avail[7] with me. I know no reason why any my private answers to the realm should serve for prologue to a subsidies book.[8] Neither yet do I understand why such audacity should be used to make, without my licence, an act of[9] my words. Are [10 my words like lawyers' books which nowadays go to the wire-drawers[10] to make subtle doings more plain? Is there no hold of[11] my speech without[12] a act compel me to confirm? Shall my princely consent be turned to strengthen my words that be not of themselves sub- [15 stantives?[13] I say no more at this time, but if these fellows were well answered and paid with lawful coin there would be fewer counterfeits[14] among them.

Notes

1. *two conceivings:* a reference to the petition's reminder that Elizabeth "rightly conceaued" that Parliament pressed the succession issue out of their duty and love, and that the Queen had agreed to name a successor

2. *my . . . given:* i.e., I can say nothing more on the subject

3. *other:* others

4. *followed not:* did not pursue

5. *would:* wished that

6. *lewd:* foolish, ill-mannered

7. *avail:* be effectual

8. *subsidies book:* bill authorizing the subsidy

9. *of:* from, out of

10. *wire-drawers:* figuratively, those parsing and extenuating the meaning. Elizabeth also uses this metaphor in Speech 9, line 21.

11. *hold of:* force in

12. *without:* unless

13. *substantives:* of independent force

14. *paid . . . counterfeits:* Elizabeth's punning metaphor suggests that if the devisers of the preamble were duly punished ("paid with lawful coin"), there would be fewer such troublemakers ("counterfeits") in Parliament.

Commentary

Elizabeth took the throne November 17, 1558, upon Queen Mary's death. In the years following she exasperated even her staunchest supporters by refusing either to marry or to declare a successor to the throne. Parliament attempted to force the issue repeatedly and by various means. She set forth her responses to some of these efforts in Speeches 3–6. A draft preamble to the subsidy bill passed by Parliament in 1566 included as its third point a formal expression of gratitude to the Queen for agreeing to "declare the Succession in suche convenient tyme as your highnes with thadvise of your counsell and assent of your Realme shold thinke most mete in suche person as in whome the right

thereof accordinge to law and Justice ought to be setled and re-
mayne." [1] Thus, by signing the bill that granted her the funding
she desperately needed, Elizabeth was legally bound to nominate
a successor to her throne. She jotted down her objection to this
ploy in the blank space at the foot of the draft preamble preserved
among the Cecil Papers. Her note was probably intended for Secretary Cecil's reading and that of his fellow privy councillors, and
it was apparently effective. In its final form, the bill's preamble
merely acknowledged that the Queen would deal with the problem of succession in due time. [2]

1. L: Lansdowne MS 1236, f. 42.
2. J. E. Neale, *Elizabeth I and Her Parliaments, 1559–1581*
(1953; reprint, London, 1969), pp. 163–64.

Textual Notes

The Queen wrote "serue for preamble," then crossed out the
last word and replaced it with "prologe" (l. 8). The bifolium is endorsed in a scribal hand on f. 43v, "Touching the declaration of a
Successor to the Crowne"; and in another hand: "Q. Elizab's running hand."

Letter 16. Elizabeth to Henry Carey, first baron Hunsdon, February 26, 1570

Scribal copy with the Queen's personal postscript added in a second, informal hand, PRO: SP 15/17, f. 113.

By the Queen

Right trusty and well-beloved Cousin we greet you well.

And right glad we are that it hath pleased God to assist you in this your late[1] service against that cankered, subtle traitor, Leonard Dacre,[2] whose force [5 being far greater in number than yours we perceive you have overthrown, and how he thereupon was the first that fled, having as it seemeth a heart readier to shew his unloyal falsehood and malice than to abide the fight. And though the best we could have desired [10 was to have had him taken, yet we thank God that he is in this sort[3] overthrown and forced to flee our realm to his like company of rebels whom we doubt not but God of His favorable justice will confound[4] with such ends as are meet for them. [15

We will not now by words express how inwardly glad we are that you have had such success, whereby both your courage in such an inequal match, your faithfulness toward us, and your wisdom is seen to the world, this your act being the very first that ever was [20 executed by fight in field in our time against any rebels. But we mean also in deeds by just reward to let the world see how much we esteem and can consider such a service as this is. And so we would have yourself also

thank God heartly,[5] as we doubt not but you do (from [25]
whom all victories do proceed), and comfort yourself
with the assurance of our most favorable acceptation.
We have also herewith sent our letters of thanks to Sir
John Forster[6] and would have you namely[7] thank our
good, faithful soldiers of Berwick, in whose worthy [30]
service we do repose no small trust. 26 February 1569.

I doubt much, my Harry, whether that the victory were
given me[8] more joyed me or that you were by God appointed the instrument of my glory, and I assure you
for my country's good the first might suffice but, for [35]
my heart's contentation,[9] the second more pleased me.
It likes me not a little[11] that with a good testimony of
your faith there is seen a stout courage of your mind
that more trusted to the goodness of your quarrel than
to the weakness of your number. Well, I can say no [40]
more, *beatus est ille seruus quem ad Dominus venerit
invenerit faciendo sua mandata.*[11] And that you may
not think that you have done nothing for your profit
though you have done much for your honor, I intend
to make this journey somewhat[12] to increase your [45]
livelihood that you may not say to yourself, *Perditur
quod factum est ingrato.*[13]

               Your loving kinswoman. Elizabeth R

Notes

    1. *late:* recent

    2. Before the rebellion began, Dacre had secured an
audience with Elizabeth at Windsor and assured her of his
loyalty. Late in 1569 he led forces against the rebels, but only
to secure towns and lands he considered due to him by

inheritance. After the defeat by Hunsdon's army, he escaped to Scotland and from there to the Continent; he died in Brussels on August 12, 1573.

3. *sort:* way, manner

4. *confound:* destroy

5. *heartly:* heartily, sincerely

6. Warden of the Middle Marches, whose forces pursued the defeated rebels north toward Scotland.

7. *namely:* particularly

8. *were . . . me:* was given to me

9. *contentation:* contentment

10. *It . . . little:* i.e., I am very pleased

11. *beatus . . . mandata:* Blessed is that servant who, when the Lord comes, shall be found carrying out his orders (Elizabeth's adaptation of Luke 12.37).

12. *journey somewhat:* expedition to some degree

13. *Perditur . . . ingrato:* It is lost because done for an ingrate.

Commentary

Henry Carey, first baron Hunsdon, was Elizabeth's first cousin, the son of Mary (née Boleyn), Anne Boleyn's sister. He spent most of his career in military service as governor of Berwick, the northern fortress that served as England's first line of defense against incursions from Scotland. The "Northern Rebellion," a Catholic uprising against the Elizabethan regime, erupted in November of 1569. On February 15 following, Hunsdon marched from Berwick with 1,500 men. On the 20th, he engaged near Carlisle a force commanded by Leonard Dacre, who had initially taken the government's side in the conflict. Hunsdon's troops defeated the enemy, who outnumbered them roughly two to one.

Letter 17. Elizabeth to William Cecil, Lord Burghley, April 11, 1572

O: Ashmole MS 1729, no. 7, f. 13, holograph.

My Lord,

Methinks that I am more beholding to the hinder part of my head than well dare trust the forwards side of the same, and therefore sent to the Lieutenant and the sheriffs,[1] as you know best, the order to defer this execution till they hear further. And that this may be [5 done, I doubt nothing without curiosity of[2] my further warrant, for that[3] their rash determination[4] upon a very unfit[5] day was countermanded by your considerate[6] admonition. The causes that move me to this are not now to be expressed lest an irrevocable deed be [10 in meanwhile committed. If they will needs[7] a warrant, let this suffice, all written with mine own hand.

Your most loving sovereign,
Elizabeth R.

Notes

1. *Lieutenant . . . sheriffs:* Sir Owen Hopton, lieutenant of the Tower of London, and the sheriffs of London and Middlesex were responsible for supervising the execution.

2. *doubt . . . curiosity of:* do not fear without scrupulous attention to

3. *for that:* because

4. *determination:* decision

5. *unfit:* unsuitable

6. *considerate:* well-considered

7. *needs:* needs have

Commentary

Thomas Howard, fourth duke of Norfolk, was condemned for high treason at Westminster Hall on January 16, 1572. He was charged with plotting a marriage with Mary, Queen of Scots, and a rebellion to overthrow Elizabeth's government and return England to Catholicism. By April 10, Elizabeth had already signed and then revoked three warrants for Howard's execution. Burghley endorsed this, the fourth reprieve, "The Queen's Majesty with her own hand, for staying of the Execution of the D. N. Received at 2 in the Morning." Norfolk was finally beheaded on Tower Hill on June 2.

Textual Notes

Elizabeth's abbreviation in l. 4, "Levetenant and the S.," perhaps designated only one of the sheriffs, but both officers received the final warrant for Norfolk's execution.[1]

1. Neville Williams, *Thomas Howard: Fourth Duke of Norfolk* (London, 1964), p. 252.

Letter 18. Elizabeth to George Talbot,
sixth earl of Shrewsbury, October 21, 1572

Scribal with the Queen's holograph subscription,
Lambeth Palace MS 3197, ff. 41–42.

Right trusty and right well-beloved cousin[1] and
counselor we greet you well. By your letters sent to us
we perceive that you had heard of some late[2] sickness
wherewith we were visited, whereof as you had cause
to be greatly grieved, so though you heard of our   [5
amendment, and was thereby recomforted, yet for a
satisfaction of your mind you are desirous to have the
state of our amendment certified by some few words
in a letter from ourself. True it is that we were about
fourteen days past distempered,[3] as commonly hap-   [10
peneth in the beginning of a fever. But after two or
three days without any great inward sickness, there
began to appear certain red spots in some part of our
face, likely to prove the smallpox.[4] But thanked be
God, contrary to the expectation of our physicians and   [15
all others about us, the same so vanished away as
within four or five days passed no token almost appeared, and at this day we thank God we are so free
from any token or mark of any such disease that none
can conjecture any such thing. So as by this you may   [20
perceive what was our sickness, and in what good estate[5] we be; thanking you, good cousin, for the care
which you had of the one and of the comfort you take
of the other, wherein we do assure ourself of as much
fidelity, duty, and love that you bear us, as of any of any [25

degree within our realm. Given at our Castle of Windsor the 22th of October 1572, the 14th year of our reign.

My faithfull Shrewsbury, let no grief touch your heart for fear of my disease, for I assure you, if my credit were not greater than my shew, there is no beholder would believe that ever I had been touched with such a malady.

[30

> Your faithful, loving sovereign,
> Elizabeth R.

Notes

1. *cousin:* a title given by princes to other princes and nobles

2. *late:* recent

3. *distempered:* afflicted with an imbalance of the bodily humors (according to medical theory of the time)

4. *smallpox:* a needless worry; the disease can be contracted only once, and Elizabeth had survived an attack in the fall of 1562

5. *estate:* condition

Commentary

Shrewsbury was sworn to the Privy Council in 1571, yet from 1569 he served almost continuously in northern England as custodian of Mary, Queen of Scots. A draft of this letter with corrections in Burghley's hand survives in PRO: SP 12/89, f. 128. This text is endorsed "21 Octb. 1572 Cop. from the Queen's Majesty to the Earl of Shrewsbury."

Textual Notes

The note that Elizabeth subscribed to this letter is in her very neatest italic script, with a square knot flourish before the left leg of the initial *M,* and flourishes on the capitals in "Shrewsbury," "I," and "Assure," as well as the *Y* of "Your faithful," and *s* of "sovereign." The letter is endorsed "To our right trusty and right welbeloued Cousin & Counsaylor the Erle of Shrewsbury and Erle Marshall of England." Burghley's draft of Letter 18 is identical with the Lambeth Palace text but lacks "we greet you well" (l. 2), the formal closing sentence and the Queen's personal note to Shrewsbury.

Letter 19. Elizabeth to Walter Devereux, first earl of Essex, August or September 1575

Scribal copy, unsigned, PRO: SP 12/45, pp. 82–84.

Right trusty etc. The honorable and most dutiful manner of writing used in your two last letters, by the which, spoiling[1] yourself altogether of your own affections,[2] you do wholly yield and submit yourself to our will and pleasure, did not a little[3] content us: whereby [5 we perceive, after that the late exercise you have had of patience sithence[4] your employment in that our realm through a most toilful struggling with sundry cross and overthwart accidents[5] you have now at the length[6] attained, to your great and singular commendation, a [10 perfect[7] conquest over such passions as heretofore bare some rule with you and would hardly be restrained within the limits of true temperance: wherewith[8] as you know, Cousin, we have heretofore been somewhat acquainted. [15

And though perhaps you may think that it hath been a dear[9] conquest unto you in respect of the great care of mind, toil of body, and the intolerable charges you have sustained to the consumption of some good portion of your patrimony, yet if the great reputation [20 that you have gained thereby be weighed in the balance[10] of just value, or tried at the touchstone[11] of true desert, it shall then appear that neither your mind's care, your body's toil, nor purse's charge was unprofitably employed. For by the decay of those things that [25 are subject to corruption and mortality you have, as it

were, invested yourself with immortal renown, the
true mark[12] that every honorable mind ought to shoot
at. And though you are to reap the chiefest fruit
thereof, yet next yourself be you right well assured that   [30
we will give place to[13] no other creature or second person living by yielding[14] that they can take like joy or
comfort therein as we do.

Now to come to your question, by the which you
desire to know whether we think that your demands   [35
made unto us were grounded upon the respect of your
own benefit or our service, you shall for answer thereof
understand that we conceive for both, interpreting (as
we do) the word benefit not to import that servile gain
that baseminded men hunt after, but a desire to live in   [40
action and to make proof of your virtue and, being
made of that mettle you are, and not unprofitably or
rather reproachfully to fester in the delights of English
Egypt where the most part of those that are bred in that
soil take greatest delight in holding their noses over the   [45
beef pots.[15] And thus much touching your question.

Now for full answer of your demands,[16] we hope
you rest contented with that[17] we made touching your
said charges as also concerning the marshalship. And
as for the latter of the two, we protest unto you in the   [50
word of a Prince that none but yourself, whose credit
we especially tender[18] and whose satisfaction we
greatly desire, could have obtained the same at our
hands. For the other two, the one concerning the entertainment[19] for 300 men to have continuance during   [55
your life, and the other touching Magnis Island,[20] these
are to let you wit[21] that for the first we are grown to a
full determination with the Deputy last sent over,[22]

both touching the government as also the charges, a
certain proportion of treasure which we mean not to [60
exceed being set down for the defraying of the same,
and therefore cannot without alteration of our full resolution therein directly answer you until we have
heard from him: notwithstanding we have some cause
to think that he will well allow of[23] our yielding to your [65
request for that[24] we are given to understand the said
number you desire may be very profitably employed at
the Ferney. And because we think it convenient for
many respects[25] that with some speed you know his allowance[26] thereof, we have directed by this bearer our [70
letters unto him requiring him to signify unto you his
opinion therein. Now touching your last demand for
Magnis Island, though we have some cause to continue
our former determination in referring the same over
unto our said Deputy's consideration, at whose hands [75
we appointed you should receive full resolution, yet
have we so great a desire to satisfy you therein that we
are content absolutely to yield that you shall have the
same.

Now to conclude: whereas you desire by your hum- [80
ble and earnest request unto us to have your said demands to pass immediately from us, to whom only you
desire to be beholding,[27] surely our meaning and intent was never otherwise, though we must (as all other
princes do) use therein the ministry[28] of others, for we [85
would be loath that any portion of that love and devotion which we mean (besides common duty) by well
using of you to deserve should be cast on others who
shall neither have that will nor power to enable them
to be sufficient competitors with us in that behalf. [90

Notes

1. *spoiling:* depriving
2. *affections:* biased feelings
3. *not a little:* i.e., very much
4. *sithence:* since
5. *cross . . . accidents:* contrary and unfavorable occurrences
6. *at the length:* at last, finally
7. *perfect:* complete, thorough
8. *wherewith:* with which
9. *dear:* costly
10. *weighed . . . balance:* weighed in the scale
11. *tried . . . touchstone:* tested by the touchstone (used figuratively to mean anything that determines genuineness)
12. *mark:* target
13. *give place to:* give way to, yield to
14. *yielding:* conceding
15. *English Egypt . . . beef pots:* Elizabeth incites Essex to continue his Irish campaign by likening her nobility who live in decadence at home to the Israelites who lived comfortably in Egypt before the Exodus. In Exodus 16.3 the Israelites, fearing starvation in the wilderness, nostalgically recall "the land of Egypt, when we sate by the flesh pottes" (Geneva Bible translation).
16. *demands:* questions
17. *that:* that which
18. *tender:* regard highly
19. *entertainment:* maintenance
20. Sir Henry Sidney, lord deputy of Ireland, wrote the Queen on September 28 urging her to grant Essex Magee (Magnis) Island and the right to command 300 men for life in Ireland (Great Britain, Public Record Office, *Calendar of the State Papers Relating to Ireland, of the Reigns of Henry VIII,*

Edward VI, Mary, and Elizabeth [London, 1860–1912],
2:80).

21. *wit:* know

22. Sir Henry Sidney was appointed lord deputy of Ireland
in August 1575; he arrived at his post in early September,
replacing Sir William Fitzwilliam.

23. *allow of:* agree to

24. *for that:* because

25. *respects:* reasons, considerations

26. *allowance:* approval

27. *beholding:* beholden

28. *ministry:* service

Commentary

Essex had sailed to Ireland in the summer of 1573, intending
to subdue the Scottish and Irish forces that controlled Ulster and
transform the area into an English colony. The Queen and her
Privy Council supported the earl's initiative, but in return demanded that he mortgage his principal estates to the Crown.
Nearly two years of fighting ensued, with English massacres of the
Scots and Irish accompanied by the decimation of Essex's own
troops. By 1575 it was clear that the project was doomed to failure. On March 9, 1575, he was nevertheless appointed earl marshal of Ireland, and on May 7 received the lordship of Ferney. On
May 22, however, Elizabeth ordered Essex to abandon the attempt
to colonize Ulster. He died in Ireland on September 22, 1576.

Textual Notes

At l. 12, "and would" is repeated. At ll. 41–42, "being . . . are" is
written in the margin with a caret after "and" in l. 41 to indicate its
placement.

Letter 20. Elizabeth to George and Elizabeth Talbot, earl and countess of Shrewsbury, June 25, 1577

Scribal, with autograph heading,
Lambeth Palace Library MS 3206, pp. 819–22.

By the Queen
    Your most assured, loving cousin[1] and sovereign,
        Elizabeth R
Our very good Cousins,
    Being given t'understand from our cousin of
Leicester how honorably he was not only lately re-   [5
ceived by you, our cousin the Countess, at Chatsworth,
and his diet[2] by you both discharged at Buxtons, but
also presented with a very rare present, we should do
him great wrong (holding him in that place of favor we
do) in case we should not let you understand in how   [10
thankful sort we accept the same at both your hands,
not as done unto him but to our own self, reputing
him as another ourself. And therefore ye may assure
yourselves that we (taking upon us the debt not as his
but our own) will take care accordingly to discharge   [15
the same in such honorable sort, as so well deserving
creditors as ye are shall never have cause to think ye
have met with an unthankful debtor.
    In this acknowledgement of new debts we may not
forget our old debt, the same being as great as a sover-   [20
eign can owe to a subject, when through your loyal and
most careful looking to the charge committed to you,
both we and our realm enjoy a peaceable government,
the best good hap that to any prince on earth can be-

fall. This good hap then, growing from you, ye might   [25
think yourselfs most unhappy if you served such a
prince as should not be as ready graciously to consider
of it as thankfully to acknowledge the same, whereof
you may make full accompt[3] to your comfort when
time shall serve. Given under our signet at our manor   [30
of Greenwich the 25th day of June 1577, and in the sixth
year of our reign.

Notes

   1. *cousin:* a title given by princes to other princes and
nobles

   2. *diet:* provision of food

   3. *accompt:* account

Commentary

   In June 1577, Leicester visited the baths at Buxton, Der-
byshire, with his brother Ambrose, earl of Warwick. On the way
they were entertained by Elizabeth Talbot (Bess of Hardwick),
countess of Shrewsbury, at Chatsworth, a Shrewsbury manor
house some fifteen miles southeast of Buxton. The countess as-
sisted her husband in his duties as the guardian of Mary, Queen of
Scots.

Textual Notes

   Only the heading that begins "Your most assured . . ." and the
signature are holograph. The letter is endorsed "To our right
trustie & right welbelouid Cousin and Counsellor th'Earle of
Shrewesburye and to or right deere and right welbelouid Cousin
Countesse his wyfe."

Letter 21. Elizabeth to William Paulet,
third marquis of Winchester,
July 1578

Scribal draft, PRO: SP 12/125, f. 89.

By the Queen

Right trusty and right welbeloved cousin,[1] we greet you well,

Where heretofore we have dealt with you for some good reconciliation between you and our cousin the Lady Marquess your wife, being induced thereunto [5 through her dutiful and earnest desire to recover your favor, her constant promise wholly to submit herself unto you and so to continue in all respects, and through her manifest sorrowfulness, and for many other causes which we then alleged unto you: foras- [10 much as we do not yet see that good fruit proceed of our dealing with you in that behalf which we most earnestly wished and looked for, and was, in effect, that you would have received our said cousin your wife into your house, reserving the increase of your furder[2] [15 favor to be obtained by desert of her good usage and behavior towards you, we are once again willing to move you herein.

And therefore to forbear many reasons which we have heretofore and could yet allege, we are content [20 only to propound unto you ourself for an example, who have been pleased to remit both great and sundry offences committed even against ourself, whereby hath ensued good unto va{rlets?};[3] much more we, in-

clining thus far, as ourself to make request unto you [25
for the receiving of our said cousin your wife again,
with some beginning of favor to your wife (and yet not
otherwise than as she shall hereafter deserve by her dutiful usage), would verily hope not to be refused at
your hands. We do now therefore eftsoons[4] entreat [30
you that if no other thing can move you to grant this
which we thus desire of you, yet that you will give
this preeminence to us as to your sovereign to yield
and be at the length overcome by us in this matter,
wherein you shall much please God who refuseth [35
none that seeketh and returneth to Him with repentance. You shall also greatly content the world and
quiet your own conscience. And for our part, as we
shall be much satisfied by conformity to yield to this
our request and take the same in as thankful part as [40
yourself can wish, so by the contrary (having thus
often moved you herein) we may have cause to conceive that you bear a harder[5] respect unto us than we
look for of you.

Given . . .[6] [45

Notes

1. *cousin:* a title given by princes to other princes and
nobles

2. *furder:* further

3. Conjectural reconstruction of the word lost in the
margin; for other emendations, see the textual notes.

4. *eftsoons:* again

5. *harder:* lesser

6. The conclusion was left to be filled in for Elizabeth's
signature in the final draft.

Commentary

Paulet had become the third marquis of Winchester upon his father's death just two years before. More than twenty years earlier he had married Agnes or Anne Howard, the daughter of William, Baron Howard of Effingham and his wife, Catherine. The Lady Marquess was thus sister to Charles Howard, a prominent courtier destined to serve the Queen as her Lord Chamberlain and, most famously, as the Lord Admiral who commanded England's repulse of the Great Armada in 1588. The exact nature of Lady Winchester's conflict with her husband is unclear, but the Queen's intervention apparently had little effect, for Paulet was not reconciled with his wife; his mistress, Jane Lambert, bore him four illegitimate sons by the time of his death in 1598.[1]

1. G. E. Cokayne, *The Complete Peerage of England, Scotland, Ireland, Great Britain, and the United Kingdom, Extant, Extinct, or Dormant,* new ed. (London, 1910–59), 12:764–65.

Textual Notes

The leaf, dated July 1578, is badly frayed along the right margin; small holes in the paper also obscure several readings. The draft includes a number of cross outs and interlinear additions presumably dictated by the Queen. Reconstructed readings include "sorrowfulness" (l. 9) and "to yield" (l. 33) ["ss" and "ield" lost in the margin] and "sundry offences" (l. 22) ["ry of" missing due to a hole in the paper]. After "reasons which" (l. 18) the scribe has written "we" twice.

Letter 22. Elizabeth to King James VI of Scotland, January 1585

Holograph, L: Add. MS 23240, f. 7.

I mind not deal,[1] my dear brother,[2] as wise men commonly counsel, to try my trust with trifles first and thereby judge of like event,[3] but have agreed to make my first assay[4] of your many promises and desires that you might know the way to please me most. And there- [5 fore do require[5] that a question may, upon allegiance,[6] be demanded by yourself of the Master Gray, whether he knoweth not the price of my blood, which should be spilled by bloody hand of a murtherer, which some of your near-akin did grant.[7] A sore question, you may [10 suppose, but no other act than such as I am assured he knows, and therefore I hope he will not dare deny you a truth. But yet I beseech you, let it not seem to come from me, to whom I made no semblance[8] but igno- rance. Let him suppose that you received it elsewhere. [15 O most wicked treacher,[9] to gush[10] the drops of inno- cent blood, yea, of such as perhaps hath saved often theirs! As this toucheth me nearest, so use it with best commodity[11] and let the answer be speeded after a three or four days after his return. It may please you [20 ask it no sooner lest he suspect it come of me from whom,[12] according to trust, let it be kept.

Your most assured sister and cousin.
God ever keep you from all dangerous attempts, and grant you many years to live and reign. [25

Notes

    1. *mind not deal:* intend not to act

    2. *brother:* like "cousin," a title of address used between monarchs. Elizabeth's aunt Margaret, sister to Henry VIII, was the mother of James V of Scotland, whose daughter was Mary, Queen of Scots, and the mother of James VI. James was thus Elizabeth's first cousin twice removed.

    3. *like event:* a similar outcome

    4. *assay:* trial

    5. *require:* request, ask

    6. *upon allegiance:* upon Gray's duty to his sovereign

    7. *grant:* agree to

    8. *semblance:* appearance

    9. *treacher:* traitor, deceiver

    10. *gush:* shed

    11. *commodity:* advantage

    12. *from whom:* i.e., from Gray

Commentary, Letters 22 and 23

King James sent Patrick, sixth Baron Gray as his ambassador to the English court during the winter of 1584–85. Gray had served in France as a confidential agent of James's mother, Mary, Queen of Scots, and remained in contact with her despite his employment by James. The English government thus believed that he knew what reward Catholic conspirators had offered for Elizabeth's assassination.

Textual Notes

The bifolium is unsigned but endorsed in the Queen's hand, "Au Roy de Escose mon bon frere & Cousin." On either side is a red seal apparently showing the arms of England over shreds of pink ribbon.

Letter 23. Elizabeth to King James VI of Scotland, January or February 1585

Holograph, L: Add. MS 23240, ff. 11–11v.

I have, right dear brother, received your friendly and affectionate letters in which I perceive the Master Gray's half limping answer which is lame in these respects: the one, for that I see not that he told you who bade him talk with Morgan[1] of the price of my blood, [5 which he knows, I am assured, right well; nor yet hath named the man that should be the murtherer of my life. You well perceive that nothing may nearlier[2] touch me than this cause, and therefore according to the bond of nature and the promise of strict friendship let [10 me conjure you that this villainy be confessed. I hope I may stand you in better stead[3] than that you will shew you uncareful[4] of such a treason.

And because I desire that no cause be given of[5] your part to make me or the lookers on to slander your [15 good will, I hear out of my realm of Ireland that Scots assemble in great troops. Give you charge immediately, I most heartily require you, that, upon pain of treason they desist from such action, and so shall you bind me to recompense such honorable treat- [20 ment.

And where I perceive that you expected the earls'[6] departure from the borders, it is true, upon my honor, that I dispatched forthwith a charge unto them which they answered after a week's leisure, that they were so [25 indebted to my subjects that they could not; but I am sure by this time they are departed. As for their not banishment out of my realm, I have, by my secretary,[7] signified to the Master Gray what reasons necessary to be considered moves me thereunto, specially since [30 they offer to submit themselves to suffer as if they were my subjects offending me and to take condign pain if, while they bide in my government, they disobey their allegiance to you. And this, with the rest, I trust will content you as one that I will take as great care of for [35 your honor and your surety as whosoever may give you more golden promise with leaden performance.

I beseech you let your answer be returned me with your best speed and most commodity.[8] Thus, not willing to molest[9] you, I, with my humblest devotion, en- [40 treat the Almighty to protect from all inconvenience and grant you many happy years.

> Your most assured sister and cousin,
> Elizabeth R.

Notes

1. The English expatriate Charles Morgan, a Catholic deeply involved in plots to free Mary, Queen of Scots, and place her on the throne of England.

2. *nearlier:* more nearly

3. *stand . . . stead:* maintain you in better circumstances

4. *you uncareful:* yourself not mindful

5. *of:* on

6. The earls of Mar and Angus had participated in the "Ruthven Raid" of August 1582, in which James was kidnapped and held captive for almost a year. In 1584 they attempted another coup; upon its failure, they fled to England.

7. Sir Francis Walsingham.

8. *commodity:* convenience

9. *molest:* annoy

Textual Notes

Endorsed in a clerk's hand: "A Monsr mon bon frere & Cousin Le Roy D'Escosse." Parts of red seals survive opposite the endorsement.

Letter 24. Elizabeth to King James VI of Scotland, after June 9, 1585

Holograph, L: Add. MS 23240, ff. 15–15v.

Right dear brother,

Your gladsome acceptance of my offered amity together with the desire you seem to have engraven in
your mind to make merits correspondent[1] makes me
in full opinion that some enemies to our goodwill shall
lose much travail[2] with making frustrate[3] their baiting   [5
stratagems, which I know to be many and by sundry
means to be explored. I cannot halt[4] with you so much
as to deny that I have seen such evident shews of your
contrarious dealings that if I made not my reckoning
the better of the months,[5] I might condemn you as un-   [10
worthy of such as I mind[6] to shew myself toward you;
and therefore, I am well pleased to take any color[7] to
defend your honor, and hope that you will remember
that who seeketh two strings to one bow, they may
shoot strong but never straight. And if you suppose   [15
that princes' causes be veiled so covertly that no intelligence may bewray[8] them, deceive not yourself: we old
foxes can find shifts[9] to save ourselves by others' malice, and come by knowledge of greatest secret, specially
if it touch our freehold.[10] It becometh, therefore, all of   [20
our rank to deal sincerely lest, if we use it not, when we
do it we be hardly believed. I write not this, my dear
brother, for doubt but for remembrances.[11]

My ambassador writes so much of your honorable
treatment of him and of Alexander that I believe they   [25

be converted Scots. You oblige me for them, for which I render you a million of most entire thanks, as she that meaneth to deserve many a good thought in your breast through good desert. And for that your request is so honorable, retaining so much reason, I were out [30 of senses if I should not suspend of any hearsay til the answer of your own action, which the actor ought best to know. And so assure yourself I mean and vow to do, with this request: that you will afford me the reciproque.[12] And thus with my many petitions to the [35 Almighty for your long life and preservation, I end these scribbled lines.

> Your very assured, loving sister and cousin,
> Elizabeth R.

Notes

1. *merits correspondent:* reciprocal qualities of true deserving

2. *travail:* labor

3. *making frustrate:* rendering ineffectual

4. *halt:* limp, here meaning "deceive" (an allusion to the maxim that "to halt before a cripple" will not deceive him)

5. *the better . . . months:* at favorable times

6. *mind:* intend

7. *color:* excuse

8. *bewray:* reveal

9. *shifts:* stratagems

10. *freehold:* office (here, her sovereignty as Queen of England)

11. *doubt . . . remembrances:* suspicion but as a reminder

12. *reciproque:* the like. Elizabeth preceded this word with a second "the," here omitted.

Commentary

By the spring of 1585, Elizabeth's government had drawn up the prospective terms of a league with Scotland. In May, Elizabeth dispatched Sir Edward Wotton as her special ambassador to the Scottish court to set forward the negotiations. Robert Alexander arrived in Scotland on June 9 with the Queen's presents of six horses for James's personal use.[1]

1. Great Britain, General Register Office, *Calendar of the State Papers Relating to Scotland and Mary, Queen of Scots, 1547–1603* (Edinburgh, 1898–1969), 7:662.

Textual Notes

A tear at "self toward you" (l. 11) removes all but the "tow" and part of the *d* in "toward," which might have read "towards." The letter is endorsed in Elizabeth's hand: "A mon bon frere Le Roy d'Escose."

Letter 25. Elizabeth to Robert Dudley, earl of Leicester, February 10, 1586

Copy, L: Cotton Galba MS C.8, f. 27.

How contemptuously we conceive ourself to have been used by you you shall by this bearer understand, whom we have expressly sent unto you to charge you withal.[1] We could never have imagined (had we not seen it fall out in experience) that a man raised up by [5 ourself and extraordinarily favored by us above any other subject of this land would have in so contemptible a sort broken our commandment in a cause that so greatly toucheth us in honor. Whereof, for that[2] although you have showed yourself to make but little [10 accompt,[3] in most undutiful sort, you may not therefore think that we have so little care of the reparation thereof as we mind to pass[4] so great a wrong in silence unredressed. And therefore our express pleasure and commandment is that, all delays and excuses laid [15 apart, you do presently,[5] upon the duty of your allegiance, obey and fulfill whatsoever the bearer hereof shall direct you to do in our name, whereof fail you not, as you will answer the contrary at your uttermost peril. [20

Notes
    1. *withal:* therewith
    2. *for that:* because
    3. *make . . . accompt:* hold in low esteem (account)

4. *mind to pass:* intend to pass over

5. *presently:* immediately

Commentary

On August 10, 1585, Elizabeth agreed by treaty to support the Dutch independence movement against Spanish military intrusion. She declined, however, to accept any responsibility of rule over her allies. Leicester, as lieutenant general of the English expeditionary force, landed in the Netherlands in December. In early 1586 he defied the Queen's instructions by accepting the title of governor of the Netherlands. Elizabeth sent Sir Thomas Heneage to Leicester with this strong rebuke (along with detailed verbal instructions for her erring favorite). On April 1, however, she urged Heneage to "comfort the Earl of Leicester, that he do not despair upon her dislike she had shewed against him, when he had accepted the absolute government." Her message went on to explain that now that she understands why the Dutch offered Leicester the appointment, she is "contented with their proceedings."[1]

1. L: Cotton Galba MS C.9, f. 204.

Textual Notes

Dated by another hand in the left margin "1585 10. Feb.," reflecting the ancient practice of beginning the new year on March 25. The date is February 10, 1586, by modern reckoning. The italicized readings "repa*ra*tion" (l. 12) and "command*ment*" (l. 15) are lost in the margin and reconstructed in the edited text.

Letter 26. Elizabeth to King James VI, March 1586

Holograph, L: Add. MS 23240, ff. 38–39v.

The expertest seamen, my dear brother, makes vaunt[1] of their best ships when they pass the highest billows without yielding, and brook nimblest[2] the roughest storms. The like proof, I suppose, may best be made, and surest boast of friends, when greatest per- [5] suasions and mightiest enemies oppose themselves for parties.[3] If then a constant, irremovable goodwill ap- pear, there is best trial made. And for that I know there is no worse orator for truth than malice, nor shrewder inveigher[4] than envy, and that I am sure you have [10] wanted[5] neither to assail your mind to win it from our friendship; if not availing all these meaners[6] you keep the hold of your promised inward affection, as Randol at length have told me and your own letters assure me, I dare thus boldly affirm that you shall have the better [15] part in this bargain.

For when you weigh in equal balance, with no palsy[7] hand, the very ground of their desires that would withdraw you, it is but root of mischief to peril yourself, with hope to harm her who ever hath pre- [20] served you. And since you may be sure that Scotland, nor yourself, be so potent, as for your greatness they seek you, nor never did,[8] but to injure a third. And if you read the histories, there is no great cause of boast for many conquest,[9] though your country served their [25] malice. This you see the beginning[10] why ever Scotland hath been sought. Now, to come to my groundwork:[11]

only natural affection *ab incunabulis*[12] stirred me to
save you from the murderers of your father and the
peril that their complices[13] might breed you. Thus, as [30
in no counterfeit mirror, you may behold without
mask the faces of both beginners. It is for you to judge
what are like to be the best event[14] of both, and thereafter I pray God you may use your best choice to your
surest good, no semblant false[15] to beguile. And as I re- [35
joice to have had, even in this hammering world, such
present proof of your sincerity, so shall you be sure to
employ it upon no guileful person nor such as will not
take as much regard of your good as of her own.

Touching an instrument, as your secretary term it, [40
that you desire to have me sign, I assure you, though I
can play of[16] some, and have been brought up to know
music, yet this discord would be so gross as were not fit
for so well-tuned music. Must so great doubt be made
of free goodwill, and gift be so mistrusted, that our [45
sign Emanual[17] must assure? No, my dear brother:
teach your new, raw counselers better manner than to
advise you such a pairing[18] of ample meaning. Who
should doubt performance of a king's offer? What dishonor may that be deemed? Follow next your own na- [50
ture, for this never came out of your shop. But for your
full satisfaction, and to pluck from the wicked the
weapon they would use to breed your doubt of my
meanings, these they be. First, I will, as long as you
with evil desert alter not your course, take care for [55
your safety, help your need, and shun all acts that may
damnify[19] you in any sort, either in present or future
time. And for the portion of relief,[20] I mind never to
lessen, though, as I see cause, I will rather augment.
And this I hope may stand you in as much assurance [60

as my name in parchment, and no less for both our honors.

I cannot omit, also, to request you, of all amity between us, to have good regard of the long-waiting expectation that all our subjects looks after, that some [65 persons be delivered into my hands for some repair of my honor though no redress for his death,[21] according as my ambassador Randol shall signify, and that there be no more delays, which have been over many already. And thus I end my troubling you. Committing [70 you to the tuition of the living God, who grant you many years of prosperous reign.

> Your most assured, loving sister and cousin,
> Elizabeth R.

Notes

1. *makes vaunt:* boast
2. *brook nimblest:* endure most nimbly
3. *for parties:* as disputants
4. *shrewder inveigher:* more malicious denouncer
5. *wanted:* lacked
6. *meaners:* those who mean or intend (editorial correction for Elizabeth's "minars")
7. *palsy:* palsied, shaking
8. *never did:* i.e., never did seek you
9. *conquest:* conquests (Elizabeth's use of a singular as plural)
10. *the beginning:* is the origin, principle cause
11. *my groundwork:* the foundation of my argument
12. *ab incunabulis:* from your cradle
13. *complices:* accomplices
14. *event:* outcome

15. *semblant false:* false seeming

16. *of:* upon

17. *sign Emanual:* sign manual, signature (Elizabeth's "Emanuel" suggests a pun on "Emmanuel/Immanuel," the prophetic name applied to Jesus)

18. *pairing:* damaging, impairing

19. *damnify:* injure, damage

20. *portion of relief:* allowance of financial assistance, i.e., the pension

21. *his death:* Sir Francis Russell, son of the earl of Bedford, had been killed in a border skirmish during a time of truce on July 27, 1585. Elizabeth continued to press James to arrest those responsible for the crime.

Commentary

Elizabeth sent Sir Thomas Randolph (her "Randol") as special ambassador to James in January 1586. This was Randolph's seventh embassy to Scotland during her reign; he soon secured James's consent to a defensive league between the two nations that would deflect Catholic pressure on Scotland from France and Spain. At issue too was James's desire that Elizabeth commit herself with a legally binding document ("instrument"), for the payment of his £4,000 pension. The Queen cajoled her royal "brother" in part because she feared that Catholic influence in Scotland, be it native or foreign, posed a grave threat to England. James, on his part, dared not alienate his "dearest sister" or her chief ministers for fear of being excluded from the succession upon Elizabeth's death.

Textual Notes

After "your selfe with" (l. 20) Elizabeth wrote "and who to," then crossed out these words, replacing them with "hope to harm."

Letter 27. Elizabeth to Robert Dudley, earl of Leicester, July 19, 1586

Scribal copy, PRO: SP 84/9, ff. 85–86.

Rob,

I am afraid you will suppose by my wandering writings that a midsummer moon hath taken large possession of my brains this month, but you must needs take things as they come in my head, though order be left behind me. When I remember your re- [5 quest to have a discreet and honest man that may carry my mind and see how all goes there, I have chosen this bearer, whom you know and have made good trial of. I have fraught him full of my conceipts of those country matters,[1] and imparted what way I mind to take and [10 what is fit for you to sue.[2] I am sure you can credit him and so I will be short with these few notes.

First, that Count Maurice and Count Hollock[3] find themselves trusted of you, esteemed of me, and to be carefully regarded if ever peace should happen, and of [15 that assure them on my word, that yet never deceived any. And for Norris[4] and other captains that voluntarily, without commandment, have many years ventured their lives and won our nation honor and themselves fame, be not discouraged by any means, neither by [20 new-come men nor by old, trained soldiers elsewhere; if there be fault in using of soldiers or making of profit by them, let them hear of it without open shame, and doubt not but I will well chasten them therefore. It frets me not a little that the poor soldiers that hourly [25

ventures life should want their due that well deserve
rather reward. And look in where[5] the fault may duly
be proved, let them smart therefore. And if the treasurer[6] be found untrue or negligent, according to
desert he shall be used, though you know my old   [30
wont,[7] that love not to discharge from office without
desert, God forbid. I pray you let this bearer know
what may be learned herein. And for this treasure I
have joined[8] Sir Thomas Shirley[9] to see all this money
discharged in due sort where it needeth and behoveth.   [35
Now will I end that do imagine I talk still with you, and
therefore loathly say farewell õõ,[10] though ever I pray
God bless you from all harm and save you from all
foes, with my million and legion of thanks for all your
pains and cares.   [40

> As you know, ever the same,
> E. R.

Let Wilkes see that he is acceptable to you.

If anything there be that Wilkes shall desire answer
of, be such as you would have but me to know, write it   [45
to myself. You know I can keep both others' counsel
and mine own. Mistrust not that anything you would
have kept shall be disclosed by me, for although this
bearer ask many things, yet may you answer him such
as you shall think meet, and write to me the rest.   [50

Notes

1. *conceipts . . . matters:* thoughts on the affairs of that
country

2. *sue:* pursue, follow

3. Maurice of Nassau, Prince of Orange, and his foremost general, Count Hohenlo.

4. Sir John Norris. For Elizabeth's condolences to his mother on his death in 1597, see Letter 43.

5. *look in where:* wherever

6. Sir Richard Huddleston, treasurer of the English army in the Low Countries.

7. *wont:* custom, policy

8. *joined:* enjoined, charged

9. Shirley replaced Huddleston as treasurer on February 1, 1587.

10. *ōō:* symbol used by Elizabeth to represent "eyes," her nickname for Leicester

Commentary

Elizabeth's fury with Leicester for accepting the governorship of the Netherlands (see Letter 25) was quelled by insistence from both her Dutch allies and her privy councillors that his authority would not compromise England's safety in the region. In July, she sent Thomas Wilkes to the Low Countries with further instructions for her fully pardoned commander.

Textual Notes

The bifolium is endorsed (f. 86v) "19 July 1586 Copie of her Mates Lre sent by w[ilkes]. to the E. of Leicester her Highnes Lieu: gnal in the Low Countrys."

Letter 28. Elizabeth to Sir Amias Paulet, mid-August (?) 1586

Scribal copy, L: Cotton Caligula MS C.9, f. 654.

Amias, my most careful and faithful servant,

God reward thee treblefold in the double for thy
most troublesome charge so well discharged. If you
knew (my Amias), how kindly besides dutifully my
grateful heart accepts your double labors and faith-
ful actions, your wise orders and safe regards, per-   [5
formed in so dangerous and crafty a charge, it would
ease your travail[1] and rejoice your heart, in which
I charge you carry this most just thought, that I cannot balance in any weight of my judgment the value
that I prize you at, and suppose no treasure to counter-   [10
vail such a faith, and shall condemn myself in that fault
which I never yet committed if I reward not such
deserts. Yea, let me lack when I have most need if I
acknowledge not such a merit with a reward *non
omnibus datum.*[2]   [15

But let your wicked murtheress[3] know how that
with hearty sorrow her vile deserts compels these orders. And bid her from me ask God forgiveness for her
treacherous dealings towards the saver of her life many
years, to the intollerable peril of our own;[4] and yet, not   [20
content with so many forgivenesses, must fall again so
horribly, far passing a woman's thought much less a
princess's, instead of excusing (whereof not one can
serve, it being so plainly confessed by the authors[5] of
my guiltless death). Let repentance take place and let   [25
not the fiend possess her so as her better part be lost,

which I pray with hands lifted up to Him that may both save and spill.

With my most loving adieu and prayer for thy long life. [30

Your most assured and loving sovereign in heart [6]
by good desert induced,
Elizabeth Regina

Notes

1. *travail:* hard work

2. *non omnibus datum:* not given to everyone

3. *murtheress:* murderess; other manuscripts read "mistress"

4. From Speech 8 (November 12, 1586), Elizabeth deleted a reference to Mary that concluded, "so void of grace, or false in faith as now to seeke my death by whome so long her life hath bene preserued with th'Intolleable perill of my owne."

5. *authors:* instigators

6. *loving . . . heart:* sovereign, loving in heart

Commentary

Paulet had served as lieutenant governor of Jersey and ambassador to France before his appointment as guardian of Mary, Queen of Scots, in 1585. In the same year he was sworn to the Privy Council. Mary's complicity in the Babington assassination plot was revealed in August of 1586, but it was late September before Elizabeth agreed that her rival should be brought to trial. In a letter to Sir Francis Walsingham dated August 22, Paulet may be referring to the Queen's letter to him when he thanks her secretary that his "partial report hath wrought in her Majesty [s]o good acceptation of my poor service, as hath appeared by her most gracious letters."[1] Copies of this letter circulated widely throughout the first half of the seventeenth century; see the textual notes for a representative listing of manuscript copies.

1. Sir Amias Poulet, *The Letter-Books of Sir Amias Poulet, Keeper of Mary Queen of Scots,* ed. John Morris (London, 1874), p. 268.

Textual Notes

I have emended the copy text only in the subscription, substituting "induced," for "and meede." Manuscript copies of this letter include L: Add. 15226, ff. 34v–35; Add. 22587, f. 18v. Add. 48027, f. 491. Add. 73087, ff. 56v–57v; Cotton Caligula B.4, f. 290; Harl. 290, f. 202; Harl. 444, ff. 1–1v; Lansdowne 1236, f. 44; Stowe 150, f. 53; Huntington Library, HM 1340, f. 94v; Inner Temple, Petyt 538.10, f. 7v; Petyt 538.18, f. 205v; O: Eng. hist. c.121, f. 3; Eng. misc. e.226, f. 19v; Rawl. D.264, f. 1; Rawl. D.352, f. 5; Tanner 78, f. 17; University College, Oxford, MS 152, pp. 121–22.

Letter 29. Elizabeth to King James VI of Scotland, before October 15, 1586

Holograph, L: Add. MS 23240, ff. 53–53v.

My dear brother,

.   It hath sufficiently informed me of your singular care of my estate[1] and breathing that you have sent one in such diligence to understand the circumstances of the treasons which lately were lewdly[2] attempted and miraculously uttered,[3] of which I had made partici-   [5 pant[4] your ambassador afore your letters came. And now am I to shew you that, as I have received many writings from you of great kindness, yet this last was fraughted with so careful passion[5] and so effectual ut- terance of all best wishes for my safety and offer of as   [10 much as I could have desired that I confess, if I should not seek to deserve it and by merits tie you to continu- ance, I were evil-worthy such a friend. And as the thanks my heart yields, my pen may scant render you, so shall the owner ever decern[6] to shew it not evil em-   [15 ployed but on such a prince as shall requite your good- will and keep a watchful eye to all doings that may concern you.

    And whereas you offer to send me any traitor of mine residing in your land, I shall not fail but expect   [20 th'accomplishment of the same in case any such shall be, and require you in the meantime that speedy deliv- ery may be made of the Carrs,[7] which toucheth both my conscience and honor.

    I thank God that you beware so soon of Jesuits, that   [25

have been the source of all these treacheries in this
realm, and will spread like an evil weed if at the first
they be not weeded out. I would I had had Prometheus
for companion, for Epimetheus[8] had like have been
mine too soon. What religion is this, that they say the   [30
way to salvation is to kill the prince for a merit merito-
rious? This is that[9] they have all confessed without torture or menace, I swear it on my word. Far be it from
Scotland to harbor any such, and therefore I wish your
good providence may be duly executed, for else laws   [35
resemble cobwebs whence great bees get out by break-
ing and small flies sticks fast for weakness.

As concerning the retarding[10] of your answers to all
points of your ambassador's charge, you had received
them or[11] now but that matters of that weight that I   [40
am sure you would willingly know cannot as yet receive a conclusion, and til then Master Douglas[12] doth
tarry; and with his return I hope you shall receive honorable requital of his amicable embassade[13] so as you
shall have no cause to regret his arrival, as knoweth the   [45
Lord, whom ever I beseech to give you many joyful
days of reign and life.

> Your most assured, loving, and faithful sister
> and cousin,
> Elizabeth R.   [50

I must give you many thanks for this poor subject of
mine,[14] for whom I will not stick to do all pleasure for
your request, and would wish him under the ground if
he should not serve you with greatest faith that any
servant may. I have willed him tell you some things   [55
from me; I beseech you hear them favorably.

Notes

1. *estate:* circumstances
2. *lewdly:* wickedly
3. *uttered:* disclosed
4. *participant:* one to whom news is imparted
5. *fraughted . . . passion:* expressed with such solicitous emotion
6. *decern:* determine, decide
7. Elizabeth issued a proclamation in August for their arrest, strictly forbidding her subjects to aid them in any way should they flee to England (see Great Britain, General Register Office, *Calendar of the State Papers Relating to Scotland and Mary, Queen of Scots, 1547–1603* [Edinburgh, 1898–1969], 8:579).
8. *Prometheus . . . Epimetheus:* figures from Greek mythology whose names mean "forethought" and "afterthought," respectively
9. *that:* that which
10. *retarding:* delaying
11. *or:* ere, before
12. Archibald Douglas, the Scottish ambassador.
13. *embassade:* ambassadorial mission
14. I have not identified Elizabeth's messenger on this occasion.

Commentary

In August 1586, the government arrested Anthony Babington and those who plotted with him to assassinate the Queen and bring Mary, Queen of Scots, to the throne. Through his ambassador at the English court, Archibald Douglas, James learned that his mother would be tried for complicity in the crime and that her life might be at stake as a result. Elizabeth stalled at giving him a definitive answer about Mary's fate. She continued, however, to press James for the surrender of William and James Carr, with other members of the Carr family and their retainers, suspected of killing Sir Francis Russell more than a year earlier (see n. 21 to Letter 26). Although James agreed to turn them in, the suspects simply went into hiding.

Textual Notes

Endorsed by Elizabeth "A mon bon frere & Cousin Le Roy D'Escose." A different hand notes the letter's reception in Scotland "the 15 of October 1586." At l. 42, Elizabeth wrote "an conclusion."

Letter 30. Elizabeth to William Cecil, Lord Burghley, and Sir Francis Walsingham, October 1586

Scribal copy, British Library,
Lansdowne MS 10, f. 213.

Sir Spirit mine and you, Master Moor,[1]

When I consider that the prisoner king may perchance deny utterly to answer and that I remember that you mean notwithstanding to proceed to judgment, methinks very convenient that some competent member went to his chamber and read some principal points of his charge. And if {s}he will not answer yet {s}he shall not say that {s}he denied not to answer those things that {s}he heard not. I pray God it be no slander in the world that the sentence be given without an answer. Consider what is best, and let this learn you at your tables,[2] in which if you find the matter sufficiently considered already you wipe them out. I have commanded this bearer to bring me word of both your healths. And so, when a fool hath spoken, {s}he hath all done.

[5

[10

[15

Such am I to you as your faiths have deserved.

E. R.

Notes

1. The Queen's nicknames for Lord Treasurer Burghley and her Principal Secretary, Sir Francis Walsingham.

2. *learn . . . tables:* teach you at your writing tablets

Commentary

This memorandum concerns the complicity of Mary, Queen of Scots, in the Babington plot that Walsingham and his agents brought to light in August 1586. Her trial by a commission of thirty-six officers and peers of the realm began at Fotheringay Castle on October 11. Elizabeth worried that Mary might be sentenced without answering to the charges against her. On October 12, the Queen wrote to Burghley ordering him to report to her in person before pronouncing sentence on Mary.[1] Insofar as the execution of a fellow sovereign was at issue, Elizabeth or the Lansdowne scribe obscured her direct involvement in the matter by referring to Mary in this note as "the prisoner king." The scribe has crossed out the initial *s* in five instances to tranform "she" into "he."

1. Copies of this letter in summary form are preserved in L: Harl. MS 290, f. 193, and Cotton Caligula MS C.9, f. 467.

Letter 31. Elizabeth to King James VI of Scotland, mid-August 1588

Holograph, L: Add. MS 23240, ff. 77–77v.

Now may appear, my dear brother, how malice joined with might strivest to make a shameful end to a villainous beginning, for by God's singular favor, having their fleet well beaten in our narrow seas and pressing with all violence to achieve some watering place to [5 continue their pretended[1] invasion, the winds have carried them to your coasts, where I doubt not they shall receive small succour and less welcome, unless those lords that so traitors-like[2] would belie[3] their own prince and promise another king relief, in your [10 name be suffered to live at liberty to dishonor you, peril you, and advance some other (which God forbid you suffer them live to do). Therefore I send you this gentleman,[4] a rare young man and a wise, to declare unto you my full opinion in this great cause as one that [15 never will abuse you to serve my own turn nor will[5] you do ought that myself would not perform if I were in your place.

You may assure yourself that, for my part, I doubt no whit but that all this tyrannical, proud, and brain-[20 sick attempt will be the beginning though not the end of the ruin of that King that, most unkingly, even in mids of treating peace, begins this wrongful war. He hath procured my greatest glory that meant my sorest wrack, and hath so dimmed the light of his sunshine [25 that who hath a will to obtain shame let them keep his

forces company. But for all this, for yourself sake, let
not the friends of Spain be suffered to yield them force,
for though I fear not in the end the sequel, yet if by
having them unhelped you may increase the English   [30
hearts unto you, you shall not do the worst deed for
your behalf, for if ought should be done, your excuse will play the *boiteux*[6] if you make not sure work
with the likely men to do it. Look well unto it, I beseech
you.   [35

The necessity of this matter makes my scribbling
the more speedy, hoping that you will measure my
good affection with the right balance of my actions,
which to you shall be ever such as I have professed, not
doubting of the reciproque of[7] your behalf, according   [40
as my last messenger unto you hath at large signified,
for the which I render you a million of grateful thanks
together for the late general prohibition to your subjects not to foster nor aid our general foe, of which I
doubt not the observation[8] if the ringleaders be safe in   [45
your hands, as knoweth God who ever have you in His
blessed keeping, with many happy years of reign.

> Your most assured, loving sister and cousin,
> Elizabeth R

Notes

1. *pretended:* intended
2. *traitors-like:* traitorously
3. *belie:* misrepresent with lies
4. Elizabeth appointed Sir Robert Sidney as her special
ambassador to Scotland on August 14.
5. *will:* urge
6. *boiteux:* cripple (French)

7. *of the reciproque of:* the like on

8. *observation:* observance, obedience (to the proclamation)

Commentary

After its defeat in the English Channel, the remnants of the Spanish Armada sailed north along the east coasts of England and Scotland. It rounded the British Isles and returned home with considerable loss of life and shipping. While Elizabeth rejoiced in her victory, she urgently reminded James not to allow the fleeing Spaniards to find refuge or resupply among his subjects, especially among the Catholic nobility about whom she warned him continuously.

Textual Notes

The letter is endorsed in Elizabeth's hand "To my verey good brother the King of Scottz," with the remains of a seal on either side of this passage.

Letter 32. Elizabeth to Lady Elizabeth Drury, 1590

Scribal copy, L: Harley MS 6986, f. 59.

Be well ware, my Bess, you strive not with divine ordinance nor grudge at irremediable harms, lest you offend the Highest and no whit amend the married hap.[1] Heap not your harms where help there is none, but since you may not that you would, wish that[2] you [5 can enjoy with comfort: a king for his power and a queen for her love, who leaves[3] not now to protect you when your case requires care, and minds[4] not to omit whatever may be best for you and yours.

Your most loving, careful[5] sovereign, E. R.

Notes

1. *married hap:* i.e., the accident that has befallen your marriage
2. *that . . . that:* obtain that which you would most desire (i.e., the life of her husband), wish for that which
3. *leaves:* ceases
4. *minds:* intends
5. *careful:* caring

Commentary

Sir William Drury died early in 1590 from wounds suffered in a duel while serving as a colonel in the Netherlands. The Queen's consolatory letter to his widow must have been especially comforting since Drury left an estate heavily indebted to the Crown.[1]

A copy of Lady Drury's grateful reply to the Queen immediately follows this letter in the manuscript.[2]

1. P. W. Hasler, *The House of Commons, 1558–1603* (London, 1981), 2:58–59.

2. The reply is printed in *Elizabeth I: Collected Works*, ed. Leah S. Marcus, Janel Mueller, and Mary Beth Rose (Chicago, 2000), p. 362.

Textual Notes

In the Harleian MS, Lady Drury's reply is a scribal draft followed by what appears to be a holograph postscript signed "E. Drury."

Letter 33. Elizabeth to William Cecil, Lord Burghley, May 10, 1591

Scribal copy, Elizabethan Club, Yale University.

Elizabetha Anglorum id est a nitores Angelorum Regina Formosissima et Felicissima.

To the disconsolate and retired Sprite, the Hermit of Theobalds: and to all other disaffected souls claiming[1] by, from, or under the said Hermit: sendeth greeting. WHERE in our high Court of Chancery it is given us to understand that you, Sir Hermit, the abandonate [5 of[2] nature's fair works and servant to heaven's wonders, have (for the space of two years and two months), possessed yourself of fair Theobalds with her sweet rosary,[3] sometime the recreation of our right trusty and right welbeloved Sir William Cecil, Knight, leav- [10 ing to him the old, rude repose wherein twice five years (at his costs) your contemplative life was relieved.[4] In which place fate inevitable hath brought griefs immeasurable (for love's grief bideth[5] no compare), suffering your solitary eye to bring into his house [15 desolation and mourning, joy's destroyers and annoy's friends, whereby paradise is grown wilderness and for green grass are comen[6] gray hairs, with cruel banishment from the fruits of long labors, the possession whereof he hath holden many years; the want of the [20 mean profits thereof (health and gladness), having been greatly to his hindrance, which cumbereth[7] as much the interest we have in his faithful services be-

sides the lament of his loving neighbors and friends
infinite as by the record of their countenances most   [25
plainly may appear.

   We, upon advised consideration have commanded
you, Hermit, to your old cave, too good for the for-
saken, too bad for our worthily beloved Counselor;
and because we greatly tender your comforts we have   [30
given power to our Chancellor to make out such and
so many writs (as to him shall be thought good), to abjure Desolation and Mourning (the consumers of
sweetness) to the frozen seas and deserts of Arabia Petrosa,[8] upon pain of five hundred despites[9] to their ter-   [35
ror and contempt of their torment, if they attempt[10]
any part of your house again. Enjoining you to the en-
joyments of your own house and delights, without
memory of any mortal accident or wretched adver-
sary. And for that you have been so good a servant to   [40
common Tranquility, we command Solace to give you
full and pacific possession of all and every part thereof,
not departing until our favor (that ever hath inclined
to your meek nature), have assured you peace in the
possessions thereof, wherein we command all causes   [45
within the prerogative of our high favor to give you no
interruption. And this under the pain aforesaid they
shall not omit. Teste meipsa apud Tybolltes decimo die
maij Anno regni tricesimo trio.[11]

Notes

   Title: Elizabeth of England, that is, the most splendid and
fortunate queen of the brilliant angels (with pun on "English,"
in Latin *Angli*).
   1. *claiming:* asserting rights

2. *the abandonate of:* one abandoned to (?)

3. *rosary:* rose garden. Burghley's elaborate gardens at Theobalds became an Elizabethan tourist attraction.

4. Burghley had begun major expansion and rebuilding of the Middle Court at Theobalds in 1571; he had completed work on the manor house by 1585. See Conyers Read, *Lord Burghley and Queen Elizabeth* (New York, 1960), p. 122.

5. *bideth:* permits, tolerates. Mildred Cecil, Lady Burghley, had died in early April 1589. A week later, Cecil, in mourning at Theobalds, was recalled to London by the Queen (Read, *Lord Burghley,* p. 449).

6. *comen:* archaic past participle of *to come*

7. *cumbereth:* hampers, confounds

8. *abjure . . . Petrosa:* banish the personified Desolation and Mourning to frozen seas and the deserts of Arabia (as opposed to the fertile Arabia Felix)

9. *despites:* outrages, scornings

10. *attempt:* attack

11. Witnessed by me at Theobalds on the tenth day of May in the thirty-third year of the reign.

Commentary

On May 10, 1591, Elizabeth traveled from Hackney to Theobalds, Burghley's country house in Hertfordshire, for a ten-day visit to her Lord Treasurer. There, presumably, she presented him with this elaborate missive addressed to her "Sprite" (spirit), her pet name for Cecil. Her epistle is in the form of letters patent, the official legal instrument by which the government granted rights and privileges to subjects. Her words were engrossed (written in a broad, legal hand) on a sheet of parchment that was signed by the Lord Chancellor, Sir Christopher Hatton, and affixed with the Great Seal of England. The Queen's fiction in this mock-patent treats Burghley as two persons, the retired and grieving hermit and her highly esteemed privy councillor. The letter grants Burghley explicit royal permission to abandon his role as hermit by ending the "desolation and mourning" he experienced since his wife's death at Theobalds some two years earlier.

Textual Notes

John Nichols published a transcript of this charter in his *Progresses and Public Processions of Queen Elizabeth,* new ed. (London, 1823), 3:75, from the copy in John Strype's *Annals of the Reformation* (first pub. 1708; 1824 ed., reprint, New York, n.d.), 4:108–9. The original is now in the collection of the Elizabethan Club at Yale University.

Letter 34. Elizabeth to Robert Devereux, second earl of Essex, October 4, 1591

Scribal copy headed with the Queen's signature,
Hatfield House, Cecil Papers 20, ff. 34–35.

Elizabeth R

Right trusty and right well-beloved cousin we greet you well,

Where by sundry our late[1] letters, some to yourself and some to our ambassador[2] and Sir Thomas Leighton,[3] we declared our pleasure to be that both   [5 you and our forces should return from thence after the end of the two months according as was accorded[4] afore your going thither, and having shewed and sent to you in writing very good cause which moved us thereto, such as if you have well weighed them with a   [10 mind and judgment not blinded with vain persuasions either of yourself or of such others as do accompany you with their glorious, windy discourses, you would have readily assented thereto; yea besides the regard of our honor, which hath been overmuch blemished by   [15 the king's actions, even for your own reputation, you would without our commandment at the end of the two months which were the time limited for your charge have returned.

But yet since our commandment sent[5] for your re-   [20 turn, which we doubt not but you have disposed yourself according to your duty to have performed, we have lately considered that since the winning of Gournay[6] in so short a time whereof we are very glad, and that we

perceive the attempt of Caudebec and the besieging [25
also of Rouen is begun and like well to succeed,[7]
wherein also we certainly understand that our people
not only with their own proper[8] forces, but with a reputation of them are[9] like to give great furtherance, and
their revocation great hindrance, and that also other [30
the forces of the king's,[10] which are promised to be
shortly brought thither by himself, as we are made to
believe might percase[11] be discomforted upon report
of the revocation of ours, and so also the enterprise
against Rouen and Newhaven might fall to the ground, [35
and the enemy's forces which are to come from sundry
places might have more comfort to come towards
Rouen to raise the siege thereof; for these considerations only, and not to pleasure the king at all, how erst
soever[12] he hath and may be to entreat us to stay[13] our [40
forces there for some longer time than by covenant we
have been bound, we are content that if the king shall
make due payment to our army there for the time
of their abode after the two months expired, then
notwithstanding our former commandments, you [45
and our forces shall and may remain for one month
longer or [blank] days, so as[14] they shall be employed
only to recover Rouen and Newhaven and for no other
services.

And yet we think it meet that such of our forces as [50
are grown by any sickness infectious unable to serve,
should be dismissed and sent home, but not to come to
our city of London, nor to populous towns, but for
avoiding of further infection. And this our contentation[15] with the causes thereof, you shall impart to the [55
Marshal Biron and to others of the king's council there,
so as they may understand that herein we have more re-

gard of the common cause to be relieved and the dangers avoided than particularly to gratify the king therein, whose strange actions towards us in many of [60 his proceedings, contrary to our many advises for his own weal,[16] hath bred in us a great misliking, such as though his affairs may hereby receive advancement, yet we will not require any thanks from him for the same.

Finally, considering the former enterprise at [65 Rouen, whereby, besides the loss of Devereux,[17] there might have happened a great loss of our people, yea of the most principal persons, was such as we had reason in our former letters to condemn it of rashness, yet now understanding that since our censure thereof [70 and the general misliking by many others, Roger Williams[18] hath presumed in an audacious and foolish manner by writing to commend, yea to extol it, as thereby apparently manifesting himself to have been the author or principal persuader thereof, so as we [75 have just cause to doubt[19] that he may, continuing in his error, commit the like offence again, the rather considering he hath the principal office of the field as marshal and thereby and by the credit he presumeth to have with you our general: we do think it very conve- [80 nient to avoid all such occasions by his dangerous advises[20] or rash directions. And therefore we will and command you that no action of any moment be attempted by his advice either privately or publicly without the assent of Sir Thomas Leighton and some other [85 of the captains of most discretion and understanding. And so we require you to observe this our commandment, for otherwise it were better for our service that he were displaced, notwithstanding we know he can serve well in his kind. [90

Given under our signet at our Manor of Oatlands the fourth day of October in the xxxiijth year of our reign. 1591.

Notes

1. *late:* recent

2. Sir Henry Unton, resident ambassador to the French court.

3. Leighton was captain and governor of Guernsey and had served on several diplomatic missions to France and the Netherlands. He was Essex's second in command at the siege of Rouen in 1591.

4. *accorded:* agreed to

5. *since . . . sent:* in the time since we sent orders

6. A combined English and French army had besieged Gournay in late September as a prelude to the siege of Rouen.

7. Caudebec had been captured without English aid by the marshal of France, Armand de Gontaut, seigneur de Biron. Biron and Essex had cooperated in taking Gournay, as they did later in the siege of Rouen.

8. *proper:* particular

9. *are:* as are

10. *other . . . king's:* other of the King's forces

11. *percase:* perchance, perhaps

12. *erst soever:* ever much before, previously

13. *stay:* keep, detain

14. *so as:* provided that

15. *contentation:* satisfaction

16. *advises . . . weal:* recommendations for his own well-being

17. Essex's brother, Walter

18. Sir Roger Williams, an enthusiastic supporter of

Henry's cause, had been fighting the French Catholics on his behalf since 1589.

19. *doubt:* fear

20. *advises:* judgments

Commentary

When the Protestant Henry of Navarre became Henry IV of France in 1589, he was forced to fight for control of his predominantly Catholic kingdom. In order to limit Spanish power in northern France, Elizabeth sent troops in Henry's support. The earl of Essex landed in August 1591, at the head of the third army that England had dispatched to help Henry, who was now preparing to besiege Rouen. The earl's brother, Walter Devereux, was killed in one of the earliest skirmishes of the deployment about the city. The Queen had ordered Essex to bring the army home within two months; but in this letter, taking note of the critical status of Henry's campaign, she agreed to a further period of engagement. Essex finally returned to England in January, having accomplished nothing substantive toward securing Henry's control over his kingdom.

Letter 35. Elizabeth to King James VI, before January 21, 1593

Holograph, L: Add. MS 23240, ff. 108–9.

My most dear Brother,

Wonders and marvels do so assail my conceits[1] as that[2] the long expecting of your needful answer to matters of such weight as my late letters carried needs not seem strange, though I know they ought be[3] more regarded and speedily performed. Yet such I see the[4]   [5 imminent danger and well-nigh ready approach of your state's ruin, your life's peril, and neighbor's wrong, as I may not (to keep you company) neglect what I should though you forget that[5] you ought. I am sorry I am driven from warning to heed,[6] and from too   [10 much trust to seek a true way how your deeds, not your words, may make me assurance that you be no way guilty of your own decay and other danger. Receive, therefore, in short, what course I mind to hold and how you may make bold of[7] my unfeigned love   [15 and ever-constant regard.

You know, my dear brother, that since you first breathed I regarded always to conserve it as mine own it had been you bare.[8] Yea, I withstood the hands and helps of a mighty king to make you safe, even gained   [20 by the blood of many my dear subjects' lives. I made myself the bulwark betwixt you and your harms when many a wile was invented to steal you from your land and making other[9] possess your soil. When your best holds[10] were in my hands, did I retain them? Nay, I   [25 both conserved them and rendered them to you.

Could I endure (though to my great expense) that foreigners should have footing in your kingdom, albeit there was then some lawful semblance to make other suppose (that cared not as I did) that there was no danger meant? No, I never left til all the French that kept their life parted from your soil. And so it pleased the Highest to bless me in that action, as you have ever since reigned void of other nation than your own. Now, to preserve this you have overslipped[11] so many sundry and dangerous attempts in neither uniting with them when you knew them nor cutting them off when you had them, that if you haste no better now than heretofore, it will be too late to help when none shall avail you.

Let me remember[12] you how well I was thanked, or he rewarded, that once brought all the letters of all those wicked conspirators of the Spanish faction, even the selfsame that yet still you have, to your imminent peril, conserved in their estates. Was I not so much doubted as it was thought an Italian invention to make you hold me dearer, and contrived of malice, not done by cause? And in that respect, the poor man that knew no other of his taking[13] but as if thieves had assailed him, he most cruelly suffered so guiltless a martyrdom as his tormentors doubted[14] his life, so sore had he the boots,[15] when they were evil-worthy life that bade it.[16] See what good encouragement I received for many watchful cares for your best safety. Well did this so discomfort my goodwill as, for all this, did I not ever serve for your true espial[17] even when you left your land and yours ready, well-nigh to receive such foreign forces as they required and were promised, which, if you had pleased to know, was and is too evident to be proved.

[30

[35

[40

[45

[50

[55

But what of all this, if he who most ought did nought [60
to assure him or to requite them?

Now of late, by a fortunate good hap, a lewd fellow[18] hath been apprehended with letters and instructions. I pray God he be so well handled as he may [65
confess all his knowledge in the Spanish conspiracy,
and that you use not this man as slightly as you have
done the ringleaders of this treason. I vow if you do
not rake it to the bottom you will verify what many a
wise man hath, viewing your proceedings, judged of
your guiltiness of your own wrack[19] with a weening[20] [70
that they will you no harm in enabling you with so rich
a protector[21] that will prove in the end a destroyer. I
have beheld of late a strange, dishonorable, and dangerous pardon which if it be true you have not only
neglected yourself but wronged me that have too [75
much procured your good to be so evil guerdoned[22]
with such a wrong as to have a free forgiveness of
ought conspired against my person and estate. Suppose you, my dear brother, that this be not rather ensigns of an enemy than the fact[23] of a friend? I require [80
therefore to all this a resolute answer which I challenge
of right that may be deeds both by speedy apprehension with heedy[24] regard, and not in sort[25] as public
rumor may precede present action, but rather that
they be entrapped or[26] they do look therefore.[27] For I [85
may make doom you would not have taken,[28] and what
will follow then you shall see when least you look.
Think me, I pray you, not ignorant what becometh a
king to do and that will I never omit, praying you to
trust Bowes in the rest as myself. [90

I am ashamed that so disordered courses makes my
pen exceed a letter,[29] and so drives me to molest your

eyes with my too long scribbling, and therefore end
with my earnest prayers to God that he will inspire you
to do in best time all for your best.   [95
                           Your loving, affectionate sister,
                           Elizabeth R

Notes

1. *conceits:* thoughts
2. *as that:* so that
3. *ought be:* ought to be
4. *Yet . . . the:* yet I see such
5. *that:* that which
6. *from . . . heed:* prior notice to careful attention, i.e.,
warning of what might happen to regard for what is about to
happen
7. *make bold of:* trust to
8. *as . . . bare:* as if it had been my own breath you bore
("mine own" is an editorial emendation for Elizabeth's "my
none")
9. *other:* others
10. *holds:* fortresses
11. *overslipped:* failed to take advantage of
12. *remember:* remind
13. *no . . . taking:* nothing about his capture
14. *doubted:* feared for
15. *had . . . boots:* was he tortured with the boots
16. *evil-worthy . . . it:* not worthy of life that commanded it
(i.e., the torture)
17. *espial:* spy, lookout
18. Ker, the intercepted agent.
19. *wrack:* destruction
20. *a weening:* mere surmise, supposing

21. *so . . . protector:* i.e., Philip of Spain

22. *guerdoned:* rewarded. I have not identified the recipient of this pardon.

23. *ensigns . . . fact:* signs of an enemy than the action

24. *heedy:* attentive

25. *sort:* such manner

26. *or:* ere, before

27. *therefore:* for it

28. *doom . . . taken:* judgment you would not have accepted

29. In the Cecil Papers draft, Elizabeth squeezed her subscription sideways into the left margin of the page.

Commentary

Elizabeth's resident ambassador to Scotland, Robert Bowes, was apparently recalled to London late in 1592. He returned to Edinburgh in January and delivered this letter to James. In it, the Queen expresses her reaction to the incident of the "Spanish Blanks," a conspiracy that came to light in December 1592. Three of James's most prominent Catholic noblemen had signed their names to blank sheets of paper that they entrusted to George Ker for delivery to Philip of Spain. Ker was presumably to fill in the papers to assure Philip of the noblemen's support in a Spanish invasion of Scotland. Ker confessed his role in the plot after being exposed to a specifically Scottish form of foot torture known as the boot. In the third paragraph, Elizabeth refers as well to an earlier, unidentified victim of the boot who brought James evidence of the ongoing subversion perpetrated by his Catholic nobility.

Textual Notes

Endorsed in a scribal hand, "For our deare Brother the K of Scotland," and below, in a different hand, "Deliuerd be Mr Bowes

Amb.or xxj Ianuar. 1593." After "wrack" (l. 70) Elizabeth wrote "wit," emended here to "with" (l. 70) A copy of this letter follows in the Additional MS on ff. 110–10v. The Queen's holograph draft is preserved at Hatfield House in Cecil Papers 133, ff. 179–80v, followed by a scribal copy on ff. 181–82.

Letter 36. Elizabeth to King James VI, March 16, 1593

Holograph, single sheet,
Folger MS X.d.397.

My Dear Brother,

The care of[1] your estate with fear of your neglect so afflicts my regard as I may not overslip the sending you a nobleman to serve you for a memorial[2] of my readiness and desire of your speed. The sliding dame[3] who, when she is turned, leaves no after step to witness her [5 arrival save repentance, that beareth too sour a record of her short abode, may make you so far awake[4] that you have never cause through too long discoursing to lose the better knowledge of hiddenest treason. One hour breeds {now?}[5] a day's gain to guileful spirits, and [10 guilty conscience skills more to shift[6] than ten wiser heads knows how to win. Let the anvil be stricken while it is warm, for if it grow cold the goldsmith mars his work and the owner his jewel.

It vexeth me to see that those of whom the very [15 fields of Scotland could, if they might speak, truly tell how their banners were displayed again[7] your person, who divers nights did sentinel[8] their acts, those self-same be but now bid to a ward[9] who long ago, God wot,[10] ought so have smarted as you need not now ex- [20 amine their treachery. All this I say not for my gaping[11] for any man's blood, God is witness, but wish you saved wherever the rest go. And this I must tell you, that if the lands of them that do deserve no breath were made but yours (as their own acts have caused), you [25

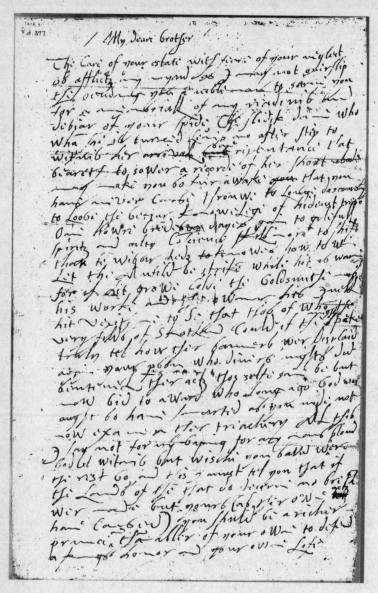

Letter 36, Folger Shakespeare Library MS. X.d.397 recto

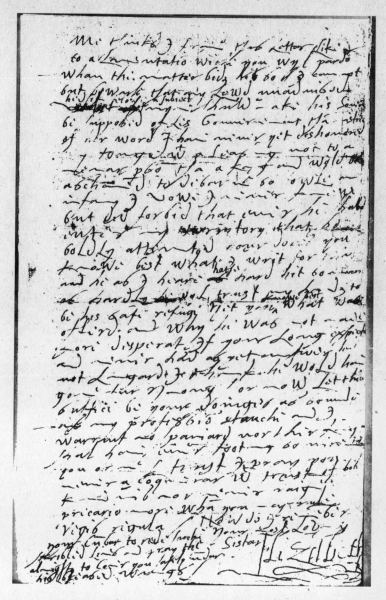

Letter 36, Folger Shakespeare Library MS. X.d.397 verso

should be a richer prince and then abler of[12] your own to defend a king's honor and your own life.

Methinks I frame this letter like to a lamentation, which you will pardon when the matter bids it so. I cannot but bewail that any lewd, unadvised, headsick [30 fellow, a subject of mine, should make his sovereign be supposed of less government than mistress of her word. I have never yet dishonored my tongue with a leasing,[13] not to a meaner person than a king, and would be ashamed to deserve so foul an infamy. I vow I [35 never knew but did forbid that ever he should enter my territory that so boldly attempted your doors.[14] You know best what I writ for that and he as I hear hath heard it so much as hardly he will trust my hands to be his safe refuge, yet you know best what was offered and [40 why he was not made more desperate. If your long ex- pected and never-had-as-yet answer had not lingered, I think he would have gone far enough or[15] now. Let this suffice: be your doings as sound as my profession[16] staunch, and I warrant no Spaniard nor their king shall [45 have ever footing so near to you or me. Trust I pray you never a conqueror with trust of his kindness nor never *reign precario*[17] more when you may rule *regis regula*.[18]

Now do I remember your cumber[19] to read such scribbled lines and pray the almighty to cover you [50 safely under His blessed wings.

Your most loving sister,

Elizabeth R

Notes

    1. *care of:* concern for

    2. *memorial:* reminder

3. *sliding dame:* Fortune or, possibly, opportunity, personified as a woman with a forelock but bald-headed behind so that she cannot be seized once she has passed by (Elizabeth's "slidik" has been emended to "sliding")

4. *make . . . awake:* so far awaken you

5. A hole in the paper has deleted this word.

6. *skills . . . shift:* knows better how to maneuver

7. *again:* against

8. *sentinel:* stand guard over (here, in the sense of "conceal")

9. *bid to a ward:* forced into a defensive position

10. *wot:* knows

11. *gaping:* longing

12. *of:* on

13. *leasing:* lie

14. During the spring of 1593, James complained that Elizabeth permitted the outlawed Francis Stewart (Hepburn), fifth earl of Bothwell, to take refuge in England. See Great Britain, General Register Office, *Calendar of the State Papers Relating to Scotland and Mary, Queen of Scots, 1547–1603* (Edinburgh, 1898–1969), 11:90, 94, and the Commentary to Letter 38. I have not identified Elizabeth's "subject of mine" whose testimony before James she found so embarrassing.

15. *or:* ere, before

16. *profession:* declaration, promise

17. *reign precario:* rule with uncertainty

18. *regis regula:* with the staff (authority) of a king

19. *cumber:* trouble

Commentary

In February 1593, Elizabeth appointed Thomas, fifth Baron Burgh, her special ambassador to the Scottish court; James wrote on March 25 to thank her for sending him as her ambassador.[1] James had just returned from a campaign against his rebellious Catholic nobility, but despite meeting little resistance he managed, again, to take no effective action against his enemies.

1. Gary M. Bell, *A Handlist of British Diplomatic Representatives, 1509–1688* (London, 1990), p. 249; HMC, *Salisbury,* 4:296–97.

Textual Notes

The smeared and faded endorsement reads "deliuered . . . the [L.] Borr[ough] xvj Marche 1592."

Letter 37. Postscript to a letter addressed to Sir Edward Norris, October 1593

Scribal copy with the postscript endorsed
"Copy of a clause written in the letter to Sir Edw.
Norris with her Majesty's own hand." PRO: SP 84/47, f. 128.

Ned,

Though you have some tainted sheep among your flock, let not that serve for excuse for the rest. We trust you are so carefully regarded[1] as nought shall be left for your excuses, but either ye lack heart or want will, for of fear we will not make mention as that our soul   [5 abhors and we assure ourselves you will never deserve suspicion of. Now or never let, for the honor of us and your nation, each man be so much of bolder heart as their cause is good and their honor must be according,[2] remembering the old goodness of our God who   [10 never yet made us fail his needful help, who ever bless you as I with my prince's hand beseech him.

Notes

1. *carefully regarded:* attentively esteemed
2. *according:* commensurate

Commentary

Norris commanded the English garrison as governor of Ostend in the Netherlands. He wrote on October 11 to Lord Burghley that the Spanish were fully resolved to capture the city. His defense was being hampered by lack of financial support from the Dutch as well as by desertions: "The daily roaming away of our soldiers is wonderfull dangerous, for the enemy knows by that means all that is done as well as ourselfs" (PRO: SP 84/47, f. 90v). Elizabeth added this personal note to the formal letter informing Norris that troops would be sent from the English garrison at Flushing to reinforce his position at Ostend. Her allusion to "tainted sheep" in his "flock" responds directly to Norris's complaint about the deserters.

Letter 38. Elizabeth to King James VI, May 1594

Holograph, L: Add. MS 23240,
ff. 132–32v.

Though by the effects I seld[1] see, my good brother,
that ever my advises[2] be followed, yet you have vouchsafed to give them the reading I well understand, having made some of them the theme of your last,[3]
though, God knows, applied far awry from their true   [5
sense or right desert.[4] For if I sin in abuse,[5] I claim you
the author of my deceit in believing more good than
sequel[6] hath told me. For I have great wrong if you
suppose that any persuasions from whomsoever can
make me have one evil opinion of your actions if   [10
themselves be not the cause. I confess that divers[7] be
the affections of many men, some to one, some to another, but my rule of trust shall never fail me when it is
grounded not on the sands of every man's humor[8] but
on the steady rock of approved fact. I should condemn   [15
my wicked disposition to found my amity promised
upon so tickle[9] ground that others' hate might break
the bonds of my love, and upon others' judgments to
build my confidence.

For Bothwell's bold and unruly entrance into my   [20
borders, I am so far from guilt of such a fault as I protest
if I had received an answer in seventeen weeks' space of
my letter[10] that contained his offer to reveal unto you
the treason of the lords with foreigners, I could soon
have banished him from thence. And next, he came   [25
with your own hand to warrant that no offence was im-

puted, which made the borderers readier to receive him. But after I had not left unpunished some of his receipters,[11] I could not have believed they durst have procured the pain due for such desert, and mind to make them afraid to venture such a crime again. And if order given now to all the wardens[12] do not suffice, I vow their bodies and purses shall well suffer therefore. [30

I will not trouble you with recital of what this gentleman[13] hath heard in all the other points, but this toucheth me so near as I must answer that my deserts to[14] you have been so sincere as shall never need a threat of hell to her that hath ever procured your bliss.[15] And that you may know I am that prince that never can endure a menace at my enemy's hand, much less of one so dearly treated, I will give you this bond, that affection and kind treatment shall ever prevail, but fear or doubt shall never procure ought from me, and do avow[16] that if you do ought by foreigners, which I know in end worst for yourself and country, it shall be the worst aid that ever king had and I fear may make me do more than you will call back in haste. Dear brother, use such a friend therefore as she is worth and give her ever cause to remain such a one as her affection hath ever merited, whose rashness is no such as[17] neglect their own so near if they will not forgo their best and shun their own mishaps whom none can at my hand procure but your own facts.[18] [35

[40

[45

[50

Thus hoping that this bearer will tell you my faithful meaning and sincere professions with all the rest that I have committed to him, I leave this scribbling, beseeching God evermore to preserve you. [55

> Your most affectionate sister and cousin,
> Elizabeth R

Edward VI (1537–1553), Elizabeth's half brother
and addressee of Letters 8, 9, and 11,
by Courtesy of the National Portrait Gallery, London

Thomas Seymour (d. 1549), Baron Seymour of Sudeley,
Lord Admiral of England,
by Courtesy of the National Portrait Gallery, London

Lady Elizabeth Drury, wife of Sir William
and recipient of Letter 32,
by Courtesy of the National Portrait Gallery, London

William Cecil, 1st Lord Burghley (d. 1598),
Secretary of State, Lord Treasurer,
and addressee of Letters 17, 30, 33,
by Courtesy of The Marquess of Salisbury

A DN 1572
Æ : SVÆ 32

VIRTVTIS · COMES · INVII

Walter Devereux, 2nd Viscount Hereford and
1st Earl of Essex (d. 1576), addressee of Letter 19,
by Courtesy of the National Portrait Gallery, London

Sir Amias Paulet (d. 1588), Guardian of Mary,
Queen of Scots and addressee of Letter 28,
by Courtesy of the National Portrait Gallery, London

James VI of Scotland, afterward James I of England (1566–1625),
addressee of Letters 22–24, 26, 29, 31, 35–36, 38–39,
by Courtesy of the National Portrait Gallery, London

George Carey, 2nd Baron Hunsdon (1547–1603),
Lord Chamberlain and addressee of Letters 48–50,
by Courtesy of Berkeley Castle

Notes

1. *seld:* seldom

2. *advises:* advice, in the sense of formal notice

3. *last:* i.e., James's letter of April 13

4. *right desert:* true worth

5. *I . . . abuse:* responding to James's charge that she was "abused by your own subjects" in their support of Bothwell (HMC, *Salisbury,* 4:510)

6. *sequel:* what followed

7. *divers:* varied

8. *humor:* whim, disposition

9. *amity . . . tickle:* promised friendship upon so unstable

10. James's letter of April 13 replied to Elizabeth's letter to him of December 22, 1593 (PRO: SP 52/51/75).

11. *receipters:* harborers of criminals or stolen goods

12. *wardens:* Elizabeth's wardens of the Marches of Scotland, charged with guarding the borderlands between the two countries

13. Robert Bowes, veteran of five ambassadorial missions to Scotland since 1579.

14. *deserts to:* good deeds toward

15. *procured . . . bliss:* brought about your felicity with great care. James's threat was couched in the guise of a quotation from Virgil's *Aeneid* 7.321, in translation: "If I cannot influence the gods, I will stir up Acheron [hell]." As Elizabeth read the allegory, James threatened to turn to foreign powers if he could not persuade Elizabeth to keep her subjects from assisting Bothwell.

16. *avow:* declare, affirm (editorial emendation for Elizabeth's "advowe")

17. *as:* editorial emendation for the minim and loop that resembles Elizabeth's "ne."

18. *facts:* actions

Commentary

Francis Stewart (Hepburn), fifth earl of Bothwell, had enjoyed James's favor and respect as a young man at court in the early 1580s. By 1589, however, he was involved in a series of plots to kidnap James and actually managed to take the King prisoner in July 1593. But Bothwell failed to press his advantage, thus allowing James to assemble a coalition of Scottish peers to oppose Bothwell and the Catholic allies with whom he later joined forces. After one final attempt against James, Bothwell fled from Scotland to England on April 3, 1594. James complained to Elizabeth that Bothwell, "my avowed traitor," not only gained refuge in her realm but was supplied with money to pay English recruits to continue his uprising.[1] The Queen responded with this mixture of exasperation and protestations of innocence, warning James not to seek help from France or Spain in his efforts to stabilize his regime.

1. HMC, *Salisbury*, 4:509–10; April 13, 1594.

Textual Notes

An earlier draft of this letter, also in the Queen's hand, is preserved at Hatfield House in Cecil Papers 133, ff. 120–20v. Elizabeth revised much of the wording and added several sentences to the Additional MS copy that she dispatched to James. The letter is endorsed in a scribal hand "To our good brother the K. of Skotts." A partially obscured annotation indicates that the letter was received in Scotland in "Maij 1594."

Letter 39. Elizabeth to King James VI, late October 1594

Holograph, L: Add. MS 23240, ff. 136–37.

My most dear brother,

Though I would have wished that your sound counsels oft given you and my many letters intercepted,[1] which made too plain a shew of that high treason that too late you believed, might have prevented your over-great peril and too much hazard, yet I rejoice [5 with who is most gladliest that at length (though I confess almost too late) it pleaseth you so kingly and valiantly to resist with your person their outrecuidant,[2] malignant attempt, in which you have honored yourself, rejoiced your friends, and confound[ed], I hope, [10 your proud rebels.

You may see, my dear brother, what danger it breeds a king to glorify too high and too suddenly a boy of years and conduct whose untimely age for discretion breeds rash consent to undecent[3] actions. Such [15 speak or[4] they weigh and attempt or they consider. The weight of a kingly state is of more poise[5] than the shallowness of a rash young man's head can weigh. Therefore, I trust that the causeless zeal that you have born[6] the head of this presumption shall rather carry [20 you to extirp[7] so ingracious[8] a root in finding so sour fruit to spring of your many favors evil-acquited,[9] rather than to suffer your goodness to be abused with his many scuses for colors[10] of his good meanings.

Though at the first your career was not the best, yet [25 I hope your stop[11] will crown all. If you now do not cut off clearly any future hope to your nobility through this example, never to combine with foreigners or compact among themselves to your danger, I vow to God you will never possess your dignity long. Weeds in [30 fields if they be suffered will quickly overgrow the corn, but subjects being dandled [12] will make their own reins, [13] and forlet [14] a other reign. My affection to your surety [15] breeds my plainness, which I doubt not but by your sour experience you will fully believe hereafter, [35 having so lately proved the sincerity of my dealings. God so prosper me in my affairs as I malign none of your subjects nor ever would exaggerate any matter but for your surety, whom I mind to take ever as great a care of as if only the interest of my life and person [40 consisted thereon.

This gentleman, the Lord of Wemys, [16] I find a most careful subject of his prince and one most curious [17] to achieve as much as you committed to him, in which I doubt not but I have satisfied you in honor, as time and [45 commodity [18] serve, with which I will not molest you more than refer me to his declaration, with this only, that no one answer to all but proceedeth from a most perfect good affection toward you, and so I desire, with most affection, that you interpret it. [50

I must not omit, for conscience sake, to speak a few words of the Master of Gray [19] with whom I have had long discourse, in which I find him the most greediest to do you acceptable service that I have ever heard any, and doth lay none of his disgraces, banishments, nor [55 loss in any part to you, but only to persuasions of such as meant his ruin, and hopes with his good endeavors to merit your former grace. And for my own, I am nothing partial to him for his particular, [20] but this I

must confess, being as honest as he is sufficient, I think [60
your realm possesseth not his second. I now speak
upon my knowledge, therefore, lose not so good an instrument for your affairs if you know no more against
him than I can learn. You will pardon my audacious
writing as one whose years teacheth more than her wit, [65
never ceasing to lift up my hands and heart with de-
vout²¹ for your most prosperous, safe, and sure success
in this voyage, for which I have sent you but to pay for
horsemeat.²²

     Your most affectionate, loving sister and cousin,
     Elizabeth R.

Notes

  1. *intercepted:* cut off, stopped; i.e., not heeded

  2. *outrecuidant:* presumptuous

  3. *undecent:* improper

  4. *or:* ere, before

  5. *poise:* gravity, importance

  6. *that . . . born:* with which you have tolerated

  7. *extirp:* extirpate, root out

  8. *ingracious:* ungracious

  9. *evil-acquited:* ill-repaid, ill-requited

  10. *scuses for colors:* excuses for outward appearances

  11. *career . . . stop:* course of action . . . conclusion.
Elizabeth's figurative language is from horsemanship: the
career is a charge or short gallop; the *stop,* a sudden reining to
a halt in the career.

  12. *dandled:* bounced up and down playfully, pampered

  13. *reins:* as if taking control of being dandled, with a pun
on *reigns*

  14. *forlet:* forsake, cease to regard

15. *surety:* security

16. James sent his "trusty and familiar servant" John Wemys, laird of Logie, as his ambassador to the English court in March 1589 (HMC, *Salisbury,* 13:408). Wemys apparently visited Elizabeth in the fall of 1594 on his return from a similar mission to France (Great Britain, General Register Office, *Calendar of the State Papers Relating to Scotland and Mary, Queen of Scots, 1547–1603* [Edinburgh, 1898–1969], 2:655, 669).

17. *curious:* careful, attentive

18. *commodity:* convenience

19. Patrick Gray had served James as his ambassador to England during the winter of 1584–85 (see the Commentary to Letters 22 and 23). In 1587 he was found guilty of treason, but suffered no worse punishment than two years of exile abroad. He returned to enjoy the King's favor, although in 1592 he joined Bothwell in another kidnapping plot.

20. *for . . . particular:* as one person among many

21. Elizabeth here failed to copy a word, probably "prayers."

22. *but . . . horsemeat:* only enough (money) to buy provender for horses

Commentary

By late summer of 1594, the earl of Bothwell had joined forces with James's primary adversaries, the Catholic earls of Huntly, Errol, and Angus. James had no choice but to oppose the united rebels. His first response, however, was to send the teenage Archibald Campbell, seventh earl of Argyll, to attack his opponents. Argyll was defeated on October 3 at the battle of Glenlivet, in part due to the treachery of his men. In her second paragraph, Elizabeth chides James for his bad judgment in entrusting his forces to this young man. The King's army gained a final victory over the earls while campaigning in the fall of 1594.

Textual Notes

The bifolium is endorsed in a scribal hand "To my deere brother the King of Scotland." Parts of two seals adhere to this part of the leaf.

Letter 40. To Frances Seymour,
countess of Hertford, November 1595

Scribal copy, PRO: SP 12/254, f. 118.

Good Frank,

We do so well understand your disposition to be
troubled with sudden impressions[1] even in matters of
little moment as we would not now forget you in this
accident of your Lord's misfortune, and therefore have
thought it not amiss, even by our own handwriting,   [5
your brother[2] being absent, whom otherwise we
would have used to assure you of the continuance of
our former grace to yourself, and to preserve your
spirits from those perturbations which love to the person offending and apprehension of the matter so far   [10
unexpected might daily have bred in your body and
mind.

To acquaint you with all the particular circumstances of his offence were not convenient, neither
could it ought avail you, who have been ignorant of all   [15
those causes. But to prevent any apprehension that this
crime is in his[3] nature more pernicious, malicious,
than as an act of lewd[4] and proud contempt against
our own direct prohibition, we have vouchsafed to
cause a ticket[5] to be shown you by this gentleman, the   [20
which may suffice to resolve you from further doubting[6] what it is not, and to satisfy your mind for caring
for that which care now remedies not, it being a matter
both proved by record and confessed with repentance.

And therefore, as you ought well to know how far it   [25

is from our desire to pick out faults in such as he is, so
believe that we (who are slow to rigor towards the
meanest), will use no more severity than is requisite
for others' caution in like cases and shall stand with
honor and necessity. And for yourself, as you will [30
quickly judge when you understand it, that his offence
can have on you no color[7] of imputation, so do we assure you that though for any his faults, you should not
be one jot the less esteemed, yet we will say that for
your sake in this or in anything else, he shall find him- [35
self without your suit[8] or { } the better used. Trust
therefore (good Frank) to this assurance as the voice of
that prince to whose pure and constant mind you are
no stranger, and comfort yourself that you have served
her who wisheth still[9] your good, and careth[10] for the [40
contrary, as much as any. And for a farewell, observe
this rule of us: that seeing grieves[11] and troubles in this
world make haste enough unsent for to surprise us,
that there can be no folly greater than, by fearing that
which is not or by overgrieving for that which needs [45
not, to overthrow at one instant the health of mind
and body, which once being lost, the rest of our life is
labor and sorrow, a work to God unacceptable and to
all our friends discomfortable.

Given under our signet at our Manor of Richmond [50
the 5th of November in the xxxvijth year of our reign.

Notes

1. *impressions:* strong effects
2. Charles, Lord Howard of Effingham, the Lord Admiral.
3. *his:* its
4. *lewd:* foolish

5. *ticket:* a short notice, document

6. *doubting:* fearing

7. *color:* tinge, semblance

8. *without . . . suit:* lacking your supplication. The following blank in the manuscript suggests that the copyist could not decipher Elizabeth's handwriting.

9. *still:* continuously, always

10. *careth for:* sorrows for

11. *grieves:* griefs

Commentary

Frances, daughter of William, Lord Howard of Effingham, had become the second wife of Edward Seymour, earl of Hertford, before 1582. The earl's first marriage to Lady Catherine Grey, younger sister of Lady Jane Grey, gave their children a claim to the throne that the government negated when it declared his marriage to Lady Grey illegal. Hertford was sent to the Tower in November 1595 for petitioning the Crown to legitimize his sons by revoking the nullification of his first marriage.

Letter 41. Elizabeth to Anne of Denmark, Queen of James VI of Scotland, January 26, 1596

Scribal with autograph conclusion and signature,
Edinburgh University MS De 1.12/9.

Right excellent, right high and noble princess, our
dearest sister and cousin,

By a servant of ours of such trust as is this Gentleman well known to you (whom now we do return to
exercise his charge of our Ambassador[1] towards the   [5
King our brother), we would not omit to salute you
with assurance of the continuance of such kindness as
we have always professed towards you although the
good intelligence[2] heretofore offered on your part
have of late passed under greater silence than we could   [10
have expected.

And yet such is our inclination still to hold a firm
correspondency[3] with you upon all occasions whereby
we may demonstrate our care either towards yourself
or the king our brother as[4] we have given in charge to   [15
this our faithful servant, sincerely affected to the
preservation of perfect amity between both kingdoms,
both freely to impart with you and carefully to deliver
[again] to us such things as you shall at any time think
meet for our understanding, who never will be found   [20
behind with any offices[5] of true kindness and affection. And so,

Right excellent, right high and noble princess, our
dearest sister and cousin, we cease further to trouble
you save with our prayers to the Almighty for your   [25

long health and prosperous estate. Given at our
Manor of Richmond the xxviijth day of January in
the xxxviijth year of our reign. 1595.

Your very affectionate sister,

Elizabeth R

Notes

   1. Elizabeth's resident ambassador to Scotland from 1589
to 1597 was Sir Robert Bowes.

   2. *intelligence:* communication

   3. *correspondency:* correspondence

   4. *as:* that

   5. *behind . . . offices:* slow in any services

Commentary

On November 23, 1589, King James VI married Anne of Denmark in Oslo, Norway. The ceremony confirmed their marriage by proxy solemnized in Copenhagen the preceding August. The royal newlyweds did not return to Scotland until May 1590. Before they left Denmark, Elizabeth had sent Anne a letter of congratulation, with profuse offers of friendship. The two queens corresponded with some regularity thereafter, in French at first, but increasingly in English after 1593.

Textual Notes

Drafts of this letter in Guildhall MS 1752 (pp. 97–98) and at Hatfield House (calendared in HMC, *Salisbury,* 6:32–33) conclude with a postscript said to be written in Elizabeth's own hand: "Sister, I beseech you let a few of your own lines satisfy me in some one point that is boasted of against you, which this bearer will tell you." At l. 19, the word before "to us" is badly faded.

Letter 42. Elizabeth to Robert Devereux, second earl of Essex, April 14, 1596

PRO: SP 12/257, f. 46. Endorsed "Copy of her Majesty's letter with her own hand to the Earl of Essex."

As distant as I am from your abode, yet my ears serves me too well to hear that terrible battery that methinks sounds for relief at my hands. Wherefore, rather than for lack of timely aid it should be wholly lost, go you on in God's blessed name as far as that place [5 where you may soonest relieve it, with as much caution as so great a trust requires. But I charge you without the mere[1] loss of it, do in no wise peril so fair an army for another prince's town.[2] God cover you under his safest wings, and let all peril go without your com- [10 pass.[3] Believe Cecil[4] in the rest.

From the *Due Repulse*,[5] where this day I have been and render a million of thanks to Grove[6] for his precious present.

E: R:[7]

Notes

1. *mere:* absolute, utter
2. *another . . . town:* i.e., Calais, which belonged to King Henry IV of France
3. *without your compass:* outside your boundary
4. Sir Robert Cecil, whom Elizabeth dispatched with the message to Essex.
5. Cecil had written to Sir Horatio Palavicino on March 5

that the *Due Repulse* was one of two royal warships launched
that week (CSPD 256/77, p. 182).

6. I have not identified Grove or his present.

7. The Queen's initials are followed by three spaced,
u-shaped loops, akin to the three triangles Sir Christopher
Hatton added to his signature in letters to the Queen in token
of her nickname for him as her "lids," in contrast with Leicester, her "eyes" (see Letter 27).

Commentary

On April 7 the Cardinal Archduke Albert of Austria, Spanish
commander of Catholic League forces in the Netherlands, began
bombardment of the French Protestants defending the port of
Calais just across the Channel from Dover. Essex was in the midst
of assembling an army and fleet for an expedition against Spain;
he proceeded to Dover, anxious to relieve the siege. Before he
could act, however, Calais surrendered on the 29th.

Letter 43. Elizabeth to Lady Margaret Norris, condoling for the death of her son, Sir John Norris, September 22, 1597

Scribal copy, L: Add. MS 38137, f. 160.

Elizabeth Reginae

Mine own Crow,[1] harm not thyself for bootless help[2] but shew a good example to comfort your dolorous yokefellow.

Although we have deferred long to represent to you our grieved thoughts because we liked full ill to yield [5 you the first reflection of misfortune, whom we have always rather sought to cherish and comfort; yet knowing now that necessity must bring it[3] to your ears, and nature consequently must move both grief and passions in your heart, we resolved no longer to [10 smother either our care for your sorrow or the sympathy of our grief for his love, wherein if it be true that society in sorrow works diminution, we do assure you by this true messenger of our mind that nature can have stirred no more dolorous affection in you as a [15 mother for a dear son than gratefulness and memory of his services past hath wrought in us his sovereign, apprehension of our miss[4] of so worthy a servant.

But now that nature's common work is done and he that was born to die hath paid his tribute,[5] let that [20 Christian discretion stay[6] the flux of your immoderate grieving, which hath instructed you both by example and knowledge that nothing of this kind hath happened but by God's divine providence. And let these

lines from your loving and gracious sovereign serve to   [25
assure you that there shall ever appear the lively characters[7] of you and yours that are left, in valuing all
their faithful and honest endeavors.

More at this time we will not write of this unsilent
subject,[8] but have dispatched[9] this gentleman to visit   [30
both your lord and you, to condole with you the true
sense[10] of your love and to pray you that the world may
see that what time cureth in weak minds, that, discretion and moderation helpeth in you in this accident,
where there is so just cause to demonstrate true pa-   [35
tience and moderation.

Given at our Manor of Richmond, the 22th of September 1597.

Notes

1. *Crow:* The Norris crest was a crow, sable. See James
Fairbairn's *Book of Crests of the Families of Great Britain and
Ireland,* 4th ed. (London, 1905), 1:414: "a raven with wings
elevated, sa."

2. *for . . . help:* pursuing relief without remedy

3. *it:* misfortune, i.e., Sir John's death

4. *miss:* loss

5. In translating Seneca in 1567, Elizabeth rendered a
passage on the willing acceptance of death, "Let equitye reigne
over thie mynde, and without bill of complyant pay the
trybute that to death thow owest" (Sir John Harington, *Nugae
Antiquae,* ed. Henry Harington [London, 1779], 2:307).

6. *stay:* stop, bring to a halt

7. *characters:* traits, characteristics

8. *unsilent subject:* matter that cannot be dealt with in
silence

9. *dispatched:* Editorial emendation from "dispathed."

10. *sense:* feeling

Commentary

Sir John Norris, second son of Sir Henry Norris and his wife Margery or Margaret, née Williams, was one of Elizabeth's ablest military commanders. He was serving in Ireland in September 1597 when he fell ill and died of gangrene.[1] Elizabeth probably dictated her condolences to a scribe, then prefixed in her own handwriting the initial greeting to "Mine own Crow" which is missing from many later copies of the text. As was customary for important and personal communications with individual subjects, the Queen entrusted a gentleman in her service to deliver her letter in person and to offer the family additional expressions of her sympathy. See Letter 46 for her condolences to the Norrises in 1599 upon the loss of two more of their sons while serving the Crown in Ireland. Copies of Letter 43 circulated widely in manuscript throughout the first half of the seventeenth century; see the textual notes for a representative listing of copies.

1. John S. Nolan, *Sir John Norreys and the Elizabethan Military World* (Exeter, 1997), p. 239. A copy of the letter was transcribed by John Nichols, *Progresses and Public Processions of Queen Elizabeth* (London, 1823), 3:420–23.

Textual Notes

Copies of this letter will be found in Chetham's Library, Manchester, MS Mun. A.4.15; Folger MSS V.b.214, f. 68; X.d.178; L: Add. MS 44848, ff. 21v–22; O: Eng. misc. MS e.226, f. 19; MS e Musaeo 18, f. 168; Tanner 82, ff. 22–22v; University College, Oxford, MS 152, pp. 1–2; PRO: SP 12/264, ff. 160, 161 (two copies), SP 12/45, p. 40.

Letter 44. Elizabeth to Sir Robert Cecil, summer (?) 1598

Holograph, Hatfield House, Cecil Papers 133, f. 187.

Let the Lords after their examination sequester him to his chamber, and let Dru Drury[1] be with him till their doings have been declared me, and then I like well these warrants, saving that three be the least that such a matter deserves. And therefore, instead of your father that never was with them,[2] the Lord Chamberlain[3] may be inserted who was one, for I like not err[4] in such a case. E. R.

[5

Notes

1. Sir Dru Drury, Gentleman Usher of the Queen's Privy Chamber, replaced Sir Michael Blunt as lieutenant of the Tower of London in 1595 but served for less than two years. It was probably this experience that recommended him as Thomas's jailer.

2. William Cecil, Lord Burghley, was in failing health in the summer of 1598 and presumably unable to attend the council meetings at which Thomas was examined. He died on August 4.

3. George Carey, second Baron Hunsdon.

4. *err:* to err

Commentary

During the winter of 1597–98, an English Catholic, Valentine Thomas, had gained an audience with James VI of Scotland. By early March he was spreading rumors in England that James had urged him to assassinate the Queen. He was arraigned in the fall of 1598 and imprisoned without trial. On December 20, Elizabeth issued a declaration denying that she gave any credence to Thomas's charges (CSPD 1598–1601, pp. 134–35). He was imprisoned but never sent to trial; Elizabeth was still justifying her treatment of him to James in a letter of May 1601 (L: Sloane MS 1786, f. 53v). When James succeeded to the throne he secured Thomas's execution. In this note, the Queen instructs Cecil on the procedure the lords of her Privy Council are to use in examining Thomas. Her note is endorsed "To the Ελφε" (Elf), Elizabeth's nickname for Sir Robert Cecil

Textual Notes

After subscribing this note with her initials, Elizabeth drew a triangle after the "R." The shape is reminiscent of those used by Christopher Hatton in his correspondence with the Queen in which he represented himself as her "lids," or eyelids, in contrast with Leicester, her "eyes." The symbol she used here could likewise represent an eyelid and presumably conveyed some private meaning to Cecil, her "Elf" (see Letter 42, n. 7).

Letter 45. Elizabeth to Edmund,
third Baron Sheffield, July 3, 1598

Scribal copy, Guildhall Library, London, MS 1752, f. 335.

Trusty and well-beloved, we greet you well. Having this occasion by the repair[1] of this bearer towards you, we have resolved to write unto you for two especial arguments,[2] wherein although we are loath to express the first in open terms, knowing that every sound [5 thereof doth but revive your wound and that arguments cannot give sudden cure to nature's passions, yet we persuade ourself that it shall comfort you to receive this gracious assurance that we acknowledge ourself to be partaker in your misfortune, not only in [10 regard of blood,[3] but in this respect, that by this untimely loss, we are deprived of that expectation of service which his towardliness[4] did promise us.

Princes' affections to their people being as deeply interested[5] in the loss of those that are like to be ser- [15 vants to their estate as natural parents in the children of their blood; which consideration being duly weighed, we doubt not but shall extinguish all excess of grief that may be hurtful to yourself, to whom we thinke it fit to deliver thus much of our care of you: that though we [20 know your zeal of our service will make you forget any particular care of your health, yet rather than you[6] should, by undertaking a journey,[7] throw yourself into further inconvenience which cannot be avoided in that unhealthful climate, we do freely give you notice that [25 we do much desire to alter[8] you from that place in that

regard, and will not fail to take some other occasion to
employ you no less to your honor and profit than this,
which course will much content us when we shall be secured[9] that those whom we desire to conserve to serve   [30
us are not hurt by desire to do us service. Dated at
Greenwich the third of July.

Notes

1. *repair:* journeying
2. *for . . . arguments:* about two particular subjects
3. *in . . . blood:* with respect to kinship
4. *towardliness:* towardness, condition of being promising
5. *interested:* concerned, involved
6. *you:* The copyist omitted this word.
7. *journey:* military expedition
8. *alter:* transfer
9. *secured:* assured

Commentary

Sheffield was knighted in 1588 for his service against the Armada. In January 1598, he was appointed governor of Brill, one of
the "cautionary towns" ceded to England by the Dutch in order to
secure Elizabeth's intervention to repel the Spanish occupation of
their country. By his first wife, Ursula Tyrwhitt, Sheffield had six
sons, all of whom predeceased him. The Queen's letter apparently
commiserates with him on the loss of a son who fell while riding
horseback and died of a broken neck.[1] The letter also explains why
Sheffield resigned his governorship shortly after he received it.

1. G. E. Cokayne, *Complete Peerage of England, Scotland,
Ireland, Great Britain, and the United Kingdom, Extant,
Extinct, or Dormant,* new ed. (London, 1910–59), 9:390.

Letter 46. Elizabeth to Sir Henry and Lady Margaret Norris, Lord and Lady Norris of Rycote, September 6, 1599

PRO: SP 12/272, f. 161.

Right trusty and well-beloved, and right dear and well-beloved we greet you well. The bitter accident lately befallen you which is the cause of our writing, being that which toucheth you both with equal smart, and our desire that all the comfort which we wish to   [5 you may reach to each of you with like effect is cause that we have coupled you together in one letter. Loath we were to have written at all because in such accidents (for the most part) the offering of comfort is but the presenting of fresh occasion of sorrow.   [10

But yet being well persuaded of your constant resolution, grounded as well on the experience of other like mishaps which your years have seen, as also chiefly upon your religious obedience to the work of His hands whose strokes are unavoidable, we could not   [15 forbear to do our part, partly because we conceive that we shall therein propose ourself for an example to you, our loss in politic[1] respect, considering the great merits, being no less than yours in natural consideration. And partly by giving you assurance that whatsoever   [20 from us may minister comfort, by demonstrating towards the admonition of you[2] the value we made of the departed, shall not fail to be employed to your best contentments, assuring you that this hard hap of yours shall rather serve us for matter to increase our care of   [25 you than any way to abate it. And because that we know it would be some stay to[3] your sorrow to have him in your eye who is in foreign parts,[4] we will give order that as soon as possibly he may leave his charge in good sort he shall be with you to yield you all duty   [30 and service he may.

Notes

1. *politic:* public, official
2. *towards . . . you:* in comparison with the grave counsel offered to you
3. *stay to:* restraint of, control of
4. Another son of Sir Henry and Lady Margaret, Sir Edward Norris, governor of Ostend in the Netherlands. He had received a personal note from the Queen in 1593 (Letter 37).

Commentary

In August 1599, both Sir Thomas and the younger Sir Henry Norris, sons of Sir Henry and Lady Margaret, died in Ireland in the course of the earl of Essex's ill-fated campaign to subdue the Irish rebels. Elizabeth's letter to their parents offers them sympathy for their loss, although it is not clear whether her letter responds to one or to both deaths. She had sent them an equally personal letter of sympathy two years earlier on the death of another son, Sir John Norris (Letter 43).

Textual Notes

This copy of the letter is primarily a scribal draft with corrections in the Queen's hand. The text above preserves her revisions, which consist of cross outs and inserted words and phrases. The endorsement on f. 161v reads, "6° Sept. 1599. To the L. Norreis & his La:" A second official draft of the letter, lacking many of Elizabeth's revisions, is preserved in the Guildhall Library, London, MS 1752, p. 450. It is subscribed "at Nonsuch the vjth of Sept. 1599." A third copy occurs in O: MS e Musaeo 18, f. 198.

Letter 47. Elizabeth to Charles Blount, eighth Lord Mountjoy, December 3, 1600

Scribal copy, Lambeth Palace, Carew Papers 604, ff. 242–42v.

Mistress Kitchen-maid,

I had not thought that precedency had been ever in question but among the higher and greater sort; but now I find by good proof that some of more dignity and greater calling may by good desert and faithful care give the upper hand to one of your faculty,[1] that [5 with your frying pan and other kitchen stuff have brought to their last home more rebels, and passed greater break-neck[2] places than those that promised more and did less. Comfort yourself therefore in this, that neither your careful endeavors nor dangerous tra- [10 vails, nor heedful regards to our service, without your own by-respects,[3] could ever have been bestowed upon a prince that more esteems them, considers and regards them, than she for whom chiefly, I know, all this hath been done, and who keeps this verdict ever in [15 store for you, that no vainglory nor popular fawning can ever advance your forward[4] but true vow of duty and reverence of prince, which two afore[5] your life I see you do prefer.

And though you lodge near papists and doubt[6] you [20 not for their infection, yet I fear you may fail[7] in an heresy, which I hereby do conjure you from: that you suppose you be backbited by some to make me think you faulty of many oversights and evil defaults in your government.[8] I would have you know for certain that [25

as there is no man can rule so great a charge without
some errors, yet you may assure yourself I have never
heard of any had[9] fewer; and such is your good luck
that I have not known them, though you were warned
of them. And learn this of me, that you must make dif-   [30
ference betwixt admonitions and charges,[10] and like of
faithful advises[11] as your most necessariest weapons to
save you from blows of princes' mislike. And so I ab-
solve you *a poena et culpa*,[12] if this you observe. And so
God bless you and prosper you as if ourself were where   [35
you are.

> Your sovereign that dearly regards you.

Notes

1. *faculty:* stature
2. *break-neck:* life-endangering
3. *by-respects:* subordinate considerations
4. *forward:* prompt, eager
5. *afore:* before
6. *doubt:* fear
7. *fail:* be at fault
8. *government:* Mountjoy's management of affairs in
Ireland
9. *had:* who had
10. *charges:* accusations
11. *advises:* consultations
12. *a . . . culpa:* from punishment and blame

Commentary

Mountjoy succeeded the earl of Essex as lord deputy of Ireland. He arrived at his post in late February 1600 and by the end

of the year had solidified English control over Munster and the Pale, that portion of central Ireland nominally ruled by England but heavily subverted by Catholic intrigue. His success failed, however, to insulate him from charges that his officers were undisciplined and that he spent far more than was necessary. Mountjoy complained bitterly and at length to Secretary Cecil in a letter of October 27: "what a miserable steward am I, that am by my mistress' expectation tied to keep a great house, yet must needs offend her with the faithful and careful expenses thereof, and of the which I see no possibility to diminish any material sum, without the unperforming that which she expects."[1] Elizabeth seems to have responded to this complaint by playfully demoting Mountjoy from steward to "Kitchen-maid."

1. Great Britain, Public Record Office, *Calendar of the State Papers Relating to Ireland, of the Reigns of Henry VIII., Edward VI., Mary, and Elizabeth* (London, 1860–1912), 9:515.

Textual Notes

Endorsed "3. Decembr. 1600 Copie of her Mates lre to the Lo: Deputy. with her owne hand." L. Cotton Titus MS c. 7, f. 125, preserves another copy of this letter.

Letter 48. To George Carey,
second Baron Hunsdon, May 1600 / August 1602 (?)

Berkeley Castle Muniments, Select Letter 8. The leaf is sealed
with the Queen's signet (with yellow ribbons attached).
Torn and damaged portions of the text are indicated with brackets.
The heading is holograph.

Your most affectionate, loving sovereign Elizabeth R

Good George, I cannot but render all laud and
thanks to God for that since your coming to Bath I understand you have so well observed all such good order   [5
both for diet and otherwise as was prescribed you before your going thither; for your performing whereof I
do not only give you my particular thanks, in that you
shew thereby a care to please me, by observing such
prescription as myself had a care to give you, but do   [10
also still[1] out of the same care and love advise you, yea
charge you, to continue the same good [c]ourse.

And glad I am to hear that you do use the advice of
such as {   } skillful and experimented[2] there, their
judgments being best to be liked {   } can [not] but   [15
wonder, considering the great number of pails of water
{   }hea[r] have been poured upon you, that you are
not rather drowned than otherwise. But I trust all shall
be for your better means to health. {   } your sending
to me upon Saturday, hath prevented[3] me, who was   [20
purposed to have sent to you upon Monday. Com-
mend me to your Lady[4] and companion whose estate,[5]
though I would were better, yet I wish yours were no
worse. Thus good George, as we receive very great con-

tentment by our hope to hear of good success to your   [25
health, so take ye comfort both you and she by my love,
which, with my continual prayers to the Almighty God
for you both, shall never fail you.

Notes

1. *still:* continuously

2. *experimented:* experienced

3. *prevented:* anticipated

4. Elizabeth, daughter of Sir John Spencer, who married George in 1574.

5. *estate:* condition

Commentary, Letters 48–50

George Carey, second Baron Hunsdon, was Elizabeth's first cousin once removed. He fought under his father's command against the Northern Rebellion of 1569–70 (see Letter 16). From 1583 he served as governor of the Isle of Wight. He succeeded his father as Lord Hunsdon in 1596, and on April 17, 1597, was sworn to the Queen's Privy Council and appointed Lord Chamberlain of her household. By the spring of 1600 he was so ill that courtiers began pressing suits for his offices. He left London in May with his family and a group of courtier friends to take the mineral waters at Bath.[1] Another journey there in late summer of 1602 left him "neither much better nor worse then when he went out."[2] He died September 8, 1603, surviving his royal cousin by scarcely five months.

Letter 48 may pertain to Hunsdon's journey to Bath in May of 1600 or to his sojourn there in late summer of 1602. In Letter 49 the Queen apparently urged George to leave Bath because she considered its air to be unhealthy. Elizabeth stayed close to London during the late spring of 1600, so Letter 50, in which the Queen offers to extend her summer progress some "twenty or thirty miles" to visit George, must date from September 1602, after his return from Bath. In that month Elizabeth traveled from Woking and Chertsey in Surrey north to West Drayton, where she visited Hunsdon on October 2.[3] These documents from the Berkeley Castle Muniments are designated Select Letters 8–10 in a gathering of papers transcribed courtesy of the Trustees of the Berkeley Will Trust.

1. HMC, *De L'Isle and Dudley,* 2:465, 471. He had returned to court by June 25.

2. *The Letters of John Chamberlain,* ed. Norman Egbert McClure (Philadelphia, 1939), 1:161; Chamberlain to Dudley Carlton, October 2, 1602.

3. E. K. Chambers, *The Elizabethan Stage* (Oxford, 1923), 4:115.

Textual Notes

The letter is endorsed "To my good George, Lord Hunsdon, my Lord Chamberlain."

Letter 49. To George Carey, second Baron Hunsdon, August 20, 1602

Berkeley Castle Muniments, Select Letter 10. This document is a copy in a cursive, mixed italic and secretary hand of the first half of the seventeenth century. The endorsement reads, "To our right trusty and wellbeloved cousin the Lord Hunsdon our Lord Chamberlain."

Your very affectionate Sovereign Elizabeth Re.

Good George. We can but give you our hearty thanks for your visiting us so often by your messengers, as being desirous out of your kind affection to hear of the continuance of our happy estate,[1] so especially in that you let us understand what alteration you [5 find in the state of your own body. For the bettering whereof, though you have experimented many and sundry means, yet is there not any medicine so sovereign and comfortable unto you as the daily apprehension and feeling you have of our earnest care and [10 longing after your good recovery, at the least the ease and mitigation of your infirmity. This indeed we hope you will ever rest most assured of, and so continue in the meditation of the manifold testimonies we have thereof given unto you. And for that[2] amongst other [15 impediments to the furtherance of your welfare we accompt[3] none to be of more importance than the want of the freeness of the air,[4] we are therefore very careful[5] and withal most earnestly wish that, as soon as you may, you would come out of that close place and make [20 trial of some better air.

And albeit my Lady be also most careful in her place to omit nothing that may tend to your good, yet seeing you were the rather drawn thither by some other occasions for which she may have cause yet to [25 make some further stay there, yet we think it needful that yourself should presently remove from thence, though my Lady remain behind some fortnight after. And this to th'end you might the sooner taste of the benefit we hope shall arise unto you by this change and [30 freshness of the air. Herein we shall be desirous to hear of your resolution. And though it hath so fallen out that hitherto we could not see you where you are, yet we nothing doubt but shortly to see you where we may. And in what place soever you be, you shall find us a [35 mother and a wife to minister unto you all the best effects of that tender and kind affection which we may possibly extend to one whom for many respects we hold so near and dear unto us. And so recommending our care and well-wishing unto you, we betake you to [40 the Almighty's keeping, and recommend us to my Lady your better part in the all-effectual sort we may. Given under our signet at our Manor of Oatlands⁶ the xxᵗʰ of August in the forty-fourth year of our reign.

[45

Notes

1. *estate:* state, condition
2. *for that:* because
3. *accompt:* account
4. *want . . . air:* lack of freely moving air
5. *careful:* full of care
6. A royal manor in Surrey.

Letter 50. To George Carey,
second Baron Hunsdon, September (?) 1602

Berkeley Castle Muniments, Select Letter 9, in the same italic hand
as Letter 8, endorsed, "To my good George, the Lord Hunsdon,
my Lord Chamberlain." The letter is sealed with the signet,
with yellow ribbon attached, and begins with a holograph heading.

Your most affectionate sovereign Elizabeth R.

Good George. Because I have heard that before
your departing from Bath, neither your speech was become much better, nor your legs any stronger, and
being still careful[1] and desirous to know that you are
rather amended since your coming from thence, I have   [5
sent this gentleman, the bearer hereof (who we know
shall not be a little welcome unto you), purposely to
see you, and to bring me word of your state how it is
since your coming from Bath, hoping by him to hear
that good effect wrought in you which is said by such   [10
as have experience of the nature and operation of that
water doth commonly ensue and more appear after
some time past of leaving the use thereof, although as
yet I somewhat still doubt that there hath been too
great abundance of the same squashed[2] upon you,   [15
which I would have restrained, if myself might have
been with you. For therein would I have been bold to
have played the part of a physician both to you and my
Lady, of whom I am very sorry that she hath received
so little benefit by the water, as I hear she hath, yet do I   [20
hope to hear of better by this gentleman.

I am glad you are no furder[3] from the way of my intended summer journey,[4] for that it may be I shall not stick[5] to make twenty or thirty miles compass to visit you, except my present choler[6] against those extreme [25 waterpourers do stay[7] me, for that indeed I would rather come to find you amended than otherwise, for which, as I will daily pray, so I assure you, good George, of all comfort that we can give both to yourself and to my Lady your second self and best companion, [30 to whom I pray you commend me, as I commend you both to God's holy protection.

Notes

1. *careful:* full of care
2. *squashed:* splashed, dashed
3. *furder:* further
4. *summer journey:* royal progress, Elizabeth's customary summer tour of various parts of her realm
5. *stick:* hesitate
6. *choler:* anger
7. *stay:* stop, inhibit

IV

Prayers

Prayer 1. On Progress at Bristol, August 15, 1574

L: Lansdowne MS 116, f. 71. Endorsed "The Queen's prayer after a Progress. Entered August 15 being then at Bristol."

I render unto Thee, O merciful and heavenly Father, most humble and hearty thanks for thy manifold mercies so abundantly bestowed upon me as well for my creation, preservation, regeneration, and all other thy benefits and great mercies exhibited in Christ [5 Jesus. But specially for thy mighty protection and defence over me in preserving me in this long and dangerous journey, as also from the beginning of my life unto this present hour from all such perils as I should most justly have fallen into for mine offenses hadst not [10 Thou, O Lord God, of thy great goodness and mercy preserved and kept me. Continue this thy favorable goodness towards me, I beseech Thee, that I may still likewise be defended from all adversity both bodily and ghostly.[1] [15

But specially, O Lord, keep me in the soundness of thy faith, fear, and love, that I never fall away from Thee, but continue in thy service all the days of my life. Stretch forth, O Lord most mighty, thy right hand over me and defend me against mine enemies that they [20 never prevail against me. Give me, O Lord, the assistance of thy Spirit and comfort of thy grace truly to know Thee, entirely to love Thee, and assuredly to trust in Thee. And that as I do acknowledge to have received the government of this Church and kingdom [25

of[2] thy hand, and to hold the same of Thee, so grant
me grace, O Lord, that in the end I may render up and
present the same again unto Thee a peaceable, quiet,
and well-ordered state and kingdom as also a perfect,
reformed Church to the furtherance of thy glory. And   [30
to my subjects, O Lord God, grant, I beseech Thee,
faithful and obedient hearts, willingly to submit themselves to the obedience of thy word and commandments, that we all together being thankful unto Thee
for thy benefits received may laud and magnify thy   [35
holy name, world without end. Grant this, O merciful
Father, for Jesus Christ's sake our only mediator and
advocate. Amen.

Notes

1. *ghostly:* spiritual
2. *of:* from

Commentary

Elizabeth composed this prayer upon reaching Bristol during
the progress of August 1574. The "perils" she had escaped included the Northern Rebellion of 1569–70 and the more recent
Ridolfi plot of 1571. Her emphasis on her personal responsibility
for a "perfect, reformed Church" acknowledges her office, confirmed by her first Parliament, as Supreme Governor of the
Church of England.

Textual Notes

A draft of this document is preserved in L: Lansdowne MS
115, f. 108. Herbert Westphaling entered a third text in his anthol-

ogy of verse and prose, C: MS Ff.5.14, f. 109.[1] These versions of the prayer are nearly identical and all three associate it with the progress of 1574.

1. Transcribed by Michael G. Brennan, "Two Private Prayers by Queen Elizabeth I," *Notes and Queries*, n.s., 32 (1985): 28.

Prayer 2. On the defeat of the Spanish Armada, August 1588

Thomas Sorocold, *Supplications of Saints* (1612),
sig. N7–8v.

Queen Elizabeth's Prayer of Thanksgiving, for the overthrow of the Spanish navy, sent to invade England. Anno 1588.

Most omnipotent Creator, Redeemer, and Con-
server: when it seemed most fit time to thy worthy
providence to bestow the workmanship of this world's
globe, with thy rare judgment thou didst divide into
four singular parts the form of all this mould,[1] which   [5
aftertime hath termed elements,[2] all they serving to
continue in orderly government the whole of all the
mass; which all, when of thy most singular bounty and
never-yerst-seen[3] care, thou hast this year made serve
for instruments to daunt our foes, and to confound   [10
their malice. I most humbly with bowed heart and
bended knees do render my humbliest[4] acknowledge-
ments and lowliest thanks. And not the least for that
the weakest sex hath been so fortified by thy strongest
help that neither my people need find lack by my   [15
weakness nor foreigners triumph at my ruin.

Such hath been thy unwonted grace in my days as,
though Satan hath never made holiday in practicing[5]
for my life and state, yet thy mighty hand hath over-
spread both with the shade of thy wings, so that nei-   [20
ther hath been overthrown nor received shame but
abide with blessing to thy most glory and their greatest

ignominy. For which, Lord, of thy mere[6] goodness
grant us grace to be hourly thankful and ever mindful.
And if it may please thee to pardon my request, give us   [25
thy continuance in my days of like goodness, that my
years never see change of such grace to me, but especially to this my kingdom, which Lord grant (for thy
Son's sake) may flourish many ages after my end.
Amen.   [30

Notes

1. *mould:* the earth or world
2. *elements:* i.e., the four elements: earth, air, fire, and water
3. *never-yerst-seen:* never-before-seen
4. *humbliest:* most humble
5. *made . . . practicing:* taken time off from plotting
6. *mere:* absolute, perfect

Commentary

In this prayer the Queen attributes the English victory to
God's providence, although the key factor in dispersing the Great
Armada was of immediate human origin. On the night of August
7, Elizabeth's commanders sailed fireships into the Spanish fleet
anchored near Calais off the French coast. The Spaniards cut their
anchors to save the ships, some of which ran aground, while the
rest were decimated at sea by violent storms. Elizabeth thus notes
in her prayer that the elements of fire, water, earth (the sandy
shoals of the English Channel), and wind all contributed to the
Armada's ruin.

Textual Notes

I have emended Sorocold's text to add "the whole" after "orderly government," from Huntington Library MS EL 2072, f. 2a. In addition to at least forty-five editions of Sorocold's *Supplications* between 1612 and 1754, the prayer was published in a broadside of 1688 headed *Queen Elizabeth's Opinion concerning Transubstantiation*.

Prayer 3. Undated, possibly written after the 1591 expedition to France

Holograph, Hatfield House, Cecil Papers 147, f. 155.

Most powerful and largest-giving God, whose ears it hath pleased so benignly to grace the petitions of us thy devoted servant, not with even measure to our desires but with far ampler favor, hath not only protected our army from foes' prey[1] and from seas' danger, but [5 hast detained malicious designs, even having force to resist us, from having power to attempt us or assail them. Let humble acknowledgment and most reverend thanks' sacrifice[2] supply our want[3] of skill to comprehend such endless goodness and unspeakable [10 liberality, even such, good Lord, as our simple tongues may not include such words as merits such lauds.[4] But this vow accept, most dear God, in lieu of better merit, that our breaths, we hope, to their last gasps shall never cease the memorial of[5] such flowing grace as thy [15 bounty fills us with, but with such thoughts shall end the world and leave to Thee. All those, with thy good grace, we trust perform we shall.

Notes

1. *foes' prey:* conquest by enemies
2. *thanks' sacrifice:* sacrificial offering of thanks
3. *want:* lack
4. *merits such lauds:* such a cause of praise deserves
5. *the memorial of:* to memorialize

Commentary

The emphasis in this prayer on the English army having escaped danger by land and sea argues against a connection with the Great Armada. The army neither went to sea nor engaged the enemy in 1588, but did so in the French campaign of 1591 and the "Cádiz Raid" of 1596. Elizabeth may have composed this prayer at the conclusion of one of these expeditions or for some similar undertaking.

Prayer 4. For the success of the expedition against Spain, June 1596

Scribal copy, L: Lansdowne MS 82, f. 161.

Most omnipotent Maker and Guider of all our world's mass, that only searchest and fathomest the bottom of all hearts' conceits,[1] and in them seest the true original of all actions intended. Thou that by thy foresight dost truly discern how no malice of revenge [5 nor quittance of injury nor desire of bloodshed nor greediness of lucre hath bred the resolution of our now set-out army, but a heedful care and wary watch that no neglect of foes nor oversurety of harm[2] might breed either danger to us or glory to them. These being [10 grounds, thou that didst inspire the mind, we humbly beseech with bended knees, prosper the work and with the best fore-winds[3] guide the journey, speed the victory, and make the return the advancement of thy glory, the trump[4] of thy fame, and surety to the realm, [15 with the least loss of English blood. To these devout petitions, Lord, give thou thy blessed grant.

Notes

1. *conceits:* thoughts
2. *oversurety of harm:* overconfidence of immunity from harm
3. *fore-winds:* winds blowing a ship on course
4. *trump:* trumpet

Commentary

Elizabeth composed this prayer to invoke her blessing upon the "Cádiz Raid," the English expedition that captured and looted the Spanish town of Cádiz. The text of the prayer in L: MS Cotton Otho E.9, f. 209, affirms that this is "Her Majesty's private meditation upon the present expedition, sent from Sir Robert Cecil to the generals of her Highness' army at Plymouth, enclosed in this letter hereunder written." A copy of this letter, addressed to the earl of Essex and Lord Admiral Howard and dated June 1596, is preserved in the Lansdowne MS (f. 161). The letter itself, addressed to the earl of Essex and Lord Admiral Howard, is preserved in O: Tanner MS 76, f. 30. In it, Cecil urges the commanders, now under protection of the enclosed prayer, to "put forth therefore, my lords, with comfort in confidence, having your sails filled with her heavenly breath for your forewind. . . . That which was only meant a secret sacrifice to one I have presumed out of trust to participate [i.e., share] with two. It came to my hands accidently; I dare scarce justify [i.e., defend as proper] the sight, much less the copy." He concludes by asking them to keep what he has shared with them in strict confidence.

Textual Notes

The copy text has been emended from "other danger" to "either danger" (l. 10), the reading of all other versions. This prayer became one of Elizabeth's most widely circulated writings. In addition to the documents cited above, manuscript versions occur in Folger MSS V.b.142, f. 20, V.b.214, f. 226; Huntington Library MS EL 1205c; Inner Temple Petyt MS 538.10, f. 6; L: Add. MS 38823, f. 96; L: Cotton MS Otho E.9, f. 209; Lambeth Palace MS 250, f. 338v; O: Add. MSS C.299, f. 67a; Cherry 36, ff. 63v–64; Rawlinson B.259, ff. 53v–54; All Souls College, Oxford MS 155,

f. 10; and Y: Osborn MS f b 9, f. 33. John Norden included it in at least three editions of his *Progresse of Pietie* (reprinted in *The Pensive Mans Practise* (1596–1600). Thomas Sorocold printed it with Prayers 2 and 5 in his *Supplications of Saints* (1612); by 1754 this book had seen an astonishing forty-five editions. Camden, *Annals* (1634), sig. V3v, John Speed, *The History of Great Britain* (1611, 1627) and a broadside of 1688 *(Queen Elizabeth's Opinion concerning Transubstantiation)* also included a text of the prayer.

Prayer 5. For the success of the 1597 naval expedition against Spain

Certaine Prayers set foorth by Authoritie
(STC 16528a.5, 1597),
sig. A3–3v.

O God all-maker, keeper, and guider: inurement
of[1] thy rare-seen, unused,[2] and seld-heard-of goodness, poured in so plentiful sort upon us full oft, breeds
now this boldness, to crave with bowed knees and
hearts of humility thy large hand of helping power to   [5
assist with wonder our just cause, not founded on
pride's motion nor begun on malice-stock[3] but, as
thou best knowest, to whom nought is hid, grounded
on just defence from wrongs, hate, and bloody desire
of conquest. For since means thou hast imparted to   [10
save that[4] thou hast given by enjoying[5] such a people
as scorns their bloodshed, where surety ours is one:
fortify (dear God) such hearts in such sort as their best
part may be worst that to the truest part meant worst,
with least loss to such a nation as despise their lives for   [15
their country's good, that all foreign lands may laud
and admire the omnipotency of thy work, a fact[6] alone
for thee only to perform. So shall thy name be spread
for wonders wrought, and the faithful encouraged to
repose in thy unfellowed[7] grace; and we that minded   [20
nought but right, enchained in thy bonds for perpetual slavery, and live and die the sacrificers of our souls
for such obtained favor. Warrant, dear Lord, all this
with thy command. Amen.

Notes

1. *inurement of:* familiarity with
2. *unused:* unusual, unaccustomed
3. *malice-stock:* a foundation of malice
4. *that:* that which
5. *enjoying:* taking delight in
6. *fact:* deed, accomplishment
7. *unfellowed:* unequaled

Commentary

As with the expedition of 1596, the "Islands Voyage" of 1597 was again commanded by the earl of Essex and Lord Admiral Howard. They initially set sail on July 10 but were forced back to port by stormy weather. The fleet set out again a month later but failed to seize the Spanish treasure flotilla or to engage the Spanish navy in any meaningful fashion. Elizabeth no doubt wrote the prayer before the initial sailing, for a copy of her work reached Archbishop John Whitgift, who included it in a volume of official prayers for the good success of the expedition. By July 11 Elizabeth was acquainted with this publication, but her reaction was not altogether favorable. Sir Robert Cecil wrote accordingly to Whitgift:

May it please your Grace,

I have presented unto the Queen your book of printed prayers, and haue read unto her three or four of them, of all which she taketh so great liking as she hath willed me to give you many thanks for the same, and hath commanded some of them to be read in the chapel, as they were. But I must tell you withal, that she is much troubled that her own prayer is in print, and therefore hath commanded me to require you in any wise to make stay of it, and that the same may be taken out of all the books that are printed. This I hope your Grace will effect, and hereof I mean (when I shall see you) to speak with you further.

In a postscript, Cecil added: "I assure you her Majesty requests this very earnestly to be done."[1] As a result, Whitgift's book of prayers survives in four different states, only two of which include Elizabeth's prayer.

1. Lambeth Palace Library, Fairhurst MS 3470, f. 195.

Textual Notes

The copy text is identical in all substantive readings with the version in L: Harl. MS 6986, f. 58, a scribal copy endorsed "The Queenes Ma prayer at the goinge out of the naveye 1597." This text of the prayer occupies a third of a folio leaf. The endorsement, verso, is followed by a later note, "Giuen by Mr. Geo. Holmes." The italic script of this text lacks Elizabeth's characteristic letter forms and spellings. For later texts see L: Add. MS 38823, f. 96; Cotton Galba MS D.12, f. 139; and O: Cherry MS 36, ff. 63v–64 (facsimile ed. Percy W. Ames, *The Mirror of the Sinful Soul,* London, 1897). In addition to the government's official publication of the work, it also appeared in the many editions of Thomas Sorocold's *Supplications of Saints,* from 1612 (STC 22932, sig. N10v–11v), until at least the forty-fifth edition ([London, 1754], pp. 114–15).

V

Essays

Essay 1

PRO: SP 12/235, f. 4.

Even such good health, my friend, as never can appair[1] is wished may fall unto your share by one even
wholly yours, if he can be such a one that scant is found to
be his own. Your curious care to know what grief encumbered my breast, together with the remedy that may cure   [5
the sore, is harder for me to utter than write. If my guest
were not worser than his lodging,[2] the rest were not
worse than the travail.[3] And lest my paraphrase agree not
with my text, I will make mine own exposition. The con-
stitution of my mind's vessel[4] is not so evil framed as   [10
whereupon grievous diseases or perilous maladies have
taken hold. I find not the mixture[5] so evil made as that
any one element of all four overruleth so his fellows, as
that the rest may envy his hap, since but one other part[6]
the Divine power hath given us for the best. It followeth   [15
then that *there* must be the plaint, or gone is all the moan.

If your request, that seldom I deny, had not enforced[7] a custom newly made, it would have pleased
me well that you should not forget how hardly[8] green
wounds suffer their toucher's hand. But since a 'nay'   [20
your firm friend can scarce be brought to make you,[9]
the upper scale you shall touch; to sound the depth
shall serve the feeler's part.[10] When I a gathering make
of common paths and trades and think upon the
sundry sorts of travailers[11] in them both, I find amuse   [25
me greater[12] when multitudes be gathered and faces
many one,[13] amongst the which not two of all be found

alike. Then wonder breeds in me how all this worldly mass so long is made to hold [14] where never a mould is framed alike nor never a mind agrees. And were it not [30 that heavenly power overcometh human philosophy, it would content me well to remember that an evil is much better the less while it endureth. [15]

Notes

1. *appair:* deteriorate

2. *If . . . lodging:* i.e., my spirit is afflicted more than its bodily "lodging"

3. *travail:* i.e., effort to explain the author's grief

4. *vessel:* capacity

5. *mixture:* mixture of the four elements in her body. An imbalance of these elements, the bodily humors, was thought to cause illness.

6. *other part:* i.e., the soul

7. *him not enforced:* did not force him (the soul) to

8. *hardly:* painfully

9. *a 'nay' . . . you:* i.e., I can hardly say "no" to you

10. *upper scale . . . part:* i.e., you shall touch or know the least part of my pain (the lighter of a pair of scales or balances); it is my part to endure the greater pain

11. *travailers:* laborers

12. *amuse me greater:* I am more greatly amused

13. *many one:* many a one

14. *hold:* endure

15. *the . . . endureth:* the shorter the time it lasts

Commentary, Essays 1 and 2

Elizabeth's responsibility for these two essays on friendship is affirmed in *Nugae Antiquae,* Henry Harington's anthology of original papers collected by his family over several centuries and first published in 1769.[1] As further evidence of Elizabeth's authorship, two copies of each essay occur in the state papers of her reign from which the texts below are taken. These documents are undated and quite tentatively assigned to 1590. The Harington family might have acquired their copies at any time during the reign, for John Harington the elder and his wife served Elizabeth before she became queen until their deaths, while their son, Sir John, was also a regular courtier who survived his sovereign.

The style of both essays suggests that they might possibly be translations, but if so, I have been unable to identify the sources. Essay 1 responds in highly figurative language to a friend's question as to how he or she might assuage the writer's grief. The Queen replies by insisting that her discomfort is spiritual, not physical, yet she does not specify its nature. Rather, she reminds her friend that it is painful to talk or write about the subject of her malaise, just as fresh wounds are painful to be touched. She suggests in her concluding sentences that her discontent relates to the diversity of people in the world, where "never a mind agrees." Essay 2 responds to the question of whether or not anything should be denied to a friend by defining true friendship: it is a relationship in which one would not ask for anything the friend could not reasonably grant.

1. See Sir John Harington, *Nugae Antiquae*, ed. Henry Harington (London, 1769), 1:11–18.

Textual Notes

"Worldly" (l. 28) is an editorial emandation for "wordly" in both manuscripts (compare "world's mass" in the opening sentence of Prayer 4).

Essay 2

PRO: SP 12/235, f. 4A.

A question once was asked me thus: must ought[1] be denied a friend's request? Answer me yea or nay. It was said, 'nothing.' And first it is best to scan[2] what a friend is, which I think nothing else but friendship's harborough.[3] Now it followeth what friendship is, [5 which I deem to be one uniform consent of two minds such as virtue links and nought but death can break. Therefore I conclude that the house that shrinketh from his[4] foundation shall down for me,[5] for friend leaves he to be that doth demand more than the giver's [10 grant, with reason's leave, may yield. And if so then, my friend no more, my foe;[6] God send the mend.[7] And if needly[8] thou must will,[9] yet at the least no power be thine to achieve thy desire. For where minds differ and opinions swerve, there is scant a friend in that com- [15 pany. But if my hap have fallen in so happy a soil as one such be found that wills but that beseems[10] and I be pleased with that[11] he so allows, I bid myself farewell. And then I am but his.

Notes

1. *ought:* anything
2. *scan:* consider
3. *harborough:* harbor, shelter
4. *his:* its
5. *down for me:* fall down, in my opinion

6. *so . . . foe:* such a person is no longer my friend, but my foe

7. *mend:* amendment

8. *needly:* necessarily

9. *will:* insist

10. *but that beseems:* only that which is fitting or appropriate

11. *that:* that which

VI

Translations

Prose 1. *Cicero's oration titled* Pro Marcello

Holograph from O: Bodleian MS 900, ff. 2–8v.

Of my long silence, P. C.,[1] which in these days my use[2] hath bred me, not for dread, but driven thereto through woe and bashfulness, this present day hath brought to end and made beginning of what I would[3] and what I meant in wonted sort to speak. For so great [5 mildness, so unused and unheard of mercy, so great a mean[4] in highest power of all things, so incredible a wisdom and almost divine, with tied tongue by no means may I pass. That Marcellus, P. C., is restored to you and to the commonwealth, I deem my speech and [10 authority, not his alone, both for you and to my country kept and returned. For sorry[5] did I much and deeply grieve to see such a man in equal cause with me not like fortune to obtain. Neither could I ween,[6] nor thought it meet that I should haunt your old, wonted [15 trade,[7] when he, the fellow and follower of my studies and my pains was bereaved me, as one deprived of my companion and fere.[8]

Therefore thou hast, O Caesar, both opened to me the interlaced[9] custom of my former life and from all [20 this audience discharged an evident sign to make them not to doubt of any hope left for common good. For I have understood[10] by many and by myself the most, yea, not long ago by all, that in granting Marcellus' life to the Senate, people, and commonwealth, specially [25 when his offenses were all told, how you preferred the authority of that order and the dignity of state before

your own griefs or suspects.[11] He sure hath this day
gathered the greatest fruit of his former days with the
Senate's full voice, but closed up with your weighty   [30
and deep judgment whereby it easily appears how
great a laud is due to the giver when the receiver gains
such glory. Rightly is he happy whose welfare is accompanied with each man's joy, which luck,[12] by right
and merit, this man hath won.   [35

For who exceeds this man in blood, in truth, in
study of best arts, in pureness, or other kind of praise?
No man whose wit hath deepest current, whose
tongue and pen have greatest force, and words may
beautify, much less enlarge, O Caesar, thy glorious   [40
acts. And this I dare affirm, and under your correction
say, among all your deeds, this day hath won you the
generalest[13] praise. Oft times have I laid afore my eyes
and sundry times used in speeches to say that all the
acts of our Emperors, other strange nations and po-   [45
tent people, yea, noblest kings, could never match
yours either for greatness of contention[14] or for number of fights, or variety of countries, or speed in ending, or unlikeness of wars.[15] No men's feet could
swiftlier[16] pass with speed the compass of far-distant   [50
soils than not only your roads[17] but your victories have
done, which all, if I did not confess to be so great as
scarce a mind or thought may all express, I must confess my wits to fail me.

And yet there are greater things than these for my   [55
warlike praises. Words be so placed as t[o] disgrace the
works, and robs from captain[s][18] their glory in equal-
ing their soldiers' lauds, lest their leaders should reap
the only honor. And true it is that in the field the soldiers value the place's fitness, the companions' help;   [60

their navy and victual do much avail. But yet the greatest part even by their right, Fortune challengest,[19] and
whatso prospers well, wellnigh she claimeth all. But in
this commendation, Gaius[20] Caesar, that lately thou
hast got, none can be thy fellow.   [65

All this how much somever, which surely exceedeth,[21] all wholly is thine; no hundred captain,[22] no
leftenaunt, no lussmen,[23] no rascal can glean from thy
triumph. Yea, Fortune, the leader of all worldly haps,
can make no proffer of title to this thy glory but gives   [70
thee place and makes profession that only and wholly
it is thine. For rashness never accompanies wit,[24] nor
chance a fellow to counsel. You have tamed nations
barbarous and cruel, numberless for multitude, infinite for places fertile in all kind of store.[25] But all these [75
be such things as by nature and by state may be conquered, for never was there so great a force, so large a
store, but sword and strength might feeble and dissever.[26] But to conquer the mind, to hedge in wrath,
temper conquest, to raise from ground thy adversary   [80
whom thou mightest dread for race,[27] for wit, for
courage, not leaving with thy help,[28] but extols and enlarges his former degree and place.[29] Whoso can frame
his will to grant to this, I marshal him not among the
greatest men but shadows[30] him nearest to mightiest   [85
God.

The lauds, therefore, thy warly[31] feats, O Caesar,
shall not alone be glorified by ours but by the writs[32]
and tongues full near of all other nations. Neither shall
any after age keep counsel of[33] thy praise. Yea, even   [90
such deeds, I wot[34] not how, even while they be heard
or read, breeds amid the soldiers shouts loud of voice
full far, joined with the blast of many a trumpet. But

when we hear or read an action wisely used with
mercy, courtesy, and temper, where wrath doth reign a [95
foe to counsel,[35] when victory is won of nature rash
and proud, how dearly do we reverence such a one not
only in true stories but in poesy, even with such passion as we love whom we never saw. But thee, O Caesar,
whom present we behold, whose mind and conditions [100
we discern to be such as look what[36] the fortune of war
hath left to commonweal, that all[37] you have saved.

What thanks may extol thee, what love may we bear
thee, what endeavors may we make thee? I assure you,
methinks the very walls of this court shake in bursting [105
out to render thankfulness, with opinion that the ancient authors[38] of their forefathers is like in them and
in their seats to be restored. When I with you beheld
Marcellus's bitter tears, a man of best sort, whose piety
and virtue deserve no dying praise, the memory of all [110
his honorable predecessors pierced my breast to
whom, though dead, in Marcellus's safety thou hast restored both dignity and blood, which being few in
number, of his life thou hast from death preserved. Of
all the innumberable multitude of thanks that thy [115
worth hath bred thee, this day's praise, let it have highest room, for this matter is only your own. Other acts
while you were leader were very great, but yet not un-
accompanied of many and great assistance of rout.[39] In
this only fact[40] you are both fellow and guide, which [120
sure is such as no age shall ever see so far as the end of
thy trophies and monuments.

For nought is so made by handicraft or work but
sometime age mars or consumes. But this thy justice
and mind's kindness each day doth help to flourish [125
more and more, in such sort as look what[41] weary age

may scant from thy acts, that it addeth to thy praise. And as tofore[42] thou hast excelled the victorers[43] of civil wars, so this day thou hast conquered thyself.

But now I dread lest the hearers' ears will not easily [130 understand what in my thoughts I mean: thou hast shewed thyself the conqueror of conquest in bereaving her her spoils and bequeving[44] them to losers' luck. For when by victory's law, by right all won, we were guilty to die by thy mercy's judgment, we be all safe, justly [135 then thou art titled invincible, by whom the state and force of victory herself are made thy prey. And how far doth reach this Caesar's judgment, P. C., listen and give ear. All we driven, I wot not how, by a wretched and deadly fate, our commonweal that took upon us thy [140 trade of arms, are freed from mischief[45] though thrall to some fault of human error. For when Caesar kept, at your requests, Marcellus safe for commonwealth, he restored me to myself and to my country without a suitor. The residue[46] of noblest sort he bestowed on [145 themselves and to their soil, whose number and worth this audience shews you.

It was not he that brought our foes in our courts, but made it plain that this civil war was by the most sort enterprised[47] more for blindness and vain fear [150 than egged[48] by covetous or cruel meaning. For my part in this bickering, I supposed it our best to treat of peace and bend thereto our ears, not a little grieved to see the citizens' voice and speakers therefore with earnest suit refused, for neither this nor any other civil [155 war would I ever have followed. My counsels did ever accompany peace and long robe,[49] not war and weapon. The man I followed was for my private love,[50] not for the common cause, and so much the faithful

memory of a grateful mind prevailed with me as for no [160
gain, no, not for hope, wittenly,[51] yea, willingly I ran as
to my bane, which determination of mine was not kept
hid as this Senate may witness, when all was safe, what
I said of peace. Yea, in the sorest war I thought the same
and made it plain with the venture of my life. [165

No man shall be found so unjust a judge as to
doubt of Caesar's mind, even in the war when he sentenced the authors of peace to be preserved, and sore
offended with the rest. And yet less marvel it had been
even at that instant when uncertain was the end and [170
doubtful luck of war, when the winner favors the
peace-makers, he surely shews a will more prompt to
leave to fight than a mind greedy to win. And for this
matter I can witness with Marcellus (for our opinions,
as in peace, so in war, were ever one), how oft have I [175
and with what grief seen him fear the pride of some,
yea the fierceness of the victory.

So much more welcome is thy[52] liberality as we
ourselves were viewers of thy merits. For now is no
time to dispute causes, but to compare victories. We [180
have seen thy victory limited with battle,[53] we have
looked of no sword in the city without his[54] scabbard.
The citizens we lost no rage of victory but[55] force of
war, to set down so as no man needs to doubt of thy
goodwill, O Caesar, even to have raised[56] from grave[57] [185
if thy power had equaled thy goodwill. Many of those
that be gone since, even of the same side and troops,
thou hast saved whom thou couldest. But of this part I
will say no more but that we all did dread lest this victory would have been too bloody. For some there were [190
that threatened not the weaponed but the loiterers
with speech that it made no matter what they thought

but where they were, so that methinks the immortal
gods, although they looked for some due punishments
at the Romans' hands upon the stirrers and raisers of   [195
such huge rebellion and woeful war, yet now either ap-
peased or satisfied, they seem to have yielded all hope
of life into the hands of the victorer's mercy and wit.

Joy thou therefore in the goodness and enjoy with
thy fortune and glory thy good nature and conditions,   [200
whence proceeds to the wise man most profit and
greatest delight. In remembering the rest of thy good
turns,[58] many may joy for thy virtue but divers[59] for thy
luck. But thy bounty in making me one of the saved
with you and my country, that can you never remem-   [205
ber without the thought of your greatest benefits, incredible liberality, and singular wisdom, which be not
to be accompted[60] the greatest good but the only. So
far shines the luster of true praise, so great state in
magnanimity of mind and content.[61] This shows   [210
virtue's rewards, the other but fortune's love.[62]

Be not weary, therefore, to preserve good men that
have faulted not for ambition or lewdness,[63] but be-
guiled with opinion of[64] duty, though false it were, yet
sure not dishonest, having a show of country's good.   [215
For your fault, it was not that some have feared you,
yea, much more thy praise that though they deserved
it, they feared thee not.

Now come I to the greatest quarrel and eagerest
suspicion[65] which not you alone but all the citizens,   [220
specially myself, with the residue that thou hast saved,
ought to force;[66] which, though I hope be got awry,[67]
yet my words shall not lessen, for your safety must ever
be our warrant even so far forth as, if I must needs
fault,[68] I had rather be too fearful than scarcely wise.   [225

Who is this mad man that breeds this doubt?[69] Is he one of your own (though none can be more yours than they that hold their life of your gift when least they looked therefore)? Was he of the number that were in your troops? Such a harebrain may hardly be found as, [230 receiving all of his captain's grace, will not prefer his life afore his own. But if your own think you no harm, beware your enemy do you none. But where find we them? All they that were, either have perished by their stubbornness or were saved by thy mercy. So it follows [235 that either none doth live or they that breathe by wone thine own.[70]

But for that[71] there be so many crooken[72] and hidden holes in men's minds, let me increase your suspect;[73] so shall you increase your heed. Who is so [240 simple an innocent, so ignorant of home matters,[74] so careless of his own and common good that knows not how on thy life and welfare alone dependeth his and so the rest of citizens? Sure, when night and day I think of thee, as duty binds me, I fear the sundry mishaps that [245 falls to men, the uncertain change of health, and slipperness[75] of man's days, and grieve I do when this commonweal, which I wish immortal, to see it depend upon the breath of one mortal person. But if to human ill lucks[76] and unlooked disease these be added to, a [250 consent of[77] mischief and a sort of treason, how may we in human reason believe that a god shall help our need?

Thou must raise up from fall, O Caesar, all such things as by force of war, which needly[78] must hap, [255 were strucken[79] and beat down, yea, that that[80] time hath loosed, laws must bind. You must appoint judgment's seats, you must stablish[81] faith, suppress lust,

confirm the lawful inheritors. It was not to be looked
for in so civil a war, in so great a broil of minds and   [260
arms, but that the shaken commonwealth, whatso[82]
the hap of war might breed, should lose many orna-
ments of her state and strength of her maintenance.
Yea, either of you both in field would bide[83] full many
actions that in Senate you would never suffer done.[84]   [265
And now all the wounds that this war hath made, thou
must be surgeon to, for no man else may heal them.
Against my will full sore I have heard thy princely and
wise voice say these:[85] "I have lived long enough both
for nature and for glory." Sufficient time for your age, if   [270
so you will add to it you list[86] for your honor; but for
that[87] is most worth for your country, surely too short.

Overslip,[88] I pray you, this wisdom of learned doctors[89] that despise death. Be not wise with[90] our peril.
Oft do I hear that you too much doth use to give out   [275
this speech, that you have lived long enough. For your-
self, I believe you well, but yet with this addition: if to
yourself alone you lived, or born were only for yourself—but when your acts have managed the safety of
your citizens and country, so far be you from the per-   [280
fection[91] of your greatest affairs that I believe you have
scant laid the foundations of them that your mind
comprehends. Will you limit the end of your days with
the pleasing of your mind, not with the care of your
country's good? What if this be not sufficient for your   [285
own glory, of which, though you be a wise man, you
cannot deny you are most greedy of? Is it a small matter to leave[92] a great glory? Yea, to others; yea, to many,
enough. But to serve your liking, too little. For how
magnific[93] soever a matter be, yet if they expect a   [290
greater fortune, the rest comes too short. For if, O Cae-

sar, of your immortal fame this only should be the end
that, winning[94] your foes, you should leave your commonweal in state as now it is. Take heed that your divine virtue carry not more wonder than praise, for   [295
your glory is noble and far spread abroad by the fame
of your deserts toward many of greatest degree and
worth, yea, to your citizens, to your country, and in
short to all kind of estates.[95]

But yet there bides behind another part for you to   [300
play, another deed to execute, and this must be your
travail: to frame a commonwealth and compound[96] it
in so quiet sort as you may enjoy with it your ease. And
then when you have answered your country his due[97]
and nature have been paid sufficient for her debt with   [305
a satisfaction of life, then, if you list,[98] say, I have lived
long enough. But what meaneth this word 'enough,' in
which there is a furder end attended[99] which, when it
haps, all passed pleasures shall seem none because
there shall be none to follow. Thy haught[100] courage   [310
was ever such as never was satisfied with the strait
bounds that nature yields all men to live in, but still[101]
inflamed with love of immortality. Neither is this to be
termed life which knits the soul and body together but
that is—that is thy life, Caesar, which shall have life in   [315
memory of many ages, which posterity shall feed, and
eternity shall look on. Be diligent in this work and
boast thyself of so good a deed. This thy country hath
beheld many things to wonder at and now doth look
for many things to praise. Our posterity will be as-   [320
tonied[102] to hear and read of all your won kingdoms,
provinces, the Rhine, the Ocean, the Nile,[103] your innumberable fights, your incredible victories, your
monuments, your rewards, and your triumphs.

But unless this city be stablished by your counsels [325
and orders, your wayfaring name shall spread far and
wide, but a stable seat and sure abode it shall never
have. There shall arise a great contention among them
that shall follow as among us that now live. Some will
extol thy deeds to sky, some other will say there was [330
somewhat undone, yea of greatest consequence except
for country's good. Then quench the flame of civil stir,
which may make plain that the one[104] was destiny and
this last thy counsel. Stand to[105] the judgments of those
that in aftertime shall be furderers[106] of your deeds, [335
perchance with clearer doom[107] than ours. For their
sentence[108] shall no love, no hate, no desire, no envy
corrupt. And though that some so falsely judge that
those days shall nothing avail you, yet this present time
no man denies but it toucheth you, to show you such a [340
one[109] as no oblivion may dim your praise.

Divers were the wills and sundry were the opinions
of the citizens, for we fought not with counsels and endeavors[110] but with armor and weapon. There fell a
darkness among us, yea, there fell quarrel among the [345
greatest captains. Many doubted what was best; some,
what was best for themselves; other, what became
them—yea, some other what was lawful. Thus was this
commonwealth afflicted with this wretched and evil-
destined war. But he won who kindled not his hate [350
with his fortune, but covered it with his mercy, nor
judged not worthy[111] death nor outlawry all such as
had offended[112] him. Such weapons as were laid down
by some, others boldly took up. Ungrateful and unjust
a citizen is he who, delivered from war's danger, keeps [355
a mind armed still,[113] so that he is better that lost his

life in the battle than he that died for the cause. For that is frowardness[114] in some, to others seems constancy.

But for that[115] this broil is broken with arms and [360 calmed with the winner's clemency, it remains now that all be of one mind, not only they that be wise but they that be not mad, for without thy safety, O Caesar, and thy good sentence,[116] which heretofore and even this day thou gave, safe can we never be. Wherefore all [365 we that wish all sure do exhort and beseech thee to care for thy life and surety.[117] And that I may speak for all others, that of myself I think,[118] because thou thinks there lies lurking something worthy thy heed, we do promise thee not only scout-watch[119] and guard but [370 the bulk[120] of our sides and carcases for thy defence.

But that my oration may take his[121] end whence his beginning rose, our thanks be great we render thee, but more by much we owe thee, for all with one counsel be of like mind, as both their wishes and tears may make [375 thee know. And for that[122] all the multitude can hardly be heard at once, they have chosen me their spokesman, to whom it becometh me obey, both for that such is their will and, chiefly, for that I know my bond[123] is such as, Marcellus being restored to the Sen- [380 ate, to the people, to the commonwealth, I ought to make this function.[124] For I may perceive an universal joy as not for his life alone but for the good of all. And to prove my friendship to him, it hath been ever known to all men so great as, but to C. M.,[125] his best [385 and dear brother, I well give place to none other,[126] which I have earned by suit, by care, by labor as long as I beheld his life in doubt. And now that I see him freed

from fear, from trouble, from woe, I ought to do as
you may hear. Therefore, O Caesar, receive my many   [390
thanks as from him that confesseth himself and all his
not only preserved by thy goodness but advanced; and
yet above all thy innumberable deserts to me alone
(which I could never have imagined) this thy fact to [127]
Marcellus hath laid the highest heap.   [395

Notes

1. *P. C.: Patres Conscripti,* senators (literally, "chosen
fathers")

2. *use:* custom

3. *would:* wished

4. *mean:* moderation

5. *sorry:* sorrow (obsolete form of the verb also used by
Elizabeth as a noun in Letter 9, l. 1)

6. *ween:* think, suppose

7. Elizabeth first wrote "the old, wonted trade," then added
"your" above the line without deleting "the." Cicero's *vetere
curriculo* refers to the old way of life that he felt guilty about
resuming while Marcellus remained in exile.

8. *fere:* partner, comrade

9. *interlaced:* linked together. The Queen translated
Meter 6, l. 16 of Boethius's *De consolatione philosophiae*
"So Interlaced looue renewes" (Caroline Pemberton, ed.,
*Queen Elizabeth's Englishings of Boethius, Plutarch, and
Horace,* Early English Text Society, original ser. 113
[London, 1899], p. 97).

10. Elizabeth wrote "understand."

11. *suspects:* suspicions

12. *luck:* good fortune

13. *generalest:* most general, most ample (for Cicero's

comparative, *ampliorem*). Elizabeth's final *t* is lost in the cropped right margin.

14. *contention:* effort

15. *unlikeness of wars:* wide variety of military engagements

16. *swiftlier:* more swiftly (Elizabeth's "swiftlar")

17. *roads:* forays, raids

18. Elizabeth wrote "the disgrace the workes and robbes from Captaine."

19. *Fortune challengest:* Fortune claims (Fortune here as the goddess of chance events)

20. For Elizabeth's "Caius."

21. *somever . . . exceedeth:* soever, which surely surpasses

22. *hundred captain:* captain of a hundred men

23. *leftenaunt, no lussmen:* lieutenant, no armed men (?). Elizabeth wrote "lussemen" in translating Cicero's *cohors,* one-tenth of a Roman legion. This may derive from the obsolete *lush,* a stroke or blow, but it is also possible that in searching for a more Latinate term for pikemen, the Queen found *luce* or *lucius,* Latin for "pike," and coined the term *lussemen* (lucemen). *Luce* refers, however, to the pike fish, not the weapon of the same spelling.

24. *wit:* intelligence

25. *store:* supplies, necessities

26. *feeble and dissever:* enfeeble and break up

27. *race:* social standing

28. *leaving with thy help:* stopping at offering help

29. *extols . . . place:* elevates and enlarges his former social rank and status

30. *shadows:* portrays

31. *thy warly:* of your valiant or warlike

32. *writs:* writings

33. *keep counsel of:* keep secret

34. *wot:* know

35. *wrath . . . counsel:* anger prevails as an opponent of good advice

36. *look what:* whatever

37. *that all:* all that

38. *authors:* ancestors (for Cicero's *auctoritas,* "reputation, authority"). Elizabeth misunderstood the passage in Cicero, which looks forward to Marcellus's return to the halls where his ancestors sat as senators.

39. *rout:* followers, retinue

40. *In this only fact:* only in this action or endeavor

41. *look what:* whatever

42. *tofore:* previously

43. *victorers:* victors

44. *bequeving:* bequeathing

45. *freed from mischief:* acquitted of evildoing

46. *residue:* remainder. Caesar had already pardoned Cicero and the assembled senators who had opposed him in the civil war.

47. *enterprised:* undertaken

48. *egged:* egged on, incited

49. *long robe:* the legal profession

50. Cicero sided with Pompey, Caesar's rival.

51. *wittenly:* wittingly

52. *thy:* i.e., Caesar's

53. *limited with battle:* restricted by its battles (?). Cicero attributes Caesar's victorious status to the outcome of many battles.

54. *looked of . . . his:* looked upon . . . its

55. *no rage . . . but:* not to revenge after victory but to

56. *raised:* Elizabeth wrote "rayse."

57. *from grave:* them from the grave

58. *good turns:* benefits

59. *divers:* many others

60. *accompted:* accounted

61. *content:* contentment

62. *This . . . love:* The contrast drawn sets true praise for virtue versus mere luck.

63. *lewdness:* wickedness

64. *opinion of:* a conception of

65. *eagerest suspicion:* fiercest, most dreadful suspicion (i.e., of assassination plots)

66. *residue . . . to force:* the rest of the citizens you have saved ought to be concerned with

67. *got awry:* go off course, go amiss (referring to plots to assassinate Caesar)

68. *fault:* commit an error

69. *doubt:* fear

70. *by wone thine own:* by custom bound to you

71. *for that:* because

72. *crooken:* crooked

73. *suspect:* suspicion

74. *home matters:* civil affairs

75. *slipperness:* slipperiness

76. *ill lucks:* bad fortune. The plural "lucks" is Elizabeth's coinage for Cicero's *humanos casus* (human chances, accidents).

77. *a consent of:* an acquiescence to

78. *needly:* necessarily

79. *strucken:* stricken

80. *that that:* that which

81. *stablish:* establish

82. *whatso:* whatever

83. *bide:* endure, tolerate

84. *done:* to be done

85. *these:* i.e., these words

86. *list:* wish. The sense of the clause is, "if you will add to your longevity your desire for honor."

87. *that:* that which

88. *Overslip:* pass over

89. *doctors:* teachers

90. *Be not wise with:* do not become philosophical about

91. *perfection:* completion

92. *leave:* leave behind, bequeath

93. *magnific:* renowned, glorious

94. *winning:* conquering

95. *estates:* social classes

96. *compound:* constitute, establish

97. *answered . . . his due:* paid your country the debt you owe it

98. *list:* desire

99. *in which . . . attended:* i.e., which is accompanied with a further finality, Caesar's death

100. *haught:* noble, exalted

101. *still:* constantly

102. *astonied:* amazed

103. *the Rhine, the Ocean, the Nile:* the principal arenas of Caesar's military campaigns

104. *the one:* Caesar's military triumphs, as opposed to his cessation of the civil war through policy or counsel

105. *Stand to:* submit yourself to

106. *furderers:* supporters (?). Elizabeth apparently wrote "verderars"; the context requires "judges," for Cicero's *iudicabunt* (they will judge).

107. *doom:* judgment

108. *sentence:* verdict

109. *show . . . one:* show you to be such a one

110. *endeavors:* strenuous efforts (for Cicero's *studiis,* "zeal, eagerness")

111. *worthy:* worthy of

112. *offended:* Elizabeth wrote "offend."

113. *still:* constantly

114. *that is frowardness:* that which is obstinacy

115. *for that:* because

116. *sentence:* judgment

117. *surety:* security

118. *that of myself I think:* that which I myself think

119. *scout-watch:* sentinel

120. *bulk:* body

121. *his:* its

122. *for that:* because

123. *bond:* duty

124. *make this function:* undertake this task

125. *C. M.:* Gaius Marcellus

126. *well . . . other:* do not well give place to anyone else;
i.e., do not willingly yield to any other

127. *fact to:* action on behalf of

Commentary

Cicero delivered this speech before the Roman Senate in 46 B.C.E. Marcus Claudius Marcellus had opposed Julius Caesar's assumption of dictatorial powers in Rome. After Caesar's victory at the Battle of Pharsalia (48 B.C.E.), Marcellus retired to Mytilene, the main city on the isle of Lesbos off the coast of modern Turkey. He declined Cicero's urgings to return to Rome and seek a pardon, yet Caesar acquiesced to the Senate's wishes and pardoned him anyway. Cicero's oration congratulates Caesar on this display of clemency. Marcellus was murdered within the year, however, not without suspicion of Caesar's complicity in the act.

Elizabeth translated Cicero's long and complicated clauses with few marks of punctuation even between sentences. The punctuation of this text is therefore nearly all editorial (and rather heavy), in an effort to clarify the meaning of this often convoluted text. For Cicero's original Latin with an English translation, see N. H. Watts, trans., *The Speeches,* by Cicero, Loeb Classical Library (London, 1931), pp. 422–51.

Textual Notes

H. H. E. Craster described the Bodleian MS in "An Unknown Translation by Queen Elizabeth," *English Historical Review* 29 (1914): 721–23. His comparison of the manuscript's watermarks with other documents in Elizabeth's hand revealed that the paper was the same as that in PRO: SP 12/289, the volume in which she transcribed her translations of Boethius, Horace, and Plutarch between 1593 and 1598. Thus her translation from Cicero probably dates from the 1590s as well.

Poetry 1. *The second chorus of* Hercules Oetaeus *(attributed to Seneca)*

Scribal copy from O: e Museo MS 55, ff. 48–49.

A Translation of Q Elizabeth

What harming hurl[1] of Fortune's arm thou dreads,
Let fraught[2] of faith the burthen[3] of care relieve,
And take thou such, to fear approved by proof,
The unpicked locks of certain trust to hold:
For geason[4] is the faith and rarely kept is trust,   [5
Where puffed sails from best fore-winds[5] be fallen.
The weight of scepter's sway if choice must bear,
Albeit the vulgar crew fill full thy gates,
And hundred thresholds with their feet be smoothed:
Though with thy gleaves[6] and axes thou be armed,   [10
And root[7] full great do glory give thy name:
Amid the view of all these sundry sorts,
One faultless faith her room even scant may claim.
The golden ledge[8] full wrathful spites besets,[9]
And where the gates their posts draw forth by breadth,[10] [15
More easy way to guiles and passed safe:[11]
Heed then the clocks[12] of warned harms with good,
And let the hidden blade no wrong thee work:[13]
For when most shew by gazers' eyen[14] is spied,
And presence great thy honor most advance[15]   [20
This gift retain as fellow to thy room:
Disdain may frown, but Envy thrust[16] thee through.
No ofter[17] doth the East the night's care release
And makes the shady dark with light abashed

Than kings be made in instant[18] short and marred,   [25
So icy[19] is their joy and hopeless woe.
The love of kingdom's rule observed with care,
But[20] for himself a king but few regard:
The court's luster a stale guest made for me,
Delighted with the shine,[21] no woe forethought.[22]   [30
And this man seeks the nearest room to prince,
To glittering view amid the streets he comes,
While broiled is with cark[23] the miser's breast,
In search of gainful grasp his name to spread,
In compass[24] of the hoarded heaps to find   [35
One bit to slake desire's craves[25] he seeks;
Not all the coast where Istrus'[26] trade doth haunt,
With gems bedecked through hue of divers kind,
Nor Lydia fair with sweetest streams, suffice
To quench ne[27] answer all such thirst by half.   [40
Ne yet the soil that bides Zephyrus' slave[28]
Abashed at golden, shining Tagus' beams,[29]
Nor Hebrus' service[30] may content at full,
Rich though Hydaspes' hedge[31] his fields throw out,
Though Ganges' course his confines all do grace[32]   [45
With filled force to water all his lands.
To greedy, grating wights enough not all
That nature well doth please his lack not so.[33]
This man doth homage owe unto kingly force,
And harbor Rome[34] adores where last he haunts,[35]   [50
Not meaning that this plowshare should advance
Like crooked hind[36] his master's gain with clots,[37]
By murdering[38] oft the ground; no ease of toil,
Though thousand leas[39] his husbandmen turn up.
Well pleased rests his search with goods even such   [55
As pleasure may by gift another need.[40]
A badder sort the prince's court regard

With foiled[41] foot that stumble[42] gives at all,
And each to lose with no avail to one.
That might may equal harm, they power achieve [60
Whose living's thread[43] drawn out is of such length
Whom hap ne takes[44] ere nature calls away.
The horned, newed moon them blessed call[45]
Whose wane, them misers judge[46] when day doth fall.
A man full rarely happy is and old; [65
Mo[47] surer sleeps thee downy turfs procure.
All Tyre[48] where purple woven is and made
Not so sound slumber doth his owner yield.
The gilted[49] roofs the quiet rest bereaves,
And waking nights the purple draws from ease. [70
O that the breasts of rich men naked were,
The smoothed dreads of lofty lucks[50] that hide.
The Brutian[51] stream more milder course doth hold
When Easty[52] wind him strikes with force's stroke.
In franched mind from care the silly soul possessed[53] [75
A pot of beechy tree[54] full sure he keeps,
With steady hand that fears no snatch from hold,[55]
No sudden fright affrays, no thief he dreads.
With ease ygot[56] and single shew he feeds,
And recks not for the girded blades to thigh.[57] [80
The golden cup of bloody mixture keeps.[58]
The wife that ytied[59] is to man of mean estate
No carking hath in order pain to set,[60]
Nor shining gift of reddy[61] sea she wears;
Her ears free from the pluck[62] of gemmy weight, [85
No stone of Eoas' waves her cumber makes:[63]
Soft wool ingrained with Sidon's purple[64] fair
Drinks not the red for use that her befalls;
No Maeon needle filleth she with sleaves[65]
By parted hues that give the shade with art: [90

The silky land that lies to sunny east⁶⁶
Needs not the fruit from eastern tree to pluck.
Every herb the colors' die may mix,
That distaff fills with yarn that skill ne spun.⁶⁷
She nursed not the doubts of wedlock bed;   [95
Of lewd suspect⁶⁸ of weary works she shuns.
The wrathful lamp Erins⁶⁹ lighteth up
The feastful day adorns by pestering rout.⁷⁰
The poor man deemeth not his happy state
Till wealthy, ruined folk by fall it show.   [100
Whoso therefore the middle way eschews,
The wry⁷¹ and crooked balks⁷² most sure to tread,
While Phaeton boy⁷³ one day of father got
To rule the reins, and eke his wain⁷⁴ to guide,
In leaving wonted walk, and worned ways⁷⁵   [105
With by slide while the uncouthed⁷⁶ skies he shears,⁷⁷
Such place as heat of Phoebus' flame ne touch⁷⁸
His ruin was, the world his fellow plain.⁷⁹
Daedalus yet more larger scope and broader took,
Who never yet a sea by name did grace,   [110
Though Icarus sought the true and living birds
By guile to pass,⁸⁰ and win the trier's right.⁸¹
His father's feathered wings despised with scorn,
To Phoebus near with swifty gait he hies,⁸²
And christened by his slip the sea was sure.⁸³   [115
Evil bought⁸⁴ the great where ill exceeds the good.
Let one full happy be and highly flee;⁸⁵
God shield⁸⁶ that mighty me the vulgar call.⁸⁷
The lee of shore my silly⁸⁸ boat shall touch.
Let no full wind to depth my bark bequeath;⁸⁹   [120
From safest creeks doth fortune⁹⁰ glide and shun,
With search in middest sea for tallest ship,
And takes it⁹¹ dearest prey the nearer to cloud.

Notes

1. *hurl:* violent cast, throw
2. *fraught:* cargo
3. *burthen:* burden
4. *geason:* rare, uncommon
5. *fore-winds:* favorable winds
6. *gleaves:* swords, halberds
7. *root:* family roots, ancestry
8. *ledge:* transverse strip across a door. It is "golden" to symbolize the luxury of rulers, in contrast with the dangers of their exalted status.
9. *full . . . besets:* encloses thoroughly malignant or injurious actions
10. *draw . . . breadth:* open wide
11. *to guiles . . . safe:* for guiles to pass in safely
12. *clocks:* clock bells
13. *no wrong thee work:* work you no wrong (harm you)
14. *eyen:* eyes
15. *most advance:* advances the most
16. *Envy thrust:* Envy (personified) will thrust
17. *ofter:* more often
18. *in instant:* in an instant
19. *icy:* slippery, uncertain
20. *But:* except
21. *shine:* glitter (of the court)
22. *forethought:* anticipated
23. *broiled . . . cark:* agitated by distress
24. *compass:* bounds, limits
25. *desire's craves:* the cravings of desire (?). (This use of *crave* as a noun predates the *OED* examples by several centuries.)
26. *Istrus':* Greek colony on the east coast of the Black Sea
27. *ne:* nor

28. *bides . . . slave:* endures as slave to the west wind

29. *Tagus' beams:* beams reflected, presumably, off the waters of the Tagus, a river in central Spain

30. *Hebrus' service:* benefit rendered by the Hebrus, a river in Thrace renowned for its golden sands

31. *Hydaspes' hedge:* limit or boundary formed by the Hydaspes, a river in India marking the easternmost point reached by Alexander the Great

32. *grace:* give pleasure or honor to

33. *grating . . . so:* irritating persons (such as him for whom) all that nature provides is not enough to appease his greed

34. *harbor Rome:* the shelter of Rome

35. *haunts:* ordinarily resides

36. *crooked hind:* a stooped-over farm servant

37. *clots:* clods of earth

38. *murdering:* tormenting

39. *leas:* open lands, plowlands

40. *As pleasure . . . need:* pleasure as another may need as a gift

41. *foiled:* trampled

42. *stumble:* a stumbling or partial fall

43. *living's thread:* thread of life

44. *hap ne takes:* accident does not take

45. *newed . . . call:* renewed moon calls them blessed

46. *them misers judge:* deems them wretches

47. *Mo:* more

48. *Tyre:* city on the coast of Phoenicia that, with Sidon, was famous for its purple dye (see l. 87)

49. *gilted:* gilded

50. *smoothed . . . lucks:* placid fears of lofty fortunes

51. *Brutian:* from Bruttium, the mountainous region of southwestern Italy

52. *Easty:* eastern. Elizabeth incorrectly translates Seneca's *Coro* (Corus, the northwest wind).

53. *franched . . . possessed:* mind freed from care the lowly, self-possessed soul

54. *pot . . . tree:* pot (carved) from beechwood

55. *hold:* grasp

56. *ygot:* gotten

57. *recks . . . thigh:* cares not for blades bound to the thigh (of those who might attack and rob him)

58. *of . . . keeps:* holds the bloody mixture

59. *ytied:* tied, wedded

60. *No . . . set:* takes no pains to set necklaces in order. "Carking" is Elizabeth's variant of *carcanet,* an ornamental necklace; the *OED* records her receiving as a New Year's gift in 1572 "one riche carkenet . . . of golde."

61. *reddy:* reddish

62. *pluck:* tug, pull

63. *of . . . makes:* from eastern waves burdens her. Eos, goddess of the dawn and thus of the east, is probably intended here, although Elizabeth's spelling argues that she had in mind Eoa, a city in Africa.

64. *ingrained . . . purple:* dyed with purple of Sidon (see l. 67 and n. 48)

65. *No Maeon . . . sleaves:* she fills no Lydian needles with thin filaments of silk thread (Lydia was known for its rich embroidery)

66. *sunny east:* i.e., China, known for silk work

67. *ne spun:* did not spin

68. *suspect:* suspicion

69. *lamp Erins:* torch of the Erinyes (the Furies)

70. *feastful . . . rout:* wedding day attended by the bothersome crowd

71. *wry:* twisted

72. *balks:* ridges of land between plowed furrows

73. *Phaeton boy:* the boy Phaeton, whose father was Phoebus, the sun god

74. *eke his wain:* also his chariot

75. *wonted . . . ways:* accustomed path and well-worn ways

76. *by slide . . . uncouthed:* unprofitable pastime while the unknown or unfamiliar

77. *shears:* cleaves

78. *ne touch:* touches not

79. *his fellow plain:* manifestly his companion (in the sense of also suffering ruin: the world was scorched when Phaeton lost control of the chariot and was killed)

80. *pass:* surpass

81. *trier's right:* what belongs rightly to one who tests something

82. *swifty . . . hies:* swift course he goes

83. Daedalus and his son, Icarus, escaped from Crete using artifical wings fashioned with wax and feathers. When Icarus flew too near the sun, the heat melted the wax and he fell into the sea, which took the name Icarian from his disaster.

84. *Evil bought:* evil balanced out

85. *highly flee:* fly the heights

86. *shield:* forbid

87. *mighty . . . call:* the crowd call me mighty

88. *lee . . . silly:* sheltered shore my humble

89. *to . . . bequeath:* consign my boat to deep waters

90. *fortune:* misfortune

91. *takes it:* takes as its

Commentary

Seneca (d. 65 C.E.) is confidently credited with eight dramas in Latin verse and two doubtful plays, *Octavia* and *Hercules Oetaeus*.

Elizabeth translated lines 600–699 from the second choric speech of the latter work. Nor was this her only rendering from the popular Roman author. In 1567 she gave a copy of a prose translation from Seneca to John Harington, gentleman of her Privy Chamber.[1] More than a decade later, Sir Thomas Heneage, writing to Sir Christopher Hatton, quoted from another of the Queen's renderings of Seneca.[2] The second chorus addresses Hercules' wife, Deianira, who plans to assassinate her husband because he has fallen in love with another woman. Elizabeth may have been attracted to this passage because of its philosophical musings about the dangers of kingship relative to the secure lives led by ordinary people. She expresses a similar discontent with her onerous duties as sovereign in Poems 5a and 5b.

1. Sir John Harington, *Nugae Antiquae,* ed. Henry Harington (London, 1779), 2:304–10.

2. "[S]o as that shall be verified of her that Seneca wrote wisely, and her Majesty translated more sweetly,—of adversity and virtue, *illustrat dum vexat,* it graces whom it grates"; Heneage to Hatton, August 12, 1579. From Sir Harris Nicolas, *Memoirs of the Life and Times of Sir Christopher Hatton* (London, 1847), p. 127.

Textual Notes

The unique text of this poem is written in a neat, late secretary hand. At l. 93 I have replaced its reading "mixt" with "mix" and reduced "wounted wounted" in l. 105 to "wonted."

Poetry 2. Plutarch, **De curiositate,** *November 1598*

Scribal copy from L: Royal MS 17 A.44, ff. 1–12v.

Perchance it might be best to shun at all that home
    Where throughout the wind passage none can get,[1]
Or[2] dimmed, dark, or subject to the cold and winds,
    Or else to sickness thrall that breedeth health's decay.
But if so one delight by custom in such place   [5
    The lights may changed be, or stairs alter case,[3]
Or doors, some for passage, some other shutted be,
    Which fairer much may frame it clear[4] with better health;
And some have served their city's turn by alterings such.
    A sample may my country make, as said it is,   [10
That bending to Zephyrus' wind,[5] and fro Parnassus[6]
        taking sun,
    That to the west his course did turn by Chaeron's help,[7]
It wryed[8] was to east, the sun's arising place;
    Empedocles[9] eke,[10] the knower well of nature's course,
Is said to stop the gaping deep of hill amid the rock,   [15
    Which grievous was and sickens full the place,
For that the northen[11] wind did beat on neighbors' fields,
    And thus the plague outcast from region's ground.
Therefore if plaguey wills there be that noyful[12] are unsound,
    A rising tempest great and dimly darks[13] the mind,   [20
Best shall it be give them repulse[14] and down fall flat to
        ground,
    So to ourselves we breed an air clear, a light and breath
        pure,

And if this may not be, yet let us labor at least thus,
    That by all means that possible make we may,[15]
Turning from us and changing all breedeth us offence,[16]   [25
    We make them serve our turn and help us the best.
A sample let us make of curious, needless care,
    Whose study is nought else but others' harms to know,
    Disease that neither wants envy nor pure from[17] *wickedness.*
Why then, O Man, with envy full on others' ills   [30
    Sharpest sight dost set, and in thine own blind?
Inward draw thy science study,[18] *and so it apply*
    That thy busy care be turned from outward to thine own.
And if thou fancy have to enter story's evils,[19]
    Thou hast enough at home that idle thou ne be:[20]   [35
    "As great a stream as waters' flood doth bring to bay,
    Or circled oak by falling leaves from tree,"
So great a store of faults in thy life shalt find.
    A heap, eke, of ill desires fraught[21] *in thy mind,*
No less neglect[22] *of that thou should by office*[23] *yield.*   [40
    For as the writ of Xenophon[24] *tells the order how*
      good, frugal men
Do part aside such laid up stuff as sacrifice needs,[25]
    And do divide from banquet's cost in sort that some
Do serve the plowshare's turn, in other place the war;
    Even so do thou divide thy evil's part that envy breeds: [45
A part let jealousy have, some for coward's fruit do leave,
    For sparing[26] *some reserve, all these do count*[27] *and know.*
Such windows as to neighbor's house gives the view,
    And curious footsteps make a way too patent,[28]
But other ways open thou must truly fit and sound   [50
    Such as to servants' rooms within thy house they bring,
Sometime into thy women's closets and where thy slaves abide.
    These be such things as asking[29] *study and busy care do*
      need,

Where neither profitless deeds nor wicked work hath room,
    But full of wealth, and wholesome counsel gives thee,   [55
When each man tells himself this tale and this accompt:[30]
    Whence slide I? What done have I that undone should be?
But now as fables tell, Lamia[31] *at home doth blinded sing,*
    Her eyes she shuts in vessels' store[32] *til forth she go;*
Then in her head they[33] *go, and open sends her looks.*   [60
    So each man abroad in other matters[34] *with hate*
    Into his thought, a curious care[35] *in his head, as eye he puts*
From faults our own and wicked acts by ignorance we slip
    On these, nor[36] *rolling eyes nor light from them receive.*
The curious more profit yields his foe than good himself,   [65
    That telleth their lacks and where they do amiss,
That better they may ware the warned to correct,[37]
    Neglects at home the deeds that need were to regard,
So stunned[38] *is his care, for that most other touch.*[39]
    Ulysses eke no word would give to mother his   [70
Til Prophet asked he had cause why to hell he went.[40]
    And after he to dame turned and women asked
What wench Tyro[41] *was, where fair Chloris bid,*[42]
    And what bred cause for reaving[43] *Epicastes' life,*
    "When woeful knot of cord she knits to highest beam."[44] [75
But we, secure and knowing nought that most us touch,[45]
    Inquires of other lives, as why our neighbor's sire
A Syrian was, and grandame why a Thracian born,
    And such man owes talents three, nor usury[46] *hath paid.*
Yea, sometime such things discourse: whence came
      home such wife,   [80
    Why he and he have in a corner talked together.
But Socrates roamed up and down with doubt full great
    What words, what speech Pythagoras used to breed belief;[47]
And Aristippus, in Olympias meeting Isomachus,[48] *asked*
    Why Socrates in disputes so win could young men   [85

Who, when he picked had, seeds and samples of his words
   So moved was that scant he steady could his pace,
And grew throughout both pale and lean until,
   Thirsty and inflamed, to Athens he hoised[49] *sail,*
And both the man and words philosophy eke[50] *he learned*   [90
   Which did contain in sum, to all conclude in short,
That all men should an audit make of all their ill
   And so them better know to make them shun the more.
Another sort there is that brook cannot a look
   On life their own, but deems it as an irksome shew.   [95
No Reason's luster bear they can, reflections hers they shun,
   But mind filled all with each man's evil, all shaking, dreads
What dwells within. Abroad it goes[51] *and gazeth round about,*
   And other sins do view, both nurse and cram their vice.
For as the hen oft in the house when food is brought   [100
   Runs to a corner straight and ground scrapes with claw,
   "*That somewhere in the dung one grain at least may find,*"
So fareth it with curious, sick man's vice, who passeth
   Institutes,[52] *lessons, and scanned matter in rhetoric guise,*[53]
And other cause[54] *such as no man grieves is asked.*[55]   [105
   In heaps they throw the house's secret evil and hid;[56]
Right well applied is the Egyptian saw[57] *to him that asked,*
   What hid was that he had? "*That*[58] *made it hid,*" *quoth he.*
Nor it the fashion was to enter other's house without he
     knock afore,
   Though now the porters add,[59] *where hammers, rings,*[60]
     do hang   [110
Untouched without, served the ear from him that enter would,
   Lest stranger might the housewife in her house surprise
Beating of her maid or chastening of her man;
   Or churls might hear that maidens gave for scourge.[61]
The prying man to all this will slyly make him one,   [115
   Such one as heeds not to behold a chaste, well-ruled house,

No, though a man in treating[62] sort would call him to that sight;
   But such as key requires, a clog, or sparred door,
Uncover list,[63] and to the vulgar sort abroad it must.[64]
     Of all the winds they grieve us most and trouble breed,   [120
Ariston[65] tells, whose turn back straws us annoy.[66]
     But curious man no neighbor's chaff[67] nor clothes esteems,
     But walls he breaks and opens doors, even to the silly[68] maid,
In sort such as wind that pierceth in and enters room
     Where Bacchus' feasts, rounds,[69] and dance he may
        behold,   [125
Even such as in the night to Diana's temple vowed were,[70]
     With heedy[71] eye espies what faults he may find there.
Besides, as Cleon says, whom comedy old reproved,
     "His mind in Clopis was, his hands in Etol bid";[72]
So mind of curious man at once in rich man's house abode
     makes,   [130
     And in self time[73] the cottage poor and court of kings,
And at a wedding lately made, to pry[74] the works of men,
     Both of the guests that bidded[75] be and of the chiefest all,
And so as not of peril void[76] he venture makes thereof,
     But like to him that henbane taste[77] with curious fault,   [135
That greedy is to know afore he feed, is reaved[78] of life.
     So whoso search the mightier's ill first die or understand.[79]
For who disdains to look on sunbeams large and wide,
     And needs will stare on body's sun itself, too bold to view
The light from him to turn,[80] are blinded stark for hire.[81]   [140
     Rightly said Philippides, poet to Lysimachus[82] King, asking,
"What of mine shall I impart as of my gift to thee?"
     "Whatso[83] thou wilt," quoth he, "so secret none thou give."
For whatso kingdom hath of pleasure and of joy
     Outward set forth be—banquets, riches, solemn shews;   [145
But if hid ought there be, nor it assist, ne[84] once it touch;
     Nor[85] covered be a kingly joy when prosperous hap arrives,

Nor scorn make at his sports, nor whom he kingly graced, deride.
What hidden is, fearful, woeful, sour, and unknown,
    The treasure of an overflowing, wasting ire,   [150
Or rather habit deep in mind to roll[86] *revenge,*
    Or jealousy of wife, or son's suspect,[87] *or doubt of friend—*
Fly thou this dark and thicky,[88] *misty, folded cloud;*
    A flash and thunder shall burst out when hidden[89] *shews.*
What way therefore for flight or shunning of the same   [155
    If straight[90] *thou do as said is yore*[91] *to spare thy busy care?*
But best of all if mind thou turn to helps and delights.
O busy Man, search what heaven, earth, air, and sea affords.
    Which doth delight thee most, the small or great to know?
If great, then care whence sun arise and where she coucheth.   [160
    Ask why the moon at times, as[92] *man, so changeth she;*
Whence she so great light took, and whence she, lost,
      repairs:[93]
    "When left she hath us seemed, how may it be
    That straight her new face fair to us appears,
    Slyly to the circle's full increasing makes   [165
    Again, when beauty hers hath shone unto the top,
    Then waning, elder grows, till none she be?" [94]
For these things be nature's secret, inward works,
    Nor doth disdain such science to the learned folks.
But great things thou despise and dost not reck[95] *for them.*   [170
    Be curious then for things of less regard and worth.
Ask thou then of things which earth brings forth,
    Why some do flourish still[96] *and green remain;*
In every season green they be as she that boasts[97] *herself;*
    Some other sort, in somewhat like to these they shew.   [175
Some other kind be bared left and lee,[98] *like husbandman*
    That thrift neglects at once, that all his goods hath spent.
Then why do divers grounds[99] *breed fruit of sundry sorts,*
    Both long, cornered, half-round, and rounded all?

Perchance of this thou carest not much, for ill none is,   [180
   If needs thou seekest in evils a curious care,
Even serpent-like, that fed and nursed in poisoned wood.[100]
   Let us such curious man bring to stories[101] read,
And gather there such stuff as doth include and tell
   A plenty great of all mishaps, abundance of all evil,   [185
For there do lie the ruin of men, the waste of goods,
   The wives' dishonor, the servants' baits,[102] the friends'
      slander,
The venom prepared, envies, jealousies, wrack[103] of friends,
   The treasons huge of kings from kingdoms thrown;
Fill thou with these thy curious, nice[104] desires,   [190
   Pleasure take in these that breed no woe
Nor dolor to such folk as thou dost dwell withal.[105]
   But as it seems the curious man cares not for passed evils,
Not such as wonted were, but sly and unfound harm
   That willingly may tragedies new behold.   [195
He recks not to fellow[106] comic cause nor merry matter.
   Then if he meet with one that talk of marriage makes,
Or sacrifice tells, or bride's return, heedless and lazy
   The curious man it hears, and tells how oft that he
      heard,
And wills the teller brief in short[107] or pass it over.   [200
   But if a sitter by do tell a tale of a dishonested[108] maid,
Or wife that wedlock brake,[109] or cartel[110] sent, or brother's
      debate,[111]
   Here he sleepeth not, nor senses makes for leisure,[112]
But seeks for more men's tongues, and listen makes his ears.
   How rightly said is this, that easilier[113] ill than good to
      mortal men arrives,   [205
And rightly said is this of curious-natured men.
   For as the boxing glass[114] the worst from flesh doth draw,
So ears of nicey[115] folks the worst speech draweth out;

And better for to say, as cities have some gates
    Unlucky, void of noise, of multitude the great,[116]   *[210*
By which condemned men to die are oft conveyed,
    And through which they throw that[117] filthy is and foul,
And nought by them there goes that pure or holy is,
    So by the ears of curious man nought good or fair doth pass;
But slaughter talk[118] into their ears have passage sure   *[215*
    And there abides, which wicked tales them brings,
    "Ever-chanting tears within my house do dwell."
This is the Muse of curious men, and siren alone,[119]
    Nor ought than this may joy him best or please at all,
For curiosity hath greedy will to hear that[120] secret is and hid, *[220*
    Nor opens eye to ought if good they have at all,
And somewhile they do feign such good as there is none.[121]
    And so the nicey man, greedy to know the evil,
Is subject to disease that joys at others' harms—
    The brother true of spite and envious folks,   *[225*
For envy sorrow is for good that others joys,[122]
    A gladness of evil, the joy conceived of wicked acts,
And both proceed of malice, vice beastlike and mad,[123]
    But irksome so to man, the opening of[124] his evils,
That many chose to die than hid disease the doctor know.[125] *[230*
    What if Herophilus, Erasistratus, Aesculapius,[126] though
      men
Carrying the cure's helps, if standing without door[127]
    Were asked if fistula[128] in thigh such man hath had,
Or a wife a canker[129] hath in secret place,
    Albeit this healthful care be needful of such art,[130]   *[235*
Yet no man, I believe, but cast off would such one as it would
      ask
    Whom for no need uncalled would seek out others' harm.[131]
The busy[132] man seeks out all these and many worse
    And with no mind[133] to cure but clatter[134] out the same,

Wherefore no nickname[135] they shall give that name them
    envious men.   [240
  For searchers[136] we disdain and hardly brook[137] we can,
Not when they find that[138] open is to view of all
  But such as hidden be in vessels and in packs;
And yet the law it bids,[139] and for neglect should smart.
  In other sort the nice[140] men lose theirs, for others' search,   [245
Nor dwell they chose[141] in country for quiet fields no care.
  But if in longed time[142] they to the country go,
They rather view their neighbors' fields and pass their own,
  And asks what oxen he hath lost in number all,
And how much soured wine he cast away with loss.   [250
  And furnished thus, he quickly to city returns.
But plowman true receive slowly will such news
  As of free will is from the city spread abroad,
And says, then will fall out my digger[143] tells me tales
  On what bargains strifes[144] have ended all their plea.   [255
For now, curious of such cause, this wicked wretch doth walk,[145]
  But busy man the clown's[146] life hates, so empty, cold,
That nurse no tragic part, woeful nor wicked cause;
  But go they will to judge's seat, to markets and to ports,
Using speech such: "Have you no news? Today were ye in
    fair?   [260
  What, do you believe cities revolt in hours three?"
And if such tale he hath, from his horse he lights,
  Taking hands, embrace the man listening, sits him by.
If meet he do a man that nought tells: "What saist thou,
  Wert thou in pleading place,[147] didst thou not pass the
    hall,   [265
Nor hast thou fallen in posts[148] that lately from Italy came?"
  Praised be therefore the Locrians'[149] law, who[150] forbids
A question once at his return be asked of any news,
  And punished was in penal sort for such a fact.[151]

For as to cooks welcome is the store great of sheep,   [270
   To fisher eke the spawn full thick of fish kind,
So curious men wish plenty of evil and business much,
   New, strange events which ever they hunt and kill.
Yea, well do Thurian[152] laws forbid a citizen's check[153]
   In comedy used, but for adulter[154] or curious men,   [275
For that desire of others' delight,[155] inquiry makes
   Of matter such as, hid, is hardly to be known.
Curiosity a palsey is, consumption eke, what covert is, disclose,
   Which makes the chatting vice fellow care of[156] knowing
     much,
And so shun cannot, but slander accompanies busy care,   [280
   Which made Pythagoras teach five years' silence to young
     men,
Which called echemythia[157] was that silence doth express.
   Yea, no choice but wicked tongue curiosity fears,
For what they gladly hear they willingly, quickly tell,
   And what from some they get, to others tell delight,   [285
Wherefore disease {blank}[158] besides more evils brings to
     boot,
   That let[159] it doth to have that[160] most they seek to get.
For all men heeds them well and hides them from all such,
   Nor will do ought or say in curious sight or ear,[161]
But counsel defers, and business care[162] for other time
     appoints,   [290
   Until such man away him get from company theirs.
And if perchance a busy man come in where secret talk
   Or earnest ought be done, no otherwise than as cat
In running hides his meat, so snatches fro[163] hand that
     ready was,
   So that oft that other[164] hear or see may to such   [295
Nor view nor ear may serve their turns.
   In fine, a curious man lacks confidence or trust,

For to slaves' and strangers' charge our letters rather we commit,
  Or epistles, or our seals, than to curious, known friends.
But Bellerophon[165] not letters born against himself did open,   [300
  But hand refrained from kingly writ with temper such
As he would do with continence from his wife.[166]
  To be a curious man lacks temper[167] no whit less
Than if adulterer's part he played, as fault no less.
  To this distemper[168] this is worst that foolish madness
    hath,   [305
For in neglect of most and common women's haunt,[169]
  To the shut and glorious one, perhaps to the deformed
Be carried to, what madness more or brainfall[170] is?
  So fareth it with curious folk who (passing by the fairest
    shows,
Letters, studies, disputes) letters he breaketh up.[171]   [310
  With ears close to neighbor's wall, and whisperers add,[172]
Where servants and women bide,[173] yet not void of danger,
  But sure ever of slander's mark and infamy,
Yea, needful for such curious ones to shake off their disease.
  Remember what their gains have been, or what their loss,   [315
For as Simonides[174] said when opened he had his desks
  Filled with rewards he found, but empty that of thanks;
So if man search and open the curious bags,
  Full of unneedful, vain, and stuffed with irksome thing,
Perchance the first will him offend when by all means   [320
  He shall make plain how void of delight and scornful all
    they be.
Now go, if any entering into ancient books and takes out
  The worst from them and book he have so invented,
As out of Homer's verse that heedless, named be
  Or[175] out of tragical solecisms, or out of such verse   [325
As Archilochus[176] against women lewdly and full saucy
    made,

In manner such himself betraying and deceiving.
Worthy do you not think him of tragical curse and bann?[177]
    "Evil may thee betide, the searcher of human woes."[178]
Yea, it shall not need tragical curse, for of itself   [330
    Unseemly and fruitless slaying,[179] *the storing of other's sin.*
Such city as that was which Philip, of wickeds,[180] wretched
    men
    First built, named therefore Poneropolis,[181] as filled full
    of ill.
Curious men therefore, while roundabout they gather and
    peep,
    Not fault of[182] *verse or poesy but crimes of other's life,*   [335
Their faults and incongruity, and about them carry
    A most unpleasing, ungraceful table of[183] *other's evils*
Which their own memory fittest instrument makes.
    For as at Rome some pictures and statues, yea, indeed
Forms sold of boys, of women they despise, about they go,   [340
    And bide in marketplace where monsters sold be,
Viewing and asking for footless men that arms have like cat,
    Or three-head men[184] or such whose neck is like to camel form,[185]
Or if there any be of kind[186] that "mixture hath of like,
    Or evil-shaped untimely birth."[187] But if daily they be
    brought   [345
To such a sight, short will their liking be, and soon will it
    abhor;
    So such as curious be of others' lives and lineage birth,
About they rabble,[188] and sins that have befallen in other's
    house,
    Such as afore they pried on,[189] comes to their mind.
Remember they do how, of the heed of others' evils   [350
    They gathered have no profit nor credit any;
It much may therefore avail such malady to drive[190]
    If first from deed may hap aloof with use ourself inure,[191]

And so may learn in this motion to temper [192] give ourself.
  For disease increase [193] hath grown by custom's use   [355
Which else would turn to worse if it had further gone.
   But how it may be done of custom [194] let us speak:
   Beginning first be made [195] of easy things and soonest done,
And such as common haps made vulgar people use. [196]
  For what mad [197] matter passing by monuments old,   [360
To disdain to read, neglect verse or writ that graven be. [198]
  Or what thing were it to pass by such scrapings
As walls in writings receive and not to read?
  In silence warning us that nothing there is written
That profit or delight may breed us, or to us give,   [365
  But doth remember a writing good he best friend
     of ours
And other like to this, full vain and filled with toys
  Which in themselves seems not to hurt in reading,
But slyly they annoy, for breeding care to know unneedful
     things.
  And as the hunters rate their hounds that useth
     change, [199]   [370
And with their lyams [200] them pluck back and withdraw,
  And keeps their scent both pure and whole in right chase
That eagerlier they firm [201] their pace, and follow firm,
  "And winding with their scent the steps of their game;" [202]
So ought it fare with curious man that runs to every gaze, [203]   [375
  In striving for to see or lift [204] his ear all to hear,
Back keep him and withdraw himself, preserve for profit more.
  For as the lions walk with covert [205] claws, and eagles
     eke their talants, [206]
Lest sharpness theirs and fierceness too much they dull,
  So, minding how all curious care have sharpest sight,   [380
And narrowly looks on knowledge of sundry sorts,
  Let us not it consume nor blunt in worser thing.

In second place let us inure[207] *if by another's house we go,*
   Nor[208] *to look in nor roll our eyes to that which is within*
In using curious search, instead of other hands,[209]   [385
   But ready have Xenocrates' saw,[210] *that did deny*
That difference any were whether feet or eyes the house did enter.
   For neither just, honest, nor pleasing were such a shew,

"For guest, it is a shame an inner evil to view."
For these be seen in house most, pots that lies on ground,   [390
   Or maidens sitting still but nothing ought worth or
      grave;[211]
Yet a shame it is with glance on such to bend our eyes,
   And hither turn our wits, sharpness, and plying[212] *mind.*
For to such things a custom make[213] *is wicked ill.*
   Diogenes once when see he did Dioxippen in Olympia
      race,[214]   [395
In chariot carried, not able withdraw his eye from woman fair
   But back wrying[215] *and turning neck in casting on her look:*
"Behold," quoth he, "a wrastler stout with wry neck by maid
      is won."
   The busy men you may behold, their head they turn about
When custom and care hath made them ready to view
      each thing;   [400
   But I suppose that no man ought his sense[216] *abroad to range*
Like maiden that no bringing up such as were meet hath had.
But when from mind's care sense is sent to business work,[217]
   Attend such things and quickly tend thy message answer,
And then again in thyself with reason make abode,[218]   [405
   And there abide, not straying out of office charge.[219]
But now haps that which Sophocles wont is tell,[220]

"And so as freed horse the bit that careless hand of holder
      did neglect,"[221]

So sense[222] as we have told, void of a guide or use,
    Forth they go and often draw the mind to that ought
        not be,   [410
At length hurls him down to break his neck,
    Which makes that falsely said and bragged is of Democritus,[223]
That of purpose he plucked out his eyes, holding them to fired
        glass,[224]
    And from the same reflection took, lest that he should
His mind keep shut and oft call back to outward cause,   [415
    Not suffering that they should him let,[225] left them at home
That he might bide in understandings good, as shutting
    From windows that[226] to highways[227] bend their light.
But most true it is that rarely they do feel what do they should,
    That vexeth oft their mind with busy, careful thought.   [420
Yea, Muses deep they far from town did place,
    And night as firmest friend to knowledge great
They titled with Euphronen[228] name, supposing that such use
    And ease whom no other care did let or hinder
Should have great help to things that seek they did;   [425
    Yea, and that is not hard nor cumber[229] hath therein.
As oft as men ban thee or cursing words afford,
    No ear to give thereto, but as a deaf man hear them,
Or when great press[230] is in the place, to sit thee still
    And if thou canst not rule thee so, arise and go thy way.   [430
For if thou follow curious folk, no good thereof thou gets,
    But profit great shall thee befall if curious part thou shun,
With violence great thou use, and use it may reason's lore.[231]
    And profit taking from this groundwork, and earnester[232]
        custom,
Right well shalt do if theater thou do pass where pleasant
        ought is played;   [435
    And if thy friends do thee entreat to comedy or game,
        deny.

Or if common shouts about the ring, witsafe not look.[233]
    For as Socrates did well warn us to take heed and beware
Of such meat as did provoke the unhungry to eat,
    Alike he said of draughts such, without thirst to take.   [440
So must we shun such shows and tales as entice and allure
    When need of them we have not at all, but remedy.
Yea, Cyrus would not Panthea behold nor view,[234]
    And when Araspas told him how she worthy was be seen,
"That is the cause," quoth he, "Why more I would refrain[235]
    her,   [445
    "Yea, if I should thy counsel follow and go to her,
"Perhaps she would persuade me again return again
    "Even when my leisure ought not be to sit by her and look,
"In leaving of more serious, heedful matter."
    In manner such nor[236] Alexander would Darius' wife[237]
    behold   [450
When fame she had of beauty great and praised much for it,
    But meeting mother hers, a woman old, the maiden fair
    denied.
We while[238] full slyly look in chamber of the wife
    Though pentish-like[239] the window built, we think no harm,
Though curious care our own we suffer slip to corners all.   [455
    It profits also sometime that justice may be done to pass over
    such deed,
That thou mayst more accustom thee to fly from that[240] is wrong,
    And that thou mayst the better inure in continent sort,[241]
Sometime forbear the lawful company of thine own wife,
    Lest another time thou be enticed to other men's,   [460
Breeding this custom in curiosity, prove sometime that,[242]
    Nor suffer once thy ear to give thereto a heed.
And if a man would tell thee ought done at thy home, defer him,[243]
    And from thy ears far set what words of thee be said.
Oedipus' busy search did wrap him in most harms,   [465

For when of himself he asked as he no Corinth[244] were
But guest, he met with Laius, who, after killed he had,
 And mother his own in marriage took with whom he
  kingdom got
With dowry hers when, then happy he thought he was,
 Again he questioned more of himself, which when his
  wife would let,[245]   [470
More earnest he the old man, as guilty he were, rebuked,
 Omitting no good means to make bewrayed that[246] was hid.
Then when suspect hereof[247] his mind had much distract,[248]
 And old man had screeched[249] out, "Woe worth me,[250]
  whom need to speak constrains,"
Yet kindled and vexed, curiosity's sting made answer: [475
 "Compelled to hear, yet hear I must."[251]
So sweet a sour it is nor may be withstood, curiosity's motion,
 As wound that bloodies itself while it is lanced.
But who is freed from this disease and is of mildy[252] spirit,
 Nor guilty is of any evil shall thus begin to say: [480
 "O goddess, how wise art thou that dost forget the ill."[253]
Wherefore against all this a custom must be made
 That straight a letter brought may not be broken up[254]
As many do, which when they think their hands too slow they
  add teeth thereto.
 Whencever[255] post do come, meet him not, nor let us
  change seat.   [485
If so it hap a friend arrive and say that somewhat he will
  tell him,
 Yea, rather,[256] if ought thou brings of profit and of help.
When once in Rome dispute I made, a clown[257] that Domitian
  after[258] killed,
 Who envied much the prince's glory, assisting to[259] my lecture,
And in the while a soldier coming, Caesar's pistle[260] gave
  him,   [490

A silence made whom none would let to read the sent,[261]
Refused[262] it, nor would it open til ended was my reading,
   And that I had dismissed my hearers and scholars,
Wherein each man did admire the gravity of this man.
   But when by all means and ways he nourish shall   *[495*
Curiosity's malady, and so shall make it strong and violent,
   Then easy it is not it refrain and rule,[263]
For that[264] by use it thrown[265] is soon to things unlawful,
   Yea, the letters tear up and friends' secrets discover,[266]
And sacred things behold whom no man's view ought see,   *[500*
   And steps sets in place unfit, and kingly words and deeds do
      search,
And tyrants too, who ought all know, are made most odious
   By those men who "ears theirs" and "flatterers" be called.[267]
Therefore, younger Darius the first,[268] ὠτακομςάσ called,[269]
   Himself mistrusting, doubting others mo,[270] and fearing.   *[505*
But Dionysians[271] foisted among the Syracusians such
      fleering[272] folk
   Whom in changedst[273] state when Syracusians found,
      destroyed;[274]
For flatterers are of kind and stock of curious line,[275]
   And southars[276] to inquire what evil another or[277] meant,
      or did.
Yea, busy men even wretched haps[278] of neighbors theirs
      do search,   *[510*
   Even such as falls unto their share, though far unlooked
      for were,
And to the vulgar folk it tell abroad, such news they have.
   And said it is that winged[279] folks bear such name of
      curious vice,
For as like it was that famine had Athens plagued, nor owners
      would their corn utter,[280]
   But in night and secret sort grind they did their store.   *[515*

These[281] *walking about, did note and mark their mill's noise,*
   To which their names were given aliterii,[282] proper for such.
Of like cause they say were sycophants called and so surnamed,
   For when by law it was forbid that no man should figs
      transport,
Such as them found and brought to light bare sycophant's
      name.[283]   [520
   Yea, that were not unfit for curious folk to shun them
      the more
If they know them[284] guilty of such and like endeavor as they
      hold,[285]
   Which hated most and grievous are to all they haunt.[286]

Notes

   1. *wind . . . get:* wind can get no passage

   2. *Or:* whether

   3. *stairs alter case:* alter the staircase

   4. *frame it clear:* shape it (i.e., the home) clearly

   5. *Zephyrus' wind:* the west wind

   6. *Parnassus:* mountain in southern Greece associated with
poetry

   7. *Chaeron's help:* Chaero was the mythical founder of
Chaeronea, Plutarch's birthplace in Boetia; he was said to have
rotated the entire city from west to east.

   8. *wryed:* moved, turned

   9. *Empedocles:* Sicilian statesman, philosopher, scientist,
and poet of the fifth century B.C.E. He allegedly blocked a
chink between two rocks to stop the unwholesome draft that
came from it.

   10. *eke:* also

   11. *northen:* northern

12. *plaguey wills . . . noyful:* pestilent passions . . . noxious

13. *darks:* darkens

14. *give . . . repulse:* to rebuff them

15. *possible . . . may:* we may possibly make

16. *all . . . offence:* all that breeds offense to us

17. *wants . . . pure from:* lacks envy nor is free of

18. *science study:* study of knowlege

19. *story's evils:* the history of evil

20. *ne be:* be not

21. *fraught:* stored

22. *neglect:* neglected

23. *office:* duty

24. *writ of Xenophon:* an allusion to book 8 of the *Oeconomicus,* Xenophon's fourth-century B.C.E. dialogue on estate management

25. *as sacrifice needs:* needful for making sacrifices

26. *For sparing:* as savings

27. *count:* take account of (all these aspects of your vices)

28. *patent:* open

29. *asking:* ask, call for

30. *accompt:* account

31. *Lamia:* a legendary monster in woman's form who preys on human beings

32. *vessels' store:* a storeplace for utensils

33. *they:* i.e., her eyes, which Lamia uses only when she goes out

34. *other matters:* the affairs of others

35. *care:* corrected, possibly in Elizabeth's handwriting, from "thought"

36. *nor:* neither

37. *they . . . correct:* they may take heed to correct the warned

38. *stunned:* dazed, astounded

39. *for . . . touch:* for that which mostly concerns others

40. In the *Odyssey,* Circe warned Odysseus (Ulysses) not to speak with other ghosts in Hades until he had spoken with the blind prophet Tiresias.

41. *Tyro:* a nymph seduced by Neptune

42. *bid:* resided. Chloris was Amphion's daughter and mother of Nestor, Ulysses' comrade in arms.

43. *reaving:* depriving. Epicaste, or Jocasta, hanged herself upon learning that she had married her son, Oedipus.

44. Quoted from the *Odyssey* 11.278.

45. *most us touch:* most concerns us

46. *usury:* interest

47. *breed belief:* persuade others to share his opinion. Pythagoras was a Greek philosopher of the sixth century B.C.E.

48. *Aristippus . . . Isomachus:* Aristippus was a friend of Socrates, but in Xenophon's *Oeconomicus,* it is Socrates himself who talks with Isomachus. Olympias is Olympia, the sacred ground on the banks of the River Alpheus where the Olympic games were held.

49. *hoised:* hoisted

50. *words philosophy eke:* words and philosophy also

51. *it goes:* they go (i.e., those who cannot stand to examine their own lives)

52. *passeth Institutes:* passes over established customs

53. *scanned . . . guise:* subjects studied in a rhetorical manner

54. *cause:* subjects, matters

55. *is asked:* (when he) is asked

56. *hid:* hidden

57. *saw:* saying

58. *That:* that which

59. *add:* have been added

60. *hammers, rings:* implements serving as knockers, doorbells

61. *that . . . scourge:* what maidens said as punishment

62. *treating:* beseeching

63. *clog . . . list:* i.e., desire to open an encumbrance, or barred door

64. *abroad it must:* it must be disclosed

65. *Ariston:* a Peripatetic philosopher of the third century B.C.E.

66. *whose . . . annoy:* Plutarch's original means "that blows open our clothing."

67. *chaff:* refuse. Perhaps Elizabeth paired this word with her mistranslated "straws" in line 121. Alternatively, the manuscript's "chaf" could be a misreading of "cloak."

68. *silly:* innocent

69. *rounds:* celebrants standing or dancing in circles (Bacchus was the god of wine)

70. *to Diana's . . . were:* sworn to the service of Diana, goddess of chastity

71. *heedy:* attentive

72. *bid:* abided. The line is quoted from Aristophanes' *The Knights* (l. 79), where the slave Demosthenes satirizes Cleon, a leader of fifth-century Athens.

73. *in self time:* at the same time

74. *pry:* examine closely

75. *bidded:* invited

76. *not . . . void:* not without peril

77. *taste:* tastes. Henbane is poisonous.

78. *reaved:* deprived

79. *whoso . . . understand:* whoever pries into faults of great persons dies before they understand

80. *to view . . . turn:* to turn himself from viewing the light

81. *for hire:* i.e., as their reward

82. *Philippides . . . Lysimachus:* Philippides of Athens, a writer of comedies in the fourth century B.C.E., was supported by Lysimachus, king of Thrace.

83. *Whatso:* whatsoever

84. *nor . . . ne:* neither . . . nor

85. *Nor:* neither

86. *roll:* consider

87. *son's suspect:* suspicion of his son

88. *thicky:* thick

89. *hidden:* that which is hidden

90. *straight:* straightway, or immediately

91. *yore:* long ago

92. *as:* as does

93. *repairs:* restores (her light)

94. Excerpt from a lost play by Sophocles.

95. *reck:* care

96. *still:* always, continuously

97. *she that boasts:* i.e., the earth (?) that boasts of

98. *left and lee:* to the left and sheltered side

99. *divers grounds:* various kinds of soil

100. *wood:* woodlands

101. *stories:* histories

102. *baits:* enticements

103. *wrack:* destruction

104. *nice:* petty

105. *withal:* with

106. *recks not to fellow:* cares not to be associated with

107. *brief in short:* abbreviate

108. *dishonested:* dishonored

109. *brake:* broke

110. *cartel:* slanderous libel

111. *debate:* quarreling, fight

112. *senses . . . leisure:* directs his senses toward inactivity

113. *easilier:* more easily

114. *boxing glass:* cupping glass (a surgical instrument used to draw blood from flesh)

115. *nicey:* wanton

116. *multitude the great:* the great multitude

117. *that:* that which

118. *slaughter talk:* talk of murders

119. *siren alone:* the only siren. The holograph PRO MS reads "Siren his alone." In Greek mythology, sirens (often equated with mermaids) used their alluring songs to entice sailors to their deaths.

120. *that:* that which

121. *feign . . . none:* pretend things good that are not

122. *others joys:* others enjoy

123. *vice . . . mad:* a beastlike and mad vice

124. *the opening of:* disclosing, making known

125. *hid . . . know:* make the hidden disease known to the doctor

126. Herophilus and Erasistratus were physicians of the third century B.C.E.; Aesculapius was the god of medicine.

127. *without door:* outside the door

128. *fistula:* a long, narrow ulcer

129. *canker:* a spreading sore or ulcer

130. *of such art:* i.e., medical skill

131. *no man . . . harm:* i.e., anyone would reject assistance offered by someone who merely searched for human suffering out of morbid curiosity

132. *busy:* prying, meddlesome

133. *mind:* intention

134. *clatter:* babble

135. *nickname:* misnomer

136. *searchers:* officers authorized to search for contraband or taxable goods

137. *brook:* tolerate

138. *that:* that which

139. *bids:* demands

140. *other . . . nice:* another instance the petty

141. *dwell they chose:* choose they to dwell

142. *in longed time:* after a long time

143. *fall . . . digger:* happen that my ditchdigger

144. *bargains strifes:* conditions controversies

145. Pemberton (*Queen Elizabeth's Englishings,* p. 130) identifies lines 254–56 as a quotation from Aristophanes.

146. *clown's:* countryman's, rustic's

147. *pleading place:* law court (?). The phrase means "marketplace" in the original Greek.

148. *fallen in posts:* fallen in with messengers

149. *Locrians':* The Locri, Greeks who colonized southern Italy. They were famed for their severe, detailed laws codified by Zaleucus.

150. *who:* which

151. *fact:* deed

152. *Thurian:* of Thurii, a Greek city in southern Italy

153. *check:* rebuke, censure

154. *but for adulter:* except for an adulterer

155. *other's delight:* the delight adulterers seek (delight that the curious man seeks to find out about)

156. *chatting . . . care of:* vice of blabbing to be associated with concern for

157. *echemythia:* Greek ἐχεμυθία, "silence, reserve" (a quality associated with Pythagoreans)

158. The scribe has left a blank between "disease" and "besides"; the PRO MS reads "Wherfor this disease besides more Iuels brings this to bote."

159. *let:* prevent

160. *that:* that which

161. *in . . . ear:* in sight or hearing of the curious person

162. *business care:* concern for occupation or duty

163. *fro:* from

164. *that other:* that which others

165. *Bellerophon:* a Greek hero who, according to Homer's *Iliad* (6.156–70), delivered a letter that called for his own death (the king's wife had falsely accused him of trying to seduce her)

166. *continence . . . wife:* i.e., self-restraint from molesting the queen

167. *temper:* moderation, equanimity

168. *this distemper:* i.e., being a curious man or busybody

169. *most . . . haunt:* residences of common women

170. *brainfall:* brain failure (?). The PRO MS reads "or brain siknis may be."

171. *letters . . . up:* he opens letters

172. *add:* join

173. *bide:* abide, wait

174. *Simonides:* Greek poet, ca. 556–468 B.C.E. He was said to have become quite greedy in old age, but I have found no other reference to the anecdote of his reward without thanks.

175. *Or:* either

176. *Archilochus:* a Greek poet of the eighth or seventh century B.C.E. with a reputation for bitter invective

177. *bann:* ban, denunciation

178. Untraced quotation from a Greek tragedy.

179. *slaying:* Editorial emendation for Elizabeth's "slyeng"; the PRO MS reads "sleing." The Greek passage concerns taking account of other men's misdeeds.

180. *of wickeds:* of wicked persons

181. *Poneropolis:* a city in Thrace founded by Philip II of Macedon and named Philippopolis after himself. Plutarch

derives the city's nickname from the Greek πονηρία, "wickedness."

182. *of:* in

183. *table of:* writing tablet listing

184. *three-head men:* error for Plutarch's three-eyed men. The PRO MS reads "thre yead men."

185. *camel form:* a camel's in form

186. *of kind:* by nature

187. Quoted from Homer.

188. *rabble:* speak confusedly. There is a blank in the MS after this word, and "sins" is spelled "since." The PRO MS reads "Sins."

189. *pried on:* pried into

190. *drive:* drive out

191. *from . . . inure:* from such activity perhaps accustom ourselves to stand aloof

192. *temper:* emotional control

193. *disease increase:* increase of disease

194. *of custom:* habitually

195. *Beginning . . . made:* The beginning is first to be made

196. *such . . . use:* such common occurrences as caused ordinary people to use ("them" is implied)

197. *mad:* "Made" in the Royal MS, but the sense seems to require "mad," the reading of the PRO text.

198. *writ . . . be:* inscriptions that are engraved

199. *rate . . . change:* reprove their hounds that stray from the scent

200. *lyams:* leashes

201. *eagerlier they firm:* more eagerly they settle into

202. Quoted from Homer.

203. *gaze:* sight gazed or stared at

204. *lift:* hold up

205. *covert:* hidden (withdrawn)

206. *talants:* talons

207. *inure:* accustom ourselves

208. *Nor:* neither

209. *instead . . . hands:* (using our eyes) in place of our hands

210. *Xenocrates' saw:* the saying of Xenocrates, a Greek philosopher of the fourth century B.C.E.

211. *ought . . . grave:* worth anything or dignified

212. *plying:* consenting

213. *to . . . make:* to make such things habitual

214. *Olympia race:* a race in the Olympic games. Diogenes was a Greek philosopher of the fifth century B.C.E.; Dioxippen (Dioxippus) was an unidentified contemporary.

215. *wrying:* craning

216. *sense:* senses

217. *business work:* impertinent activity (lit., busyness)

218. *make abode:* dwell

219. *office charge:* dutiful responsibility

220. *Sophocles . . . tell:* Sophocles is accustomed to tell. Plutarch frequently quotes from the plays of Sophocles, a Greek tragedian of the fifth century B.C.E.

221. Quoted from Sophocles, *Electra* 724–25.

222. *sense:* the senses

223. *bragged . . . Democritus:* boastfully attributed to Democritus (a Greek philosopher of the fifth century B.C.E.)

224. *holding . . . glass:* fixing them on a fiery-bright mirror

225. *let:* prevent

226. *that:* that which

227. *highways:* public or main roads

228. *Euphronen:* Greek εὐφρόνη, "night" (a euphemism: lit., "the kindly time")

229. *cumber:* impediment

230. *great press:* a great crowd

231. *thou . . . lore:* i.e., you use (curiosity), and it may obey the lore of reason

232. *earnester:* more earnest

233. *ring . . . look:* arena, don't give a look

234. After capturing Panthea, the beautiful wife of Abradates, Cyrus, king of Persia, entrusted her care to Araspas.

235. *refrain:* keep back from

236. *nor:* neither

237. Alexander the Great defeated Darius III, king of Persia, and captured his family during the invasion of 331–330 B.C.E.

238. *We while:* while we

239. *pentish-like:* penthouse-like, i.e., hidden by a sloping roof

240. *that:* that which

241. *inure in continent sort:* accustom yourself in temperate fashion

242. *prove sometime that:* try that sometime

243. *defer him:* put him off to another time

244. *Corinth:* Corinthian. In Sophocles' play *Oedipus Rex*, Oedipus pursues the murderer of the former king, only to discover that it was he—and that he has killed his father and married his mother. The "old man" key to revealing his identity was a shepherd who had exposed the infant Oedipus.

245. *let:* prevent

246. *make bewrayed that:* expose what

247. *suspect hereof:* suspicion of it (his actual relationship to his wife)

248. *distract:* distracted

249. *screeched:* The Royal MS reads "skeekt"; the PRO MS reads "skrigd."

250. *Woe worth me:* cursed shall I be

251. Quoted from Sophocles, *Oedipus Rex* 1169–70.

252. *mildy:* mild

253. Quoted from Euripides, *Orestes* 213.

254. *straight . . . broken up:* immediately . . . opened

255. *Whencever:* from whatever place

256. *rather:* i.e., it would be better

257. *clown:* simple countryman. This is Elizabeth's translation of Plutarch's "Rusticus," a man's name. The Queen probably worked from an edition that did not capitalize Rusticus to mark it as a proper noun.

258. *after:* afterward. The emperor Domitian was assassinated in 96 C.E.

259. *assisting to:* attending to

260. *Caesar's pistle:* the emperor's letter

261. *let . . . sent:* prevent from reading the letter

262. *Refused:* Both MSS read "Refuse."

263. *it refrain and rule:* to shun and control it.

264. *For that:* because

265. *thrown:* directed

266. *discover:* reveal

267. *who . . . called:* who are called their ears and flatterers

268. King of Persia, 521–486 B.C.E.

269. ὠτακομςάσ *called:* called upon "listeners"

270. *mo:* more

271. *Dionysians:* both Dionysius I (ca. 430–367 B.C.E.) and his son, Dionysius II (reigned 366–344), tyrants of Syracuse

272. *fleering:* smiling obsequiously

273. *changedst:* most altered

274. *Whom . . . destroyed:* i.e., the Syracusans killed the disguised spies sent among them by the Dionysian tyrants

275. *of kind . . . line:* by nature and heritage of an inquisitive disposition

276. *southars:* perhaps "souters"—cobblers, used as a term of abuse. Transcribed by Pemberton in *Queen Elizabeth's Englishings* as "Senthars" in the PRO MS.

277. *or:* either

278. *haps:* happenings, occurrences

279. *winged:* error for "wicked." The PRO MS reads "wrongged."

280. *their corn utter:* put their grain up for sale

281. *These:* i.e., the curious, busybodies

282. *To which . . . aliterii:* which were named contraries or others

283. *bare . . . name:* bore the name of sycophant. The Greek word *sykophantes* literally means "one who shows a fig."

284. *them:* themselves

285. *hold:* practice

286. *haunt:* associate with

Commentary

Plutarch (fl. ca. 90–120 C.E.), philosopher and teacher, was educated in Greece. His *Lives of the Noble Grecians and Romans* is his most influential work; as translated by Thomas North in 1579, its biographies furnished both broad outlines and specific scenes for Shakespeare's Roman plays. "Of Curiosity," translated here by Elizabeth, belongs to Plutarch's *Moralia,* a collection of sixty-odd essays translated and first published in a complete English edition by Philemon Holland in 1603.[1] By "curiosity," Plutarch means not a healthy intellectual interest but a perverse snooping into the lives of other people. Elizabeth's translation from the Greek includes Plutarch's quotations from other writers, indented and set forth in Roman script in the Royal MS, and here placed in quotation marks. Many of these excerpts remain unidentifed because Plutarch frequently quotes from works no longer extant. Remarkably, the Queen has transformed Plutarch's Greek prose into a rough six-stress meter.

The existence of this text in the Royal collection argues that it was sanctioned by the Queen and thus copied from her original translation of the work, now housed among the State Papers in the PRO (SP 12/289, ff. 90–99v, the text edited by Caroline Pemberton). The PRO document is subscribed in the hand of her trusted amanuensis Thomas Windebank, "3° November. 1598 . . . Her Majestie's translation of a treatise of Curiositie written by Plutark. & putt into English miter [meter] . . . copied out by her Majestie's order to me the xiij$_{to}$ [13th] of No[vember]."[2] The Royal MS is the heretofore unidentified result of that royal command. Further evidence of Elizabeth's personal involvement with this text occurs at line 62, where the reading "curious thought" has been corrected: "thought" is crossed out and "care" has been written above the line in a different ink and in a different hand from the main text. While the sample is too small to permit positive identification of the revising hand, its letter forms are entirely compatible with the Queen's practice.

In many important respects, the Royal MS text is not simply a fair copy of the Queen's holograph manuscript. The scribal version incorporates scores of readings that differ from her original draft. Line 388 is the foremost example, an addition to the text not found in the PRO manuscript. Some of the variant readings simply correct damaged or illegible portions of the original text, but many others are purposeful corrections of the Queen's draft. It is unlikely that a court copyist would have presumed to alter his sovereign's words so radically. And there is a discernible pattern among the alterations, as illustrated by the different versions of line 252. In the PRO text it reads, "but he that is a plowman right, receve ful slowly wyl suche newes." The Royal MS version of the line is five syllables shorter: "But plowman true receive slowly will such news." Similarly, at line 132, "the works of men" replaces "the businis of eache man," and in line 276, "For that desire of others' delight" replaces "for adultry desiar of other pleasur." As these examples indicate, many of the revisions seem expressly designed to shorten the lines and make them fit more nearly into a six-stress rhythm. The Queen apparently tried not only to convert Plutarch's Greek prose to verse but also, in her revisions, to make her unrhymed lines more specifically resemble the hexameter rhythms of classical poetry.

1. This translation is available in the Everyman's Library edition, *Plutarch's "Moralia": Twenty Essays,* trans. Philemon Holland (London, [1911]), pp. 133–52.

2. Caroline Pemberton, ed., *Queen Elizabeth's Englishings of Boethius, Plutarch, and Horace,* Early English Text Society, original ser. 113 (London, 1899), p. 141. All quotations of the PRO MS are from this edition.

Wrongly Attributed Works

Poems

1. As Christ willed it and spake it. Variant first lines begin "Christ was the word," "It was the word," " 'Twas Christ the word." The stanza was printed in the 1635 edition of John Donne's *Poems*. The earliest attribution to Elizabeth occurs in Thomas Fuller's *The Holy State* (1642), repeated in many subsequent seventeenth-century manuscripts and printed sources. The quatrain's earliest appearance occurs in L: Royal MS 12 B.18, f. 200, where the poem is titled "Of the Euchariste/ D. C." and subscribed "1568." The poem is also subscribed "D: C:" in O: Rawl. poet. MS 219, f. 15, a text transcribed ca. 1603. These initials may refer to Dr. Richard Cox, who tutored Princess Elizabeth before 1550 and became bishop of Ely during her reign. Another early candidate for the poem's authorship is Dr. Nicholas Heath, to whom it is attributed in Oscott College MS Case B II / RNN 3, c., p. 138. This anthology dates from the mid-1590s; its scribe, Peter Mowle, titled his version of the poem "Docter Heath. vppon ye Blessed Sacrament of the Avlter." A third early candidate for the authorship of the poem is "Mr h: Biston" to whom it is ascribed (ca. 1581) by John Fitzjames, compiler of Guildhall, London, MS 777 (f. 93). Elizabeth's claim is much too late, and contested by too many earlier candidates, to be credible.

2. When the warrior Phoebus goeth to make his round. Classified by Leicester Bradner (*The Poems of Queen Elizabeth I* [Providence, R.I., 1964]) among the Queen's "Poems of Doubtful Authorship," this sonnet is almost certainly the work of John Soowthern, in whose verse anthology, *Pandora* (1584), the sole text was printed. See Steven W. May, "The Countess of Oxford's Sonnets: A Caveat," *English Language Notes* 29 (1992): 9–19, and Rosalind Smith, "The Sonnets of the Countess of Oxford and Elizabeth I: Translations from Desportes," *Notes and Queries*, n.s., 41 (1994): 446–50.

Translations

1. Fools that true faith never had. This translation of Psalm 14 (Psalm 13 in the Vulgate) was printed in 1548 at the end of Elizabeth's *A Godly Medytacyon of the christen sowle,* her translation of the Queen of Navarre's *Miroir* (see the Commentary to Letter 1). Ruth Hughey argued that the poem was probably written by the book's editor, John Bale (Hughey, "A Note on Queen Elizabeth's 'Godly Meditation,'" *Library,* 4th ser., 15 [1934]: 237–40). David Scott Kastan argued the same point in "An Early English Metrical Psalm: Elizabeth's or John Bale's?" *Notes and Queries,* n.s., 21 (1974): 404–5.

2. "A Dialogue out of Xenophon," *Gentleman's Magazine,* Miscellaneous Correspondence, no. 2 (1743): 139–57 (reprint, London, 1998). Introduced as "a Translation made by Queen Elizabeth and in her own Hand-writing," the dialogue's style does not resemble the Queen's other translations nor does the text preserve her characteristic spellings. The facsimile handwriting of this lost MS (p. 157) is in an italic script that does not match Elizabeth's.

For Further Reading

Biographical Studies

Doran, Susan. *Monarchy and Matrimony: The Courtships of Elizabeth I.* London, 1996.

MacCaffrey, Wallace. *Elizabeth I.* London, 1993.

Perry, Maria. *The Word of a Prince: A Life of Elizabeth I from Contemporary Documents.* Woodbridge, Eng., 1990.

Somerset, Anne. *Elizabeth I.* New York, 1991.

Starkey, David. *Elizabeth: The Struggle for the Throne.* New York, 2001.

Editions

Elizabeth I: Collected Works. Ed. Leah S. Marcus, Janel Mueller, and Mary Beth Rose. Chicago, 2000.

Elizabeth's Glass. Marc Shell. Lincoln, Neb., 1993. A modern edition of Princess Elizabeth's 'The glasse of the synnefull soule,' from the text in O: MS Cherry 36.

Letters of Queen Elizabeth I and James VI. Ed. John Bruce. Camden Society Publications 46. [London], 1849.

Poems of Queen Elizabeth I. Ed. Leicester Bradner. Providence, R.I., 1964.

Queen Elizabeth's Englishings of Boethius, Plutarch, and Horace. Ed. Caroline Pemberton. Early English Text Society, original ser. 113. London, 1899.

The Letters of Queen Elizabeth. Ed. G. B. Harrison. London, 1935.

Critical Studies

Bell, Ilona. "Elizabeth I—Always Her Own Free Woman." In *Political Rhetoric, Power, and Renaissance Women,* ed. Carole Levin and Patricia A. Sullivan, pp. 57–82. Albany, N.Y., 1995.

Cavanagh, Sheila. "The Bad Seed: Princess Elizabeth and the Seymour Incident." In *Dissing Elizabeth: Negative Representations of Gloriana,* ed. Julia M. Walker, pp. 9–29. Durham, N.C., 1998.

Crane, Mary Thomas. " 'Video et Taceo': Elizabeth I and the Rhetoric of Counsel." *Studies in English Literature* 28 (1988): 1–15.

Doran, Susan. "Elizabeth I's Religion: The Evidence of Her Letters." *Journal of Ecclesiastical History* 51 (2000): 699–720.

Frye, Susan. *Elizabeth I: The Competition for Representation.* New York, 1993.

Hackett, Helen. *Virgin Mother, Maiden Queen: Elizabeth I and the Cult of the Virgin Mary.* New York, 1995.

Heisch, Allison. "Queen Elizabeth I: Parliamentary Rhetoric and the Exercise of Power." *Signs* 1 (1975): 31–55.

Jordan, Constance. "States of Blindness: Doubt, Justice, and Constancy in Elizabeth I's 'Avec l'aveugler si estrange.' " In *Reading Monarch's Writing: The Poetry of Henry VIII, Mary Stuart, Elizabeth I, and James VI/I,* ed. Peter C. Herman and Ray G. Siemens, pp. 109–33. Tempe, Ariz., 2002.

King, John N. "Queen Elizabeth I: Representations of the Virgin Queen." *Renaissance Quarterly* 43 (1990): 30–74.

———. *Tudor Royal Iconography: Literature and Art in an Age of Religious Crisis.* Princeton, 1989.

Levin, Carole. *The Heart and Stomach of a King: Elizabeth I and the Politics of Sex and Power.* Philadelphia, 1994.

Marcus, Leah. "Queen Elizabeth I as Public and Private Poet: Notes toward a New Edition." In *Reading Monarch's Writing: The Poetry of Henry VIII, Mary Stuart, Elizabeth I, and James VI/I,* ed. Peter C. Herman and Ray G. Siemens, pp. 135–53. Tempe, Ariz., 2002.

Mueller, Janel. "Textualism, Contextualism, and the Writings of Queen Elizabeth I." In *English Studies and History,* ed. David Robertson, pp. 11–38. Tampere, Finland, 1994.

Orlin, Lena Cowen. "The Fictional Families of Elizabeth I." In *Po-*

litical Rhetoric, Power, and Renaissance Women, ed. Carole Levin and Patricia A. Sullivan, pp. 84–110. Albany, N.Y., 1995.

Teague, Frances. "Elizabeth I." In *Women Writers of the Renaissance and Reformation,* ed. Katharina M. Wilson, pp. 522–47. Athens, Ga., 1987.

————. "Princess Elizabeth's Hand in *The Glass of the Sinful Soul.*" *English Manuscript Studies* 9 (2000): 33–48.

Index

About the Cover Portrait

The Plimpton Sieve Portrait of Elizabeth I, painted in 1579 by George Gower, was bequeathed to the Folger Shakespeare Library in 1997. Known as the "Sieve" portrait, it is the earliest of several paintings that show Elizabeth holding a sieve (a classical symbol of the Roman vestal virgin Tuccia, who proved her chastity by carrying water in a sieve). This painting is considered one of the finest portraits executed of the queen in her lifetime.